# ADVENTIST MAVERICK

## A Celebration of George R. Knight's Contribution to Adventist Thought

Gilbert M. Valentine and Woodrow Whidden, Editors

## Pacific Press®
### Publishing Association

Nampa, Idaho | Oshawa, Ontario, Canada
www.pacificpress.com

Cover design by Gerald Lee Monks
Cover design resources provided by George R. Knight
Inside design by Kristin Hansen-Mellish

The authors assume full responsibility for the accuracy of all facts and quotations as cited in this book.

Scriptures marked NIV are quoted from the HOLY BIBLE, NEW INTERNATIONAL VERSION®, NIV®. Copyright © 1973, 1978, 1984, 2011 by Biblica, Inc.® Used by permission. All rights reserved worldwide.

Scriptures quoted from RSV are from the Revised Standard Version of the Bible, copyright © 1946, 1952, 1971 by the Division of Christian Education of the National Council of the Churches of Christ in the U.S.A. Used by permission.

Additional copies of this book can be obtained by calling toll-free 1-800-765-6955 or by visiting http://www.adventistbookcenter.com.

Library of Congress Cataloging-in-Publication Data:

Adventist maverick : a celebration of George R. Knight's contribution to Adventist thought / Gilbert M. Valentine and Woodrow Whidden, editors.
     pages cm
   Includes bibliographical references.
   ISBN 13: 978-0-8163-5613-3 (pbk.)
   ISBN 10: 0-8163-5613-0 (pbk.)
   1. Knight, George R. 2. Seventh-day Adventists—Doctrines. I. Knight, George R. II. Valentine, Gilbert M., editor.
   BX6193.K555A68 2014
   286.7092—dc23
                              2014032890

October 2014

# Contents

# Preface

In the thirty-eight years since George Knight formally began his involvement in Adventist higher education (he joined the faculty at Andrews University in late 1976), his scholarship, preaching, and teaching has helped focus and shape the discourse within his church in a number of important areas. His probing inquiry into the foundations of Christian education have helped clarify issues of objectives and methods and made a significant contribution both inside the Adventist Church and in the wider Christian community. His scholarly interests in a wide range of biblical and theological studies have enabled him to make a highly valued contribution to a more accurate and richer understanding of the origins of the Adventist Church and of the theological and organizational developments that have shaped it into the vibrant and dynamic international religious community it is today. His pastoral concern for the spiritual well-being of his community and his deep passion that the riches of the grace of God in Christ be a lived experience by all motivated him to make biblical scholarship accessible to the church. Knight's distinctive approach in his scholarship has been to undertake it and write about it in ways that are easily accessible to pastors, scholars, and laypersons. He has provided analysis and interpretation, which have enabled many in his community of faith to better understand their religious experience and theology and more deeply appreciate their sense of religious identity.

This volume is a response of gratitude and recognition for that significant scholarly contribution. It is also an acknowledgment of its helpfulness to the church. The purpose of this volume is to explore and assess Dr. Knight's distinctive contribution to Adventist publishing and to celebrate the giftedness and the labor of love that over many years have generated such an enormous body of work.

The broad range of key issues that have engaged Knight's scholarly endeavor across almost four decades while diverse, are not unconnected. In theological terms, they can be seen to be grounded in soteriological concerns and have almost inevitably spilled over into a variety of related issues in ecclesiology, eschatology, and missiology, touching on core issues in Christology, Revelation and Inspiration, and on anthropology along the way. Dr. Knight's early interest in educational philosophy led him first into an in-depth study of Adventist Christian education, its beginnings and its development, and its goals and objectives. The results of this inquiry led to a recognition of the importance of the theological conflicts that troubled Adventism in the late 1880s that subsequently had such a large impact on shaping an understanding of what was or at least what should be Christian about Adventist education. The growing awareness of the importance of this period led, in turn, to the need to more fully understand the nature of the profound theological conflicts that erupted so publicly in 1888, the issues and the people involved, the background that led up to the crisis, and the implications of the conflicts as they impacted almost every subsequent development in the shaping of Adventist self-understanding and mission. This investigation highlighted the necessity of a clearer understanding of Adventism's origins both of its theology and its institutional structure. In turn, it involved reflections on its continuing mission and the organizational issues and mission priorities that should determine matters of church structure and allocation of resources. Knight's research in all of these areas and his often provocative observations about what Adventist history had to teach the present generation of Adventist leaders, have themselves become important contributions and influences in the theological development of the Seventh-day Adventist community.

Dr. Knight's particular giftedness as a scholar and a communicator has manifested itself in his ability to engage the wider church in thinking through theological issues. His edgy style of writing and his courageous but engaging approach to sensitive topics brought an increasingly appreciative response from readers. They bought his books in large numbers and persuaded publishers that here was a writer who could talk about serious topics and also ensure that his books would sell. Knight's study and research have not been characterized by highly specialized esoteric conversations in technical language with a small cluster of like-minded and narrowly specialized academics within the cloistered and narrow confines of a discipline. Rather, he has adopted a more interdisciplinary and wide-ranging approach interacting with a range of voices and perspectives. Knight acknowledges the limitations of such an approach and self-deprecatingly refers to himself in a humorous way as an academic "Mutt," meaning that his background and interests are drawn from a mixed academic or disciplinary parentage. But his giftedness in this approach is that though he might be understood as a "jack-of-all-trades," the rejoinder epithet "but master of none" is quite unfounded. As historians of language have noted, the original usage of the "jack-of-all-trades" epigram when first coined was completely complimentary. Some individuals have the unique ability to be able to master skills in a number of trades in addition to their deeper mastery of one or more. It was nearly two centuries later that common usage attached the second part of the epigram to the moniker. In George Knight's case, the ability to reach across boundaries and see connections where others could not has been especially helpful. To understand not only the inner connectedness of things but to be able to contribute to a richer understanding of a specialized discipline is indeed something of great value. At a time when knowledge is exploding, the mastery of highly specialized knowledge and skill in a disciplinary field is vital, but equally valuable is the contribution of those who enable us to see the connections. The ability to discuss the connectedness of things makes his contribution exceedingly helpful. Knight's commitment to researching and writing in a way that embraces both specialist and nonspecialist and involves them in the conversation is a powerful legacy.

One only has to briefly scan the large bibliography at the end of this book to form a grasp of the wide-ranging contribution Knight has made to Adventist scholarship and to the life and understanding of his faith community. Knight possesses a restless pencil. It constantly pursues inquiry across boundaries and into new fields. Even in retirement it seems scarcely to have slowed its range or its pace. It seems quite unable to stop. Thus, any accounting of the publication status of Knight's writing is a fairly inexact science and is soon out of date. As of mid-2014, Knight has scribed forty-one published titles with many translated into foreign languages. In addition, he has authored more than forty chapters for books edited sometimes by himself, but mostly by others, seven articles for various reference works and twenty-four for the new *Ellen G. White Encyclopedia*.[1] So highly and widely is his credibility as a scholar recognized that he has been invited to write forewords for books by seventeen other authors. On occasion when some new volume by a former student or colleague was probing new territory, it was only the provision of an endorsement in a foreword by Dr. Knight that would embolden a publisher to weather potential criticism and proceed with a project.

It is true that four or five of the titles in Knight's list of publications represent the reworking or reissuing of former titles. And some might cite the joke that circulates from time to time in academia about well-publicized scholars. A colleague, when informed that an aged scholarly friend was reporting on the publication of another new book, inquired, "What did he call it this time?" It is true that scholars keep coming back to familiar themes, revisiting them from different perspectives or recasting the content in a fresh garb to catch a new or wider audience. Authors who write for a wider readership than just an academic specialist field often follow this path. But while there is some overlap in Knight's publication list with some titles being reissued in a new dress and while some articles evolved into books, his writing nevertheless spans a very wide range of subject matter, and where he revisits familiar territory, it is to add a new perspective or incorporate new findings. His intuitive entrepreneurial spirit in the field of publishing and the reissuing of titles was not driven by a need to derive personal income but rather to generate a sufficiently wide distribution to sustain the cost of publication. Undergirding this motivation was a passion to help his church grow in faith and understanding. Encouraging critical thinking and cultivating an engaged and thoughtful readership that was as wide as possible were his goals.

Knight also served as general editor of four scholarly multivolume series, contributed penetrating analysis and synthesis articles to nine authoritative encyclopedias, and has accumulated a total of forty published book reviews in scholarly journals. In addition, he has authored approximately 150 articles for a variety of scholarly journals and magazines. The value and helpfulness of many of these contributions can be gauged by the frequency with which his papers and articles were either translated for foreign language publications (sometimes unbeknownst to him) or republished in different regional or international publications. It is safe to say that no other writer in Adventism since Ellen White has been more widely translated. Knight has been able to engage an incredibly wide readership in his church, and his influence has been profound.

It is an awareness of this distinctive legacy that has shaped the particular form of this *festschrift*. In the normal course of things academic, a *festschrift* is a volume of specialized studies in which the students and colleagues of a scholar or teacher extend the work of the scholar by further testing their ideas or perhaps examining the implications of the scholar's ideas in a new unexplored setting. Although such essays are written in honor and acknowledgment of a scholar's contribution, they are usually highly technical and are designed to be read by a narrow group of fellow academics who understand the technical issues and have the skills and expertise to understand the disciplinary jargon.

On occasion, however, a different approach is used in scholarly circles to respond to a scholar's work and celebrate its contribution, particularly if that contribution has had a significant impact on a wider audience. The original inspiration for the format that we have adopted came from Woodrow's participation in a *festschrift* in honor of the noted Wesleyan-Evangelical historian Donald W. Dayton, published in the Princeton Theological Monograph Series in 2007.[2] Participants in that volume were assigned a key article, book, or portions of Dayton's wide-ranging scholarship in order to reflect on how these differing pieces contributed to the rich mosaic of his work. Dayton himself then contributed a retrospective chapter. Professional or scholarly societies also from time to time adopt this innovative approach in oral form to assess and celebrate the work of noted scholars. One such session at a recent meeting of the Society of Biblical Literature (SBL) that the editors attended in Baltimore, Maryland, involved a number of scholars joining together in reflecting on the thirty-fifth anniversary of the publication of Walter Brueggemann's *The Prophetic Imagination*. Noted scholars reflected on the significance of the work from their scholarly perspective and then tried to assess the impact of the work on their fields of study and on themselves personally. They told of the impact of the work on their own spiritual journeys and academic careers. Brueggemann himself then responded to the authors and offered a personal perspective of his own. In essence, the session functioned as an oral *festschrift*. It is this kind of more innovative and personal approach that we have adopted in the preparation of this *festschrift* for George Knight. Our objective is to embrace as wide a readership as possible. We also adopted this approach because we felt it to be a more appropriate and effective way of recognizing the broader range, interdisciplinarity, and popular orientation of the large portion of

Knight's scholarship and writing that has made it so valuable to his community. This book, therefore, embraces a variety of approaches to acknowledging the value of Knight's contribution. One of our contributors, Barry Oliver, for example, has followed the traditional *festschrift* approach and taken the opportunity to extend a particular thesis of Knight's in the field of ecclesiology and apply it to a current critical leadership dilemma. How will the church relate to the challenge of women's ordination? What might the church's history of development in the area of church structure and mission suggest as a way forward? Other authors reflect on a particular book or perhaps a cluster of Knight's publications on a given topic, analyzing, assessing, and critiquing them. The purpose in the approach adopted in these particular chapters is to explain how these publications from George's pencil have contributed to a deeper and broader understanding of the themes they discuss. Other authors were invited to reflect on particular theological themes that have been a focus of Knight's contribution. Still others addressed his contribution as a teacher or as an editor. All have been invited to muse on the contribution that George Knight has made to their own personal or spiritual development or the shaping of their career.\*

The idea of a *festschrift* to honor Dr. Knight was first discussed in late 2009 when a number of Knight's former students and colleagues found themselves attending and participating in a scholarly conference on the life and work of Ellen G. White held in Portland, Maine. The late Gary Land, Ronald Numbers, and Terrie Aamodt together with Julius Nam had convened the Portland Conference for the purpose of preparing a scholarly biography on the life of Ellen White for a readership beyond the confines of Adventism. (The hope that such a volume involving Adventist and non-Adventist scholars would be published by a leading academic press was realized in May 2014 when Oxford University Press published the title *Ellen Harmon White: American Prophet*.) The number of participants in the 2009 conference who had either worked with Knight or had been his students was substantial. It brought a new awareness of the seminal contribution he had made to the general field of Ellen White studies and to the study of denominational history through his work with students and colleagues. Beyond that, Knight had cultivated new attitudes of openness to research on the part of church authorities and in securing accessibility to historical sources within Adventism.

---

\* This approach has meant some inevitable repetition. Readers may also note stylistic unevenness in the discussions.

As George notes in his biographical reflection at the end of this volume, much of his work on Ellen White had been undertaken in the context of the debate between "her admirers and her detractors" in which he sought to be a "moderate voice that was both revisionist and constructive." As Ben McArthur perceptively notes, George "is essentially a moderate on nearly all theological positions" and his approach to history is to be seen as "rooted in pastoral concern." McArthur further suggests that historiographically, Knight served to "domesticate the troubling historical findings" about Ellen White by the historians of the 1970s and brought into Adventist mainstream at least the spirit of their inquiry if not always the same conclusions. That did not mean, however, that George's history was "without an edge."

George's readers from a more critical perspective still see him as being too much of an apologist who idealizes Ellen White and is unable to "really" cross-examine her "critically" or "find fault with her."[3] And perhaps George does too easily downplay the implications of such difficult episodes as the Israel Dammon trial or the lack of full disclosure about sources and the timing of Ellen White's reading of the health reformers of her day, given the mythical picture of her that had been constructed within the community. But as he acknowledges, his "pastoral concern for the church" was paramount and he needed to be sensitive to the needs of the church and also concerned about survival. Jim Walters has noted appreciatively that Knight has "mentored a new generation of Adventist church historians" but also observed that given the denominational context, their church histories would "understandably continue to engage in some shade of apologetics."[4] Denis Fortin, former Andrews University seminary dean, notes concerning the recent efforts in the field of Ellen White studies that "any interpretive work about an author or church leader is bound to combine historical facts with ideas and opinions, and in the end present a portrait of this person that may more or less resemble the reality." And for all historians, "integrity and honesty in the analysis of Ellen White's contribution" is essential.[5]

Among the group of George's students and colleagues participating in the 2009 conference, Julius Nam initiated the idea of developing a *festschrift* to honor Knight's work. Subsequently, during the conference a group of George's Andrews University colleagues, Jerry Moon, Woodrow Whidden, and Merlin Burt, and some former students, met to explore the value and possibility of developing such a volume. The meeting scoped out a plan and suggested possible authors.

Woodrow Whidden signed on for the task and persuaded Gil Valentine to help take a lead in the editorial role.

Almost inevitably, the project has taken longer than originally intended, because the writing and editing has had to be fitted in and around other duties. During the gestation period, Gil made yet another international move from Australia to California to establish a new home and take on new responsibilities as chair of the Department of Administration and Leadership at La Sierra University. Woodrow found himself making a transition from teaching in the Philippines to retirement in Berrien Springs and more retirement teaching than he had anticipated. It is fitting perhaps that this volume eventually makes its appearance soon after the Oxford University Press publication of the Ellen White biography and after the publication of the *Ellen G. White Encyclopedia*. This latter groundbreaking publication has also been a lengthy project first initiated by George and then passed on to Denis Fortin and Jerry Moon.

As editors, we would like to acknowledge our gratitude to the various authors for their contributions to this volume. Their willingness to participate in the project has made it possible to express our gratitude to George in a more permanent way than just saying "Thank you" at a retirement party. The assistance of Gerald Wheeler who with his editorial expertise undertook a careful reading of the final draft has been very greatly appreciated. His willingness to contribute in this way on an honorary basis is part of his tribute to long years of working in a similar capacity with George and to the warm collegiality they enjoy. Kendra Haloviak Valentine read earlier drafts and made helpful suggestions, enabling us to catch various infelicities of expression, a contribution greatly appreciated. The editors also wish to acknowledge Jerry D. Thomas of Pacific Press® for his enthusiasm and seeing the potential in this project. We are very thankful for his advocacy and willingness to work with us in getting the volume into print.

Our hope is that this volume has conveyed to George just how grateful we all are for the impact he has had on us individually and on the church which we love. We also hope that this volume with its affirmations and assessments will encourage others to benefit from reading his books.

Gilbert Valentine and Woodrow Whidden
July 2014

## Endnotes

1. Denis Fortin and Jerry Moon, eds., *Ellen G. White Encyclopedia* (Hagerstown, Md.: Review and Herald® Publishing Association, 2014.)

2. Christian T. Collins Winn, ed., *From the Margins: A Celebration of the Theological Work of Donald W. Dayton* (Eugene, Ore.: Pickwick Publications, 2007).

3. Jonathan Butler and Ronald L. Numbers, "The Hedgehog, the Fox and Ellen G. White," *Spectrum* 42, no. 2 (Spring 2014): 56.

4. "Ronald L. Numbers and the New Quest for the Historical Ellen G. White," *Adventist Today* (Summer 2014): 8.

5. "A Historical Inquiry: Review of Ellen Harmon White: American Prophet," *Spectrum* 42, no. 2 (Spring 2014): 4. Fortin believes that the Oxford University Press volume falls into that category.

# Introduction

# Historian and Provocateur

Benjamin McArthur

Historians are seldom the prophets of our age. Scientists, sociologists, and soothsayers of various stripes more often assume that role. Opinions and theories *de jour* appear and evanesce with the speed of the Web blog postings on which they are promulgated. In this intellectual environment, it is all the more remarkable that George Knight, a historian of the old school, stands as an influential commentator on the Adventist experience. His many books reach wide audiences within Adventism. Indeed, his works are as certain a commercial bet for Adventist publishing as any author of recent decades. Knight has firmly established himself as the leading interpreter of our past, not just because of his command of Adventist sources but also because of his commitment to the idea that examining our history is the surest path to understanding our collective self.

Part of Knight's influence resides in his sheer output. He is the most prolific author on Adventist history in denominational history. His total output of books has few equals in Adventist publishing. It would be dangerous here to attempt to specify an exact number, for it is a moving target. But a count as of 2014 finds at least forty-one titles. This number must be compounded by their many translations. *Reading Ellen White,* for example, has since its appearance in 1997 been published in German, Czech, French, Latvian, Hungarian, Korean, Bulgarian, Spanish, Japanese, and Dutch. Other books have been even more widely translated. A listing of his articles, chapters in books, encyclopedia entries, and other scholarly effort comprise a bibliography nearly thirty pages long.

It is true that Knight has produced no volumes with the heft of LeRoy Froom's several tomes. But I think the readability of his writings and the variety of outlets he has used, along with his active speaking calendar at lay and professional gatherings, has given him an impact upon the general Adventist reading public more substantial than any other Adventist historian. Moreover, unlike some earlier scholars, Knight has not taken upon himself the role of gatekeeper to the Adventist public. To the contrary, he has promoted the publication of historical documents and facilitated the long-overdue publication of Everett Dick's pioneering work on Millerism by Andrews University Press.

Knight's role as entrepreneur of Adventist history may not be fully appreciated by those outside academia. Again, a stroll through his *curriculum vitae* is instructive. He directed the Andrews University Press for some years. He has served on the board of Adventist Historic Properties, which has done a vital job of preserving the Adventist past. He has been a fixture at conferences on Adventist history. He helped initiate the Review and Herald Publishing's series on Adventist pioneers, which has produced wonderfully candid biographies of church leaders. He has nurtured a new generation of Adventist historians by serving as their doctoral supervisor in the church history program at Andrews. Knight has become, in short, the face of Adventist history.

It is interesting to note (and perhaps encouraging to late bloomers everywhere) that George was not a youthful publishing prodigy. His first book did not appear until fifteen years after he graduated from college. And he essentially changed fields of study in midcareer. A pastor, teacher, and school principal initially, he later earned a doctorate in education at the University of Houston. His first work concerned philosophy of education. From there, he made a smooth segue to Adventist Church history with *Myths in Adventism* (1985), a study of Ellen White's writings on education, and sundry other topics. He never looked back. From his post at Andrews University, first in the School of Education, then in the

Seventh-day Adventist Theological Seminary, he produced a flood of publications on Adventist history and theology and—later—biblical commentaries.

What has characterized Knight's writings? One sees three noteworthy qualities: a willingness to pose tough questions; a passion for his subject; and an insistence that a study of Adventist history will produce a more nuanced interpretation of Ellen White's role in the church.

Knight's fondness for raising tough questions about our history might seem at first glance unexceptional. Isn't that what historians are supposed to do? One can concede that point while also recognizing that Adventist historiography— essentially apologetic in function—long avoided tackling difficult and potentially embarrassing issues, at least in any meaningful sense. Times when such could not be avoided usually were prompted by either outsider or lapsed Adventists' attacks on Millerism, Adventist doctrine, or Ellen White. Thus, F. D. Nichols's *The Midnight Cry* (1944), which was essentially an extended rebuttal to Clara Sears's *Days of Delusion* (1924). But Adventist historians rarely raised criticisms, expressed doubt, or second-guessed church mothers or fathers. Enough of that came from the outside. From within, the call was to close ranks.

No one can accuse George Knight of not being supportive of the organized church. But his definition of support includes the necessary task of self-scrutiny. It begins with an assumption that all human institutions are fallible; further, that every prophet who ever lived was fallible. To point out errors of judgment, or even of motive, partakes of the highest level of loyalty. This is not the work of a "loyal opposition" but, quite simply, of a loyal member.

Loyalty does not preclude impertinent questions. Knight asks if Adventists are subject to the same laws of institutional evolution as other groups—and concludes that we are. He wonders out loud what Adventism and Communism might have in common as ideologies and social movements, and finds disturbing parallels between Marxism's shortcomings and Adventism's future. Most threateningly, he asks whether we will necessarily be the end-time people.

Knight takes pleasure, I think, in arousing his readership with shock statements (and shocking titles for which he is infamous). He notes that our church began in a movement "up to its armpits in fanaticism by early 1845." *Myths in Adventism* demolishes an armload of hoary "truths" that generations of Adventists grew up with. They include such examples as the highly influential notion that Ellen White prescribed a "blueprint" for education that we are bound to follow.

Or that she had a carefully devised philosophy about the study of literature. Or that accreditation of Adventist schools runs counter to divine counsel.

But Knight always has a didactic purpose to his egg heaving. He does not seek revisionism for its own sake. His statement about Millerite fanaticism, for example, makes the point of how truth can arise out of zealotry. He seeks to replace a prevailing two-dimensional, whiggish view of our past with a more complex model. That is, Adventist history has not been a story of steady improvement; rather, we have had tendencies (especially theological tendencies) that have reoccurred and show little promise of not reoccurring in the future. In his *A Search for Identity: The Development of Seventh-day Adventist Beliefs* (2000), he notes that debates regarding the inspiration of Ellen White, the relationship of law and grace, and the intertwined doctrines of the nature of Christ and belief that a last generation of Adventists will reach perfection, recycle through our church with distressing regularity.

George treats potentially explosive topics, such as the Israel Dammon episode in the immediate post-Disappointment months, with a disarming matter-of-factness, as if these revelations should have been untroubling to begin with. He can get away with this because, again, he writes with obvious loyalty to the church. Which illustrates the second quality of his work: his engagement with Adventist history. His tone is neither antiquarian nor devotional nor simply narrative. Instead—in the spirit of 1960s New Left historians—he seeks a "usable past." He asks, for example, what the agitation of 1888 means to our church today. And he finds in the meteoric—and finally tragic—career of A. T. Jones a cautionary tale for today. Knight both challenges the Adventist community by sweeping away comfortable but enervating myths of our past, while also providing reassurance that the task of rebuilding is not beyond our means.

Knight seems particularly burdened to nudge us away from the triumphalism that always lies just beneath the surface of popular Adventism. He insists upon restoring a sense of contingency to the Adventist experience. His is clearly a prophetic voice, warning that history makes clear our fate without revitalization. In a series of articles he did for *Ministry* (the Adventist Church's professional publication for its clergy) in the 1990s, he assumes the tone of a gentle jeremiad, firmly but lovingly tracing the arc of other denominations and our similar trajectory. He pokes the institutional church in the ribs about its chasing the secular gods of "community wages," bureaucratic layering, and the privileging of the medical field. In earlier decades, such concerns were spoken of in denominational publications by vague allusions to "Laodicean" conditions. Knight tolerates no such evasive cant.

Of course, in assessing Knight's courage in speaking his mind, one must remember that he represents the second generation of Adventist revisionists. He profits from and builds upon the work of Jonathan Butler, Ronald Numbers, Donald McAdams, Ron Graybill, and more recently Malcolm Bull and Keith Lockhart. Their having gone ahead and pioneered in forbidden historical terrain (especially Ellen White studies) has liberated him to pose questions that several decades earlier would not have been permitted. Without a Ron Numbers, so to speak, there would not be a George Knight. This is true both in terms of particular understandings, say, of Ellen White's borrowings, but more generally in fostering an openness to questioning hitherto untouchable issues. In historiographical terms, he has served to domesticate the troubling historical findings of these earlier men, bringing into the Adventist mainstream something of the spirit (if not exactly the same conclusions) of their 1970s research. That Knight can travel these same roads and still maintain a lively commitment to the denomination has encouraged other Adventist scholars to do likewise.

Finally, Knight's history is suffused with an ardent desire to help church members understand and properly use the gift of prophecy. This concern runs through many of his pages, and he documents repeated appropriation of Ellen White's words for political and theological purposes by various individuals. But he most directly deals with the prophetic issue in the quartet of volumes, *Meeting Ellen White* (1996), *Reading Ellen White* (1997), *Ellen White's World* (1998), and *Walking With Ellen White* (1999). The second volume is the key one, in which Knight makes his appeal for restraint and common sense principles in the use of her writings.

And what were such principles? Some were truly common sense: understand context (both literary and historical), avoid preconceptions and extreme interpretations, and always search for the underlying principle. But Knight ventures into terrain seldom visited by earlier Adventist writers. He makes the point that the inherent difficulties of human communication did not exempt prophets. White's efforts to resolve conflicts or reform behaviors led her to use language that seemed appropriate to the nuances of the situation but which was interpreted by others—in her day and ours—in absolute ways. Readers must understand that White used hyperbole, metaphor, and other figures of speech. Knight is not quite advocating a deconstruction of White's writings, but he certainly is saying that a naive, uninformed literalism is dangerous (which is why he further warns about the numerous compilations of her writings).

A major plank of Knight's hermeneutic is Ellen White's repeated request that she not be made the controlling authority in resolving major church disputes. Had she once publicly advocated a particular understanding of which law the apostle Paul had been referring to in Galatians? No matter. The church's reexamination of the issue in the late 1880s (and after) should proceed on its own merits. Had not White interpreted other texts this way or that in printed sermons earlier? Perhaps. But she insisted she was not to be the sole lens through which Scripture was to be understood. Indeed, Knight sees White's preferred role less as prophetic dictator than as reluctant mediator, seeking a principled harmony among factions. And there were many squabbling factions in nineteenth-century Adventism. (As Knight points out elsewhere, there is no golden age in early Adventism for us to pine for.) The hundreds of pages that comprise the printed *Testimonies* betray a people continually calling upon her for counsel.

Any overview of George Knight's writings must include reference to his autobiographical confessions about his own religious and intellectual growth. These appealing *mea culpas* help tie him to his readership. Certain titles, *I Used to Be Perfect* (1994) and *My Gripe With God* (1990), invite readers to explore issues they may well have struggled with. Likewise, his decades of experience within Adventism and his passion for its mission impart similar passion to his work. Knight's writings betray a sensibility less scholarly (perhaps excepting *Millennial Fever and the End of the World: A Study of Millerite Adventism* [1993]) than pastoral. This is unsurprising when one recalls that his early career included stints in the ministry. There is a sermonizing quality to some of his writings. And his interest in creating a true "on the ground" exposure to Adventist history was realized in a daily devotional book, *Lest We Forget* (2008).

But a history rooted in pastoral concern does not mean a history without an edge. Knight, in his writings and in the lectern (he has long been in demand as a keynote speaker at Adventist gatherings), does not shy away from organizational rebuke. In *Search for Identity*, among his most candid works, he bemoans the tendency of Adventist leaders in the 1920s and 1930s to fall into the trap of fundamentalist views on inspiration and of theological rigidity in general. In *If I*

*Were the Devil* (2007), which was an expanded version of a notable presentation to the church's General Conference Session in 2000, Knight pulled no punches in taking on institutional shibboleths. His *Organizing for Mission and Growth* (2006) had the temerity to suggest a restructured, streamlined church organization. Knight can write such things and be invited back for more because his comments are always said with a smile and with a clear sense of his church loyalties. His fervent rhetoric notwithstanding, George is essentially a moderate on nearly all theological positions. He seeks reconciliation among various Adventist theological camps, extolling the virtues of balance and calling on all parties to appreciate the particular strength of others' positions. Despite this, there are pockets within the church that see him as too edgy for comfort, too outspoken about the institution, or too contextualizing of Ellen White's writings.

Which of Knight's books will have the greatest staying power? For my money, *Millennial Fever* promises to long remain the finest volume on the Millerite and early Adventist movement. *Angry Saints: Tensions and Possibilities in the Adventist Struggle Over Righteousness by Faith* (1989) endures as the best overview of the much-studied 1888 theological controversy. And *From 1888 to Apostasy: The Case of A. T. Jones* (1987) stands among the best Adventist biographies. (Knight is not through with Jones; he continues to rethink this complex figure.)

How does Knight evaluate his own work? As he nears the end of that portion of his career focused on Adventist history (his publishing interests have moved toward biblical and theological commentary), Knight offers neither apologies for stepping on historical toes nor admissions of doubt about his interpretations. There were a few topics he never found time to explore in the depth he wished. But some of these areas he directed his doctoral students and other protégés to.

If prophets are generally without honor in their own home, George Knight is a happy exception. He has received a clutch of academic honors and accolades of various sorts—including this volume. But will his salutary influence on our denomination's historical consciousness endure? Has our church reached a point where its ability to learn from its own history will end the cycle of doctrinal advance and regress? If not, the next generation will require another George Knight.

# Chapter 1

# Adventist Educational Historian

Arnold C. Reye

D r. George R. Knight is Adventism's "Renaissance man." By this I mean that through his teaching and writing, Knight consistently reveals a mastery of a number of academic disciplines: philosophy, history, theology, social theory, and cultural anthropology. A prolific writer and a craftsman with words, he is also an accomplished public speaker and presenter. As a balance to the academic life, he is a lover of the outdoors and is always ready for a new adventure, be it hiking, rafting, or sailing. Widely read, he respects the thoughts and ideas of others. Couched in terms of the English game of cricket: he is a superb batsman, a fearsome bowler, and a consummate fieldsman—a genuine all-rounder.

The problem, therefore, when tasked with analyzing Dr. Knight's contribution to a specific academic field is that at all times the Renaissance man draws upon all his interests and experiences to frame his work. It is a daunting task to discuss George Knight, teacher and researcher of the history of Seventh-day Adventist education, without being acutely aware of the contributions other disciplines have made to the Knight gestalt.

## Andrews University School of Education: 1976–1985

Having just been awarded his doctorate at the University of Houston, Texas, Dr. Knight joined the faculty of Andrews University School of Education in 1976 with the rank of assistant professor. It is of interest to note that within six years he had progressed in academic standing from assistant to associate to full professorship. Knight's prime responsibility in the School of Education was teaching Educational Foundations, specifically educational philosophy, the history of American education, and the history of Adventist education. He was also responsible for teaching documentary methods in research to both masters and doctoral students. His qualifications lay in two master's degrees from Andrews in which he had majored in theology and Christian philosophy, and in his doctoral program at the University of Houston, where his focus included both the history and philosophy of education.[1]

## Teacher

At the time George Knight took up his appointment, no definitive book yet existed on the history of Adventist education. Not surprising, therefore, the outline for the course EDUC517 in 1981 stated, "no textbook will be required." Rather, it asked students to "utilize resource materials contained in books, periodicals, and both private and public documents."[2] For the benefit of his students, however, George had commenced the compilation of a bibliography of secondary and unpublished sources. Eventually, he published it as an addendum to *Early Adventist Educators*.[3] A perusal of the works cited reveals that only three purported to address the scope of Adventist educational history. George, therefore, had precious little to work with! But it was a challenge he grasped with enthusiasm.

Knight approached the challenge in three ways. First, he prepared formal lectures that provided the historical context in which Adventist education emerged, traced the contours of the Adventist search for appropriate educational models for its elementary, secondary, and college institutions, drew attention to turning points in Adventist educational history, and identified some of the key issues in understanding Adventist educational history. Second, at that time he had several doctoral students sufficiently advanced in their research to make presentations on significant figures involved in the evolution of Adventist education: Allan Lindsay on Goodloe Harper Bell, Gil Valentine on W. W. Prescott, and Warren Ashworth on E. A. Sutherland. Third, he set assignments that required students to utilize two valuable resources on campus, namely the Ellen G. White Resource Center and the Andrews University Heritage Room. Thus, he forced them to identify primary materials and to make historical judgments from those materials. Furthermore, George contributed to the development of these resource centers by passing on primary resources and copies of worthwhile term papers, such as Craig Willis's identification of the Harbor Springs Institute of 1891 as a pivotal point in our educational history.[4]

## Dissertation chairman

Knight interpreted his role as going beyond the teaching of educational history to include the identification and encouragement of potential researchers into Adventist educational history. During his tenure in the School of Education, he chaired the doctoral committees of four students whose dissertations dealt with early Adventist educators. Allan Lindsay had written a term paper on Goodloe Harper Bell. "By then," Lindsay recalls, "I was getting intrigued by the life of this man [Bell] and suggested to George, when thinking of my dissertation topic, that I'd like to delve much more into Bell's life. He encouraged me and I remember him saying that even if you write only 100 pages, so long as it is exhaustive and you have covered all that is available on the man, that would be OK." Lindsay added, "That it finally ended with more than 400 pages is a tribute to his direction."[5]

In the case of Warren Ashworth, a class assignment led him to read E. A. Sutherland's book *Living Fountains and Broken Cisterns*. The more he read, the more fascinated he became with this educational reformer. George encouraged him to turn his interest into a dissertation.[6] Gilbert Valentine had become aware of George's growing "reputation of being rigorous in expectations and of good value" as a dissertation chairman. Meanwhile, Gil had become somewhat interested in W. W. Prescott from reading Vande Vere's history of Battle Creek College–Andrews University.[7] That interest increased when a chance meeting with George led to a discussion of Prescott. George opined that there were gaps in our knowledge of Prescott, but warned that Vande Vere had experienced difficulty in finding sources. Challenged by the unknowns in Prescott's life, Gil requested that George take him on as a doctoral student. Knight agreed and the subsequent dissertation ran to two volumes.[8]

I was the fourth student to complete a doctoral dissertation under George's guidance. Like Allan and Warren, my topic emerged from the course in Adventist educational history. For the term paper, Knight provided the class with a list several pages long of potential topics he wanted researched. One item caught my attention, namely "Griggs papers." It transpired that a carton of papers belonging to Frederick Griggs, one time president of Emmanuel Missionary College, had been found in the attic of a campus building being demolished. The carton's contents finally ended up in the Heritage Room. My task was to take these miscellaneous papers and to place them in the context of Griggs's work as an educator. Following his assessment of my paper, George asked whether I saw Griggs, a moderate on the Adventist spectrum, as a dissertation topic. If so, he would be happy to be my supervisor. Concurring with Gil's assessment of George as a demanding but supportive teacher, I, too, grasped the opportunity to have him guide my dissertation.

Another Australian, John Waters, wrote a term paper on Warren Howell. Again, Knight saw the potential for a dissertation, this time an educational administrator who might be seen as conservative, even reactionary. Regrettably, while a member of John's dissertation committee, George was not permitted to serve as chairman. This highlighted a problem for him. As professor of Educational Foundations, he supported a number of departments within the School of Education—religious education, educational administration, curriculum and supervision, and psychology and counseling—but was not himself part of a major department. Beginning about 1984, the Educational Administration Department objected to George chairing the committee of a student majoring in their discipline. This development contributed to the eventual ending of his relationship with the School of Education and the cessation of mentoring of further doctoral dissertations in the history of Adventist education within the School of Education.

## Writer

In addition to teaching, George developed a passion for writing. In 1979, he wrote "Battle Creek College: Academic Development and Curriculum Struggles," in which he analyzed early Adventist efforts to clarify educational goals and practices. He highlighted the tensions between the classical traditionalists led by Sidney Brownsberger and the reformists championed by Ellen White. His paper does not appear to have been published at that time, but a copy was placed in the Heritage Room.

E. M. Cadwallader, in his *History of Seventh-day Adventist Education,* focused principally on institutions. George, on the other hand, perceived the importance and significance of thought leaders—those who influenced the course of events. He, therefore, conceived the idea of a book highlighting the role of significant persons. Hence, in 1983, *Early Adventist Educators*[9] was published. George as editor called upon nine other scholars to write on key persons whom he perceived had influenced Adventist education. He, himself, wrote three of the twelve chapters. (George graciously listed me as co-author of the chapter on Frederick Griggs, but as I recall, my contribution was limited to offering suggestions as to the structure of the chapter and providing the documents that supported it. He did the writing.) As editor, George also provided the one-word descriptors designated for each educator, such as "James White: Initiator," "Edward A. Sutherland: Reformer," and "Frederick Griggs: Moderate." Two of George's chapters were particularly important. His first chapter, "Early Adventists and Education: Attitudes and Context," outlined the social, educational, and religious milieu in which the selected educators functioned. His second chapter dealt with "Ellen G. White: Prophet" and remains the most succinct and balanced presentation of Ellen White's role in and influence upon Adventist education. In addition, in this chapter, George hinted at what he considered a crucial historical linkage. He wrote: "The revival in Christian education went hand in hand with the revival of Christocentric theology."[10] Later he would state this with greater emphasis. "Minneapolis, with its stress on Christ's righteousness, Harbor Springs, Avondale, and the elementary school movement were not unrelated. Each event led to the next, and resulted in vigor and growth throughout the system."[11]

In 1983, *Adventist Heritage* published an article by George in which he explored the possible links between Oberlin College and the Adventist search for an educational model.[12] Earlier Adventist historians, such as Cadwallader and Vande Vere, had perceived a connection between Oberlin and Adventist education through Goodloe Bell. George, on the other hand, saw E. A. Sutherland as a more plausible link between Oberlin and Adventism. In *Studies in Christian Education,*[13] Sutherland made extensive references to Oberlin in articulating his reformist platform. Furthermore, George perceived a broader picture. While he identified seven points of agreement between the early Oberlin philosophy and Adventists, he also drew attention to a significant difference, namely the "theological underpinnings" that drove the reform programs at Oberlin and Battle Creek.

Knight correctly placed the Adventist search for educational theory within the context of an era of educational reform evident across the northeastern United States during the period from 1830 to 1860. George concluded that "the early leaders of Adventism were on the cutting edge of reform even though their reforms were neither unique nor ahead of their times." Also, in the flow of time he saw Oberlin as being in the initial phase of educational reform and Adventism occupying a place in its later phase. Furthermore, in an interpretive comment, he made two interesting observations. First, that Adventism's response to social reform in the nineteenth century reveals a reforming impulse deep in the church's psyche and to deny that would be to alter the nature of the Advent movement itself. Second, that in a healthy way our Adventist forefathers were very much aware of the social issues of their times. The caution to contemporary Adventism is that we "cannot afford to remain in the nineteenth century. . . . The church is continually challenged to come to grips with issues of the present within the framework of its heritage."[14] Inherent in this statement was a justification for the study of Adventist history.

Early in his tenure in the School of Education, George conceived one of his most important books for Adventist educators, namely *Myths in Adventism*.[15] The volume reveals several things about George Knight as a scholar. First, his capacity to grasp quickly the ideas of another and to reframe them from his own perspective. As he explained in the preface to *Myths in Adventism*, in 1979 he had received a copy of Arthur W. Comb's book, *Myths in Education*. Although written from a humanistic perspective, George immediately saw its possibilities for examining problem areas in Adventist education. "His [Comb's] treatment of myths in general inspired me to critique Adventist education using the myth format. Within twenty-four hours after receiving the book, I had my 'myths book' outlined in essentially its present form."[16] In that twenty-four-hour period, Knight had identified eighteen significant Adventist educational myths (literary myths required two chapters).

Second, his book reveals his skill in bringing to bear his wealth of knowledge across several disciplines. *Myths in Adventism* is an excellent example of the masterful way in which George draws on the fields of philosophy, theology, sociology, and history to present his case. A third point we might make is that the book reveals his fearlessness as a scholar. Once armed with irrefutable evidence, George does not hesitate to explode a myth. That might mean that he was merely being an honest scholar, but we must not forget that myths come with strong emotional baggage. As he explained in the foreword to his twenty-fifth anniversary reprinting of the volume in 2009, the book "almost suffered a still birth" as his publisher was unwilling to consider the work, telling him "that Adventists wouldn't buy that kind of book." The fact that "Myth" was in the title and served as the organizing theme was problematic, but George dug his heels in and insisted that the title stay as he had proposed it. Exploding a myth can be as dangerous as defusing a mine.[17] That George did not explode just one mine, but a complete minefield, and lived to tell the story, says much about his skill in identifying, analyzing, and refuting myth. And his hunch proved right. The time was right, the book caught the Adventist imagination, and sales were brisk right from the start.

Probably George's last major contribution to Adventist educational studies while in the School of Education was to write a chapter for a book edited by Gary Land.[18] The intent of the book was to sketch the social and historical context in which Ellen White wrote, preached, and guided the emerging Adventist Church. In fourteen pages, George provided a comprehensive overview of nineteenth-century education in the United States. He made clear the issues and deficiencies in American education that stimulated Ellen White's reforming zeal. Implicitly he placed Ellen White in that line of nineteenth-century educational reformers extending from Horace Mann and John Oberlin to Francis Parker and John Dewey. This chapter again emphasized the importance Knight placed on the issue of historical, social, and cultural context. Neither Adventism in general nor individual thought leaders acted independently of a wider context.

# Department of Church History, Theological Seminary: 1985–2006

Mid-1985 saw George move from the School of Education to professor of church history in the Andrews University Theological Seminary. The transfer provided George with a far broader canvas upon which to develop his interests in the roots of Adventism. It also ushered in a period of more than twenty years in which he published prolifically on Adventist Church history. He did not, however, neglect his earlier interest in the church's educational history.

During the period 1986–2008, George wrote ten articles for the *Journal of Adventist Education*. They dealt with important themes in Adventist educational history: the search for a distinctive identity, the role of agriculture in Adventist schools in terms of the church's mission, the motivating factors that led to the dynamic educational expansion, the relationship between curriculum and educational purposes, Adventist educational essentials, service (the ultimate aim in Adventist education), the importance of the underlying philosophy to educational outcomes, the role and function of Adventist education in the light of the Apocalyptic, and the missiological roots of Adventist higher education.[19] In each of the articles, Knight moved from historical development to present-day opportunities. A proper understanding of history is to inform the present.

In 2001, George provided two lengthy articles to the *Journal of Research on Christian Education*. The first article used the provocative title "The Devil Takes a Look at Adventist Education" to explore a range of pitfalls into which Adventist education has or might fall into. At one point, rather wistfully, George asked the question: "How many people does Adventism have employed full time or even most of the time on the philosophy of Adventist education and its sister discipline, history of Adventist education?" His estimation was that the number is "zero," a neglect that he implied played into the devil's hand. Although primarily an examination of philosophical issues, the article is important from a historical perspective, for it reinforced the emphasis Adventist educators have placed on the school as a redemptive agent. George opined that Ellen White's linking of "redemption and the *imago Dei*" might in fact be her major contribution to Christian education. The second article traced in detail the emergence of Adventist educational aims from a shaky start in 1872 to bolder clarification by 1900 and a fully shaped system by the 1940s.[20]

George has published widely on the broad canvas of Adventism. Many of his books, such as *If I Were the Devil*,[21] have included sections that explore the history of Adventist education within the context of other developments within the church. Although such explorations of our educational history have of necessity been more general, they have been important, however, because they have kept Adventist education before the general Adventist reader and have reinforced the idea that, within the mature Adventist Church, education is an important component.

A well-published historian within Adventist circles, George has also been called upon to contribute to several books intended for a broader Christian readership. Beginning in 1984, a series of six books edited principally by Thomas C. Hunt and James C. Carper explored religious schools and schooling in America at elementary through tertiary levels including religious seminaries. George provided six articles in which he outlined the historical development of Adventist schooling within the given categories. The first of these was particularly important, for it revealed that he had by 1984 identified four distinct periods in the development of Adventist education: Adventist educational roots, 1853–1891; a reform period, 1891–1903; a period of growth and organizational development, 1903–1940; and a period of maturity and clear identity, 1940–1982.[22] It is interesting to speculate whether he would now add a post-1982 period in which Adventist education has been engaged in redefining its educational goals and basic principles in the context of the twenty-first century. However, through his contributions to these six books, George served to inform the broader American public on the nature and purposes of Adventist schools and tertiary institutions.

In 1993, George proudly advised that Andrews University had established a PhD program in Adventist studies. It had been available at the Theological Seminary since about 1985, and he transferred into this to help give it more rigor. His 1993 advertising brochure announced that the avowed purpose of the program was to "expand the frontiers of knowledge regarding Adventism."[23] The development during a twenty-year period of massive archival holdings at the Heritage Centers at Andrews and Loma Linda Universities, and at the General Conference Archives had made the program possible. While quick to commend the many who contributed to the development of those archival holdings, Knight would be reticent to play up the dynamic his own enthusiasm for Adventist history played. Although Adventist studies is a broad field, there may yet be persons and issues in Adventist education that will warrant attention by a new generation of PhD students.

## A personal note

My prior tertiary study had been at two Australian universities. What struck me early was how much George was like my Australian professors. Knight lectured in-depth, sharing with his students the extent of his knowledge on the subject. He was, however, thoroughly American. Somewhat proud of my English language background, my first assignment for him I wrote in British English. George's red pen underscored each occasion where I had failed to use American spellings and usages. When I remonstrated that I was using "correct" English, he politely pointed out that was a moot point. More emphatically, he reminded me that I was attending an American university and would in the future meet American literary standards. The clincher came when he said, "Down the track you will write your dissertation and will definitely need to comply with American standards." QED!

Over the three years I wrote term papers and a dissertation under his tutelage, I found my writing skills greatly enhanced. George would not tolerate sloppy sentence construction or ideas lacking clarity. I well recall the draft of my first dissertation chapter. It was returned to me with red ink comments filling every page. It took me several days to recover from this blow to my ego, but recover I did, and the red-ink medicine stood me well. John Waters shared with me his similar experience and confided that initially he felt so discouraged he almost made the mistake of asking George to step down from his dissertation committee. Waters also made an observation that held true for me. While George's written comments could be ego-deflating, his oral observations were always supportive and encouraging.[24] Both John and I share an indebtedness to Knight for making us better writers.

George was instrumental in my receiving high honor. Evidently, in conversation with then Andrews president, Joseph Smoot, he mentioned my writing on Frederick Griggs, a former president of Emmanuel Missionary College. He must have presented me in good light, for Dr. Smoot extended an invitation to present a formal paper on Griggs as part of the 1983 Founders Weekend. For me that was one of the highs of my sojourn at Andrews. Thank you, George, for that honor.

During the course of my Andrews years, my relationship with Knight progressed from teacher-student to colleague-friend. That friendship has continued well beyond Andrews. On one occasion in 1983, George and I were talking about the church we love in the context of Ellen White's counsel that people should be taught to think rather than be reflectors of other people's thoughts and Solomon's admonition on getting wisdom and understanding. I made an off-the-cuff comment, "In Adventist circles, thinking has often been treated as a virtue in rhetoric and a sin in practice," when George cut in and said, "Hold it a minute, I want to write that down!" To my surprise, the comment later appeared in the frontispiece of *Myths in Adventism*. Thank you, George, for immortalizing what may be the only occasion in which I have expressed an original thought.

Apart from his formative influence upon my academic life, he also pushed me to undertake activities that were both physically and mentally stimulating. On one of his early visits to Australia, he inveigled me to go with him to New Zealand and there climb one of the challenging alpine trails. On another occasion, he introduced me to black-water rafting, a surreal speleological experience, and white-water rafting which produced an incredible adrenaline rush. I later enticed him into crewing for a sail on Sydney Harbor. George has been equally at home in the cloistered study, the dynamic classroom, and the wholesome outdoors.

## Concluding comment

How might we remember Dr. George Knight's considerable contribution to our understanding of Adventist educational history? In summary form, I make ten points—a neat number. First, he took the study of Adventist educational history beyond the narrative to rigorous historical analysis. In this, he searched for patterns and basic themes. Second, he focused on the identification of key turning points and thought leaders and explained how those events and persons influenced the formation of Adventist education. Third, he continually forced his students and others to consider the foundational reasons for Adventist Christian education—that point at which philosophy, history, and practice meet. Fourth, he confirmed the study of Adventist educational history as a worthwhile and productive field of research, analysis, and writing at doctoral level. Fifth, George encouraged the development of major repositories of Adventist historical collections and directed his students in their use. It is perhaps no coincidence that during the last decades of the twentieth century, there has been a worldwide impetus to develop research centers in Adventist studies. Sixth, he has trained several generations of scholars in the discipline of historical research, analysis, and writing. Such scholars are better equipped to undertake historiography. Seventh, Knight has set an example of the fearlessness with which each generation of Adventist scholars must reevaluate past interpretations, hold what is secure, and prune what is myth. And do this with commitment and loyalty to the Adventist Church. Eighth, George, through his writing and teaching, continually stressed the importance of context. Be it a single document or a corpus of work, it may only be rightly interpreted when context is understood. Ninth, he has demonstrated that philosophy, history, and theology can and should co-exist and work together to inform the life and work of the scholar. Tenth, and my last point, the definitive history of Adventist education has yet to be written. Whether George himself or someone else undertakes the task, he has provided the framework for it.

### Endnotes

1. For a very brief comment on his own intellectual journey, see George R. Knight, "The Devil Takes

a Look at Adventist Education," special ed., *Journal of Research on Christian Education* 10 (Summer 2001): 181, 182.

2. Somehow my copy of the course outline and schedule of events for EDUC517 has survived several relocations and the periodic culling of files.

3. George R. Knight, ed., *Early Adventist Educators* (Berrien Springs, Mich.: Andrews University Press, 1983), 239–243. The three secondary sources that directly addressed Adventist educational history were Walton J. Brown, comp., *Chronology of Seventh-day Adventist Education*, 2nd ed. (Washington, D.C.: General Conference of Seventh-day Adventists, Department of Education, 1979); E. M. Cadwallader, *A History of Seventh-day Adventist Education*, 4th ed. (Payson, Ariz.: Leaves-of-Autumn Books, 1975); and Maurice Hodgen, *School Bells and Gospel Trumpets: A Documentary History of Seventh-day Adventist Education in North America* (Loma, Linda, Calif.: Loma Linda University Press, 1978). Of the remainder of the published sources, fifteen were biographies, fourteen the histories of educational institutions, nine were general church histories, two were biographies of educational leaders, and eight fell into other categories. Of the unpublished sources, ten were doctoral dissertations, twelve master's theses, and there were four others.

4. Craig S. Willis, "Harbor Springs Institute of 1891: A Turning Point in Our Educational Concepts" (term paper, Andrews University, 1979. Document File 60a EGWRC-AU).

5. E-mail, Allan Lindsay to Arnold Reye, May 22, 2012.

6. E-mail, Warren Ashworth to Arnold Reye, June 12, 2012.

7. Emmett K. Vande Vere, *The Wisdom Seekers* (Nashville, Tenn.: Southern Publishing Association, 1972).

8. E-mail, Gilbert Valentine to Arnold Reye, April 14, 2012.

9. Knight, *Early Adventist Educators*.

10. George R. Knight, "Ellen G. White: Prophet," in *Early Adventist Educators*, 33.

11. George R. Knight, "The Dynamics of Educational Expansion: A Lesson From Adventist History," *Journal of Adventist Education* (April–May 1990): 15.

12. George Knight, "Oberlin College and Adventist Educational Reforms," *Adventist Heritage* 8, no. 2 (Spring 1983): 3–9.

13. E.A. Sutherland, *Studies in Christian Education* (published in tract form, 1915.)

14. Knight, "Oberlin College and Adventist Educational Reforms."

15. George R. Knight, *Myths in Adventism* (Hagerstown, Md.: Review and Herald®, 1985).

16. Ibid., 13.

17. Milton R. Hook, another careful church historian, exploded the myth of the furrow story associated with the establishment of Avondale College. As a consequence, he was perceived by some as disloyal. See Milton R. Hook, "The Avondale School and Adventist Educational Goals, 1894–1900" (EdD diss., Andrews University, 1978).

18. George R. Knight, "The Transformation of Education," in Gary Land, ed., *The World of Ellen White* (Hagerstown, Md.: Review and Herald®, 1987), 161–175.

19. George R. Knight, "A System in Search of Identity: Historical Perspectives on SDA Higher Education," *Journal of Adventist Education* 48, no. 4 (April–May 1986); George R. Knight, "SDA Agricultural Programs: Symbols of Corporate Guilt or Unlimited Opportunities," *Adventist Education*, February–March 1986; George R. Knight, "The Dynamics of Educational Expansion: A Lesson From Adventist History," *Adventist Education*, April–May 1990; George R. Knight, "What Knowledge Is of Most Worth," *Adventist Education*, December 1991–January 1992; George R. Knight, "Adventist

Educational Essentials," *Adventist Education*, October–November 1998; George R. Knight, "The Aims of Adventist Education: A Historical Perspective," *Adventist Education*, General Conference 2000; George R. Knight, "Adolf Hitler and Ellen White 'Agree' on the Purposes of Education," *Journal of Adventist Education* (October–November 2002); George R. Knight, "Adventist Education and the Apocalyptic, Part I," *Journal of Adventist Education* (April–May 2007); George R. Knight, "Adventist Education and the Apocalyptic, Part II," *Journal of Adventist Education* (Summer 2007); and George R. Knight, "The Missiological Roots of Adventist Higher Education and the Ongoing Tension Between Adventist Mission and Academic Vision," *Journal of Adventist Education* (April–May 2008).

20. George R. Knight, "The Aims of Adventist Education in Historical Perspective," special ed., *Journal of Research on Christian Education* 10 (Summer 2001): 195–225; and George R. Knight, "The Devil Takes a Look at Adventist Education," special ed., *Journal of Research on Christian Education* 10 (Summer 2001): 175–194.

21. George R. Knight, *If I Were the Devil* (Hagerstown, Md.: Review and Herald®, 2007), 201–208.

22. George R. Knight, "Seventh-day Adventist Education: A Historical Sketch and Profile," in James C. Carper and Thomas C. Hunt, eds., *Religious Schooling in America* (Birmingham, Ala.: Religious Education Press, 1984), 85–109.

23. George R. Knight, "Andrews University Offers Ph.D. in Adventist Studies," *Adventist Today*, November–December 1993.

24. Telephone conversation, John Waters with Arnold Reye, June 3, 2012.

# Chapter 2

# A Cheshire Cat in the World of Christian Education

John V. G. Matthews

## Introduction

This chapter considers George Knight's contribution as an Adventist educational philosopher, particularly through his two publications: *Issues and Alternatives in Educational Philosophy* (Berrien Springs, Mich.: Andrews University Press, 1982, 1989, 1998, 2008), and *Philosophy and Education: An Introduction in Christian Perspective* (Berrien Springs, Mich.: Andrews University Press, 1980, 1989, 1998, 2006).

This essay attributes the roots of Knight's interest in things theological to his insight into Adventist education as being a product of Adventist history and theology. Knight has become an important voice, not just in Adventist education, but also as a leading provocateur in revisiting Adventist doctrinal controversies.[1] For George, the two areas were inseparably linked. To understand the field in which he started his professorship (Adventist education), he needed to explore what undergirded it and shaped it.

## George Knight and the Cheshire cat

In 1970, I preached one of my first sermons. While the topic has been lost in the fog of time, I still remember an illustration that I used in it. Alice, in her travels through Wonderland, became acquainted with an unusual Cheshire cat who had a huge grin and an annoying habit of appearing and disappearing at the most unlikely times. On one occasion, Alice reached a fork in the road and was confused about which direction to take. The Cheshire cat made an unexpected appearance in a tree above her head and Alice timidly sought his advice on which pathway to follow. The cat replied, "That depends a good deal on where you want to get to." When Alice said that she did not much care, the cat observed with great insight, "Then it doesn't matter which way you go."[2]

A decade following the delivery of that sermon, George Knight gave me a signed copy of his new publication, *Philosophy and Education* (*Philosophy*). The preface begins: "The basic premise underlying this book is the seemingly obvious proposition that one cannot arrive at his destination unless he knows where he is going."[3] Knight's book had as its theme the wisdom of Alice's Cheshire cat. "Knight's Law," as this wisdom is now presented, has changed a little over time to include gender-neutral language, but its basic theme remains through the various editions of both *Philosophy* and *Issues and Alternatives* (*Issues*). He challenges educators to recognize an important principle: What you think affects what you do. "Seemingly obvious" it may be, but that does not make it any easier to implement.[4] It is an unfortunate reality that educational practitioners—Adventists included—have tended to hurry down new pathways before considering where they might lead. Ideas have shaped practice, but sadly we have not always tested these ideas in the crucible of an integrated educational philosophy.[5]

Knight challenges both individuals and institutions to take seriously the importance of adopting a coherent philosophy before taking on the onerous task of planning a pathway for the education of future generations. If it is true that "to educate is to redeem,"[6] then teaching "your children and their children after them" (Deuteronomy 6:2, NIV) requires careful thought. In his two books on educational philosophy, Knight urges his readers to take seriously the admonition to be leaders rather than followers in the field of education.[7] In reminding educators "that they cannot arrive at their destination unless they know where they are going,"[8] Knight has proven himself to be an astute Cheshire cat who appeared on the scene at a most appropriate time.

## *Philosophy and Education* and *Issues and Alternatives*

George Knight's two major works on educational philosophy have both gone through four editions. *Philosophy and Education* has copyright dates of 1980, 1989, 1998, and 2006. The various editions of *Issues and Alternatives* have copyright dates of 1982, 1989, 1998, and 2006. *Issues* is essentially a shortened version of *Philosophy*, mirroring the first two parts of *Philosophy* in terms of content and structure, but Knight rewrote the critiques of the various philosophical positions from a secular perspective, removing matters specifically evangelical yet retaining things generically Christian. Part 3 is also a revision that focuses on the need to develop a personal philosophy of education. The third edition of *Philosophy* in 1998 added a chapter on postmodernism and this was also added to *Issues*. In the fourth edition, Knight added a further chapter on Christian teachers in the public school. This did not affect the outline and structure of the 2008 publication of *Issues*. Parts 3 and 4 of *Philosophy* focus on a Christian understanding and application of educational philosophy. By omitting these sections, George aimed *Issues* at a secular rather than a Christian audience. In the first two sections, both publications lay out the parameters of educational philosophy and present an overview of traditional and modern philosophies. The impact of educational philosophy on educational practice is the major theme, which in *Philosophy*, Knight applies from a Christian perspective in parts 3 and 4 of the book. In *Issues*, part 3 is a short section, with no theistic terminology, on the importance of developing a personal philosophy of education.

Since the early 1980s, Andrews University Press has sold about fifty thousand copies of *Philosophy*, and forty thousand copies of *Issues* to a variety of Adventist and non-Adventist clients. The sales of these two books have played an important role in maintaining the financial stability of the press.[9]

## George Knight: Scholar on a journey

George Knight's journey to a professorship at Andrews University included two MA degrees, a PhD, and periods in pastoral work, K–12 classrooms, and school principalship. His first assignment at Andrews in 1976 was in the Department of Education, where he taught courses on the history and philosophy of education. In 1985, he transitioned to the Church History Department in the Seventh-day Adventist Theological Seminary, also on the Andrews campus.

This transition is fairly remarkable. In spite of the importance of Adventist education to the denominational mission,[10] it is striking how little the worlds of Adventist education and Adventist theology have dialogued with each other.[11] Knight is one of a small number of scholars who have bridged the undeniable chasm between Adventist education and theology. I venture to propose that he began the journey toward integration because of his study of Adventist history. Knight's research into Adventist education led to his first publications, the two books featured in this article. While these books are not about Adventist educational history, nor even specifically presented as Adventist educational philosophy, their underlying foundation is a biblical synthesis of Ellen White's educational ideas. It is not really possible to understand the development of White's view on education without a study of the historical context in which she constructed her ideas. Adventist education is a product of Adventist history and White's experience of that history.[12] Knight, as he studied Adventist educational philosophy, soon realized that the educational initiatives of the church are bound up with the history and theology of the church. His educational publications led him toward new and broader scholarly endeavors. George Knight the Adventist educator was becoming George Knight the Adventist scholar, a leading thinker in three major domains: denominational education, history, and theology.

Following his two major educational works, Knight published *Early Adventist Educators* (1983), and *Myths in Adventism* (1985).[13] As the reader peruses these two books, it becomes clear that George is not merely interested in Adventist education, but that he understands Adventist education to be inextricably entwined with denominational history and biblical interpretation. *Myths in Adventism* is an in-depth analysis of misconceptions about White's views on education. However, the subtitle of the work identifies a developing interest in "related issues," that is, in more than just White's notions on education. Knight explores the myths with a focus on historical context, and with a clear understanding of the impact on education of the theological issues the church was facing. In this sense, *Philosophy* and its companion, *Issues,* provided the springboard from which Knight launched the second phase of his professorial career.[14] It was not long before Knight published *From 1888 to Apostasy.*[15] While the rest of his journey does not exclude education, his interest in the 1888 controversies shows that he was centering his attention on the most prominent theological issue faced by Adventism, one that has profoundly shaped the identity and mission of the Adventist Church from its origins in the 1840s to the present.[16] In retirement, George returned to the philosophy of education and for the first time wrote with the specific aim of developing an Adventist perspective rather than an evangelical approach as he had done in *Philosophy.* The material first appeared as the entire content of an oversized issue of the *Journal of Adventist Education* (October/November 2010) under the title "Redemptive Education." It has since been submitted for publication as a book entitled, *Educating for Eternity: An Adventist Philosophy of Education.*

## In the wider educational arena

When George Knight first taught educational philosophy at Andrews University in the late 1970s, he used textbooks by Van Cleve Morris and Young Pai (joint authors), and George Kneller.[17] These were interesting choices. Neither textbook presented a theistic perspective. Morris and Pai is a scholarly presentation of much the same material that Knight later published in the first two sections of *Philosophy.* However, students new to philosophy who consider Knight's book to be a challenge would likely give up in despair if they had to read Morris. The book is filled with important information and analysis, but the organizational structure does not lend itself to an easy grasp of the overall philosophical schema.[18] Kneller, shorter and easier to read, provides neither the depth nor insight needed in a graduate class.[19]

In the Christian world, one can find many classics on education and educational philosophy, but they are often scholarly in the extreme. John Henry Newman's seminal *Idea of a University*[20] is neither Protestant nor easy to read. Introducing a student to educational philosophy through Newman would be akin to having someone begin their study of theology by reading Karl Barth. Horace Bushnell's *Christian Nurture,*[21] an important source for understanding education from a biblical perspective, is not a book on educational philosophy and is written in the same archaic style as Newman's opus.

In the mid-twentieth century, the evangelical world awakened to the challenges of formal Christian education in contrast to Sunday School education that had been its focus through the 1800s and early 1900s.[22] Among the first recognized evangelical authors on education were Lois LeBar and Frank Gaebelein.[23] Though these authors, writing in the mid-twentieth century, were much more accessible to their readers in terms of style, their focus was more on educational practice than philosophy. Both authors wrote from a strong biblical base, but neither presented materials in the form of an educational philosophy that could do justice to an Adventist educational perspective.[24]

With no textbook that adequately addressed education in a way that he could easily use to present an Adventist educational philosophy, Knight's choice of Morris and Kneller was likely his best option. As one who sat in Knight's class in the 1970s, I find the well-preserved notes I have on my shelf very informative. Knight was not teaching primarily from Morris or Kneller. His lectures were the genesis of *Philosophy and Education*. In the absence of an appropriate text, he was sharing his own thoughtful and thought-provoking ideas—ideas that would eventually find their way into his first publications.

## Reader responses to *Philosophy and Education*

I teach a course in the Andrews University School of Education in which I assume that students have a background in Adventist educational philosophy. Any students who have not read Knight's *Philosophy* and White's *Education,* I require to do so. Each semester I read a goodly number of reviews on Knight written by students whose background in philosophy, with a few exceptions, range from nil to not much better. The overwhelming majority write in appreciation of Knight's scholarship and how, each step of the way, he lays down a base from which to explore the next big idea. Let the students speak for themselves:

One especially useful feature of the book is its logical progression from basic premises, through succinct descriptions of various philosophical concepts, to the application of these concepts to educational practice. The detailed descriptions of traditional and modern philosophies and how they impact education is [*sic*] essential in revealing how philosophical thought has progressed and the implications of various changes in thought have had on actual educational practice. Knight offers a stirring case for why an educator . . . [should] make the effort to sort through their philosophical foundations. . . . Each chapter of the book is a building block on which the next section is laid, making it possible to grasp each concept and quickly see how it fits into the bigger picture.[25]

[Knight's] style is characterized by the use of exceptionally precise language. This makes his thesis clear and his presentation unambiguous. Considering the limited [size] of the book, his presentation is surprisingly deep. How does he accomplish this? It is through his ability to go to the core of the problem, to recognize what is the most important and leave out nonessentials. The strong part of the book is that it does not merely discuss Christian philosophy of education, but it does so in the large context of general human thought. . . .

. . . The book serves as a wakeup call for Christian educators to develop their personal philosophy that would enable them to see clearly the purpose of their vocation. It brings hope that the identity crisis in Christian education is caused by our neglect, as opposed to an argument that the problem is inherent in Christian philosophy.[26]

Comments of this sort could be duplicated ad infinitum. There are, of course, more critical assessments, which is to be expected in a graduate class. But even these are generally positive.

Perhaps the most telling comments on the impact of Knight's book have come from colleagues in the North American Professors of Christian Education (NAPCE). Many of these scholars are professors at the premier evangelical institutions in North America. Often, as soon as they hear I am from Andrews University, they will ask if I know George Knight. Then they will extol the virtues of *Philosophy and Education*. On one occasion, a leading figure among them mentioned how he had published a volume he hoped would replace Knight's book as the textbook of choice. The book was published in 2003, but it apparently did not achieve the goal of its authors.[27] The sales of *Philosophy* have remained relatively even since its publication. I do know that the number of appreciative comments I hear at NAPCE about Knight has not diminished.

## Personal appreciation of George Knight

In 1977, at the end of the second quarter of my doctoral studies at Andrews University, I filled out an application for the University of Michigan. About that time, Knight happened to ask me how things were going with my studies. I responded that I felt poorer but no wiser as I walked out of most classes, and added that I planned to transfer to the U of M to read history under Charles Trinkhaus. Knight sat me down, outlined a plan of studies, and encouraged me to give Andrews one more quarter. I ended up graduating with a PhD in Religious Education, Knight's first doctoral advisee (though—no blame on George—not the first to graduate).

Knight likes to banter that he started out in education and ended up in church history, and I started out in church history and ended up in education. The reality is, he must take the blame for both those transitions. The impact of a good teacher cannot be quantified. I had outstanding history teachers in high school and college, hence my interest in church history. But Knight introduced me to a new world and showed me how the two worlds are connected. He also gave me the opportunity to teach my first class, a good way to engage a student. While he was on sabbatical, I had the privilege to substitute for him in several courses, which was pivotal in expanding and redirecting my interests. At the appropriate time, the Cheshire cat sat in a tree above my head and, with his ever-present wry smile, pointed me down a different pathway. Thanks, George, the pathway has given me opportunities for a life of service in education around the world, and though church history is still an interest, I am glad we swapped careers.

### Endnotes

1. While *provocateur* may have negative connotations, the intent here is positive. Knight has not been reticent to confront issues that needed addressing. The Adventist Church has a fairly interesting, circuitous, and—in some instances—checkered history. Knight has provided a challenge to those in the church who agree with him and those who do not to revisit constructively some of the issues Adventism has been wont to "sweep under the carpet."

2. Lewis Carroll, *Alice's Adventures in Wonderland* (1866; repr., New York: Appleton, 1927), 86, 87.

3. George R. Knight, *Philosophy and Education: An Introduction in Christian Perspective* (Berrien Springs, Mich.: Andrews University Press, 1980), v.

4. Ibid., v.

5. For example, in the Andrews University graduate programs in education since the 1990s, there has not been a core degree requirement that focuses specifically on Adventist educational philosophy.

6. Andrews University School of Education maxim, based on Ellen G. White, *Education* (Mountain View, Calif.: Pacific Press®, 1903), 30.

7. "The Lord shall make thee the head, and not the tail" (Deuteronomy 28:13). Ellen White cited Deuteronomy 28:8–13 to encourage obedience to God so the denomination would produce leaders in thought and practice. See Ellen G. White, *The Ministry of Healing* (Nampa, Idaho: Pacific Press®, 1942), 284.

8. George R. Knight, *Philosophy and Education: An Introduction in Christian Perspective* (Berrien Springs, Mich.: Andrews University Press, 2008), xiii.

9. Andrews University Press, e-mail from aupress@andrews.edu to johnmatt@andrews.edu, August 15, 2012.

10. In addition to extensive nonformal educational initiatives, the Adventist Church operates 7,806 formal educational institutions in over one hundred countries (with 1.7 million students in 111 tertiary, 1,823 secondary, and 5,813 elementary institutions). General Conference of Seventh-day Adventists, *148th Annual Statistical Report–2010*, 6, 64, accessed July 17, 2012, http://www. adventistarchives.org/docs/ASR/ASR2010 .pdf.

11. "As a [religious educator] . . . I have become painfully aware that our educators have not really understood our theologians, and our theologians have not been too good at understanding the educators. It appears . . . that our theistic worldview must more fully, understandably, and intentionally inform our philosophy of education." John Matthews, "Thoughts Regarding Two Papers on 'Unique and Defining Themes as Suggested by Adventist Theology' " (response, International Conference on the Seventh-day Adventist Philosophy of Education, Andrews University, Berrien Springs, Mich., April 7–9, 2001). The response was to papers presented by a leading Adventist theologian and a leading Adventist educator.

12. "The full implications of her [Ellen White's] counsel on education and related issues are impossible to grasp without understanding the historical situation in which she wrote." Knight, *Myths in Adventism*, 13.

13. George R. Knight, ed., *Early Adventist Educators* (Berrien Springs, Mich.: Andrews University Press, 1983); Knight, *Myths in Adventism*. A number of authors prepared chapters for *Early Adventist Educators*. Knight contributed a chapter on historical context in Adventist education and a study on White's prophetic role in Adventist education.

14. Knight, *Myths in Adventism*, 13. The second paragraph on page 13 describes Knight's own view of the journey he was taking.

15. George R. Knight, *From 1888 to Apostasy: The Case of A. T. Jones* (Hagerstown, Md.: Review and Herald®, 1987). Also George R. Knight, *Angry Saints: Tensions and Possibilities in the Adventist Struggle Over Righteousness by Faith* (Hagerstown, Md.: Review and Herald®, 1989).

16. The meeting of the General Conference of Seventh-day Adventists in Minneapolis in 1888 was the venue in which concerns in Adventist theology over law and grace were first seriously addressed. Knight sees this meeting as an important factor leading to the rapid expansion of the Adventist educational system in the 1890s (see, e.g., Knight, *Early Adventist Educators*, 33). Some of Knight's writings focus directly on the theological issues of concern at the 1888 conference. See, e.g., note 16 above, and George R. Knight, *I Used to Be Perfect: A Study of Sin and Salvation* (Berrien Springs, Mich.: Andrews University Press, 2001).

17. Van Cleve Morris and Young Pai, *Philosophy and the American School: An Introduction to the Philosophy of Education*, 2nd ed. (Boston: Houghton Mifflin, 1976); George F. Kneller, *Introduction to*

*the Philosophy of Education,* 2nd ed. (New York: John Wiley, 1971).

18. For example, metaphysics is introduced, and then a wide array of approaches to metaphysics is explored before epistemology is considered in any detail. It is not easy to fathom the structure of philosophy by exploring the details of metaphysics without first understanding the nature of the other two major philosophical questions. Morris and Pai, *Philosophy and the American School,* 26–102.

19. In the arena of secular educational philosophy, the writings of John Dewey, Robert Hutchins, George Counts, and the like cannot be ignored. However, none of these authors produced works appropriate for a course in Adventist educational philosophy.

20. John Henry (Cardinal) Newman, *The Idea of a University Defined and Illustrated* (London: Longmans, 1907). The book was first published in two volumes, in 1853 and 1858.

21. Horace Bushnell, *Christian Nurture* (New Haven: Yale University Press, 1916). The book was first published in 1847, and in 1861 it was revised and enlarged.

22. Michael J. Anthony and Warren S. Benson, *Exploring the History and Philosophy of Christian Education: Principles for the 21st Century* (Grand Rapids: Kregel, 2003), 259–283.

23. Lois LeBar, *Education That Is Christian* (Colorado Springs: Chariot Victor, 1995); Frank E. Gaebelein, *The Pattern of God's Truth: The Integration of Faith and Learning* (Chicago: Moody Press, 1968).

24. In the mid-1970s, Arthur F. Holmes published some definitive works that, like Gaebelein's classic, focused on the integration of faith and learning. Another evangelical scholar of importance was Lawrence Richards, whose main interest was the theological rather than philosophical foundations for Christian education. Scholars from the mainline denominations include the renowned George Albert Coe, Randolph Crump Miller, Iris V. Cully, and D. Campbell Wyckoff. By the mid-1970s, none of these authors had published a text appropriate for use in an Adventist course on educational philosophy.

25. Jody Washburn, "Book Review on *Philosophy and Education* by George Knight" (assignment for EDFN500, Andrews University, Berrien Springs, Mich., Fall 2009).

26. Rafal Toczylowski, "Book Review on *Philosophy and Education* by George Knight" (assignment for EDFN500, Andrews University, Berrien Springs, Mich., Summer 2012).

27. Michael J. Anthony and Warren S. Benson, *Exploring the History and Philosophy of Christian Education* (Grand Rapids, Mich.: Kregel Publications, 2003), 12. The hope was expressed that the Anthony and Benson volume in combining the themes of two existing standard books, history and philosophy (Knight's work), in one volume, the subject would seem less "fragmented and disjointed" for students.

# Chapter 3

# George R. Knight and the *Journal of Adventist Education*

Beverly J. Robinson-Rumble

'm not sure when I first met George Knight—it was so long ago. Perhaps it was when I attended one of his fascinating presentations about the early leaders of the Seventh-day Adventist Church. At one of them, I remember hearing him say that he initially viewed the founders of the church as nearly perfect, and became very discouraged about his own failed "attempt to become the first perfect Christian since Christ."[1] But then he began to read the primary sources that have informed much of his historical work over the years, and he found that those pioneers often failed at their undertakings, disagreed among themselves, and made some serious blunders. George's take-away lesson, which has been a continuing source of inspiration to me ever since, was this: *Though they weren't perfect, God still used them in important ways to accomplish His work—and He can use us likewise today!*

George and I started to work together in a formally defined relationship around 1980, shortly after the *Journal of Adventist Education* began to be printed at University Printers on the campus of Andrews University in Berrien Springs, Michigan. Administrators at the university and General Conference Department of Education decided that someone at Andrews should be designated to make decisions about urgent matters relating to the printing of the *Journal* if the editorial staff in Maryland weren't available. Though I don't recall that he was ever called upon to jump in and resolve any such crises (rendering his position largely ceremonial), he cheerfully allowed us to expand his role to that of an official "Advisor" for the publication.

When it came time to visit Andrews University each year to appeal to the professors to write for the *Journal,* I would be sure to schedule an appointment with Knight, knowing that it would produce several hours of stimulating conversation about a wide range of topics, even if it meant sometimes running right through supper! During those discussions, George would offer witty and thoughtful insights about the future of Adventist education and suggest topics he thought the *Journal* ought to tackle. In between my visits to Andrews, I heard from him regularly by letter and phone, and later by e-mail, though usually his secretary, and later his wife, Bonnie, would type the e-mails.

George has always been somewhat technophobic—why, I'm not sure. During most of the time I have known him, he's done his writing on lined yellow legal pads, which then gets transcribed into word-processing documents. I still get handwritten peer reviews from him, however, which I occasionally have to ask my secretary to help me "translate"! Once, I remember, when he was still at Andrews University, he fell off his bicycle and fractured both elbows—disastrous for a writer. It put a serious crimp on his production of handwritten documents for quite a while!

On a number of occasions, our discussions led to his agreement to write for the *Journal,* although sometimes I did have to twist his arm. Not only was he willing to tackle a variety of subjects, he was also always generous about suggesting other potential authors and topics that would be helpful to *Journal* readers.

On one memorable winter day, when I entered the seminary building and trudged down the steps to Knight's basement office, the ground outside was bare, but over the course of a couple of hours, the campus was quietly transformed into a solid blanket of snow with no identifiable landmarks. By the time I emerged from the lively discussion in George's windowless office, I found myself thrust into the whiteout conditions of a blizzard! I recall being terrified that I'd never be able to find my way back to my rental car or even identify it. There were no cell phones in those days, so George had no idea I was in danger of getting lost trying to navigate a couple of hundred feet of campus.

Because the *Journal of Adventist Education* has no travel budget for its advisory board members, and George has never lived in Maryland, we have been unable to invite him to serve on its board. I regret this—his contributions would have been invaluable. His "official advisor" classification lasted only a few years at Andrews but since then, on an unofficial basis, he has expressed consistent and tangible support for the magazine, lauding its virtues publically as a high-quality periodical with the potential for shaping the worldwide work of education by the Seventh-day Adventist Church.

Over the years, George has been one of the *Journal of Adventist Education*'s most published authors. He has written twenty-nine articles, book reviews, and guest editorials for the *Journal*. A sampling reveals their diversity: "The Great Disappearance—Adventism and Noncombatancy," "Jesus—The Teacher Who Failed," "Work Experience in the Elementary School," "A System in Search of Identity," "Teaching a Theology of the Center Versus a Theology of the Edges," "Adventist Agricultural Programs," and "The Missiological Roots of Adventist Higher Education and the Ongoing Tension Between Adventist Mission and Academic Vision."

Prompted by observations made during his wide travels, Knight himself sometimes suggested the topics. Some originated from his lectures to diverse audiences in the church or to his seminary classes, and others resulted from the research for his many books. Occasionally, he adapted presentations he had made to teacher conventions or local meetings, such as the one titled "Two Ministries, One Mission" from the Atlantic Union Conference Pastor/Teacher Convention held in Providence, Rhode Island, in August 2009, which *Ministry* magazine also published.

The editorial staff of the *Journal* has occasionally asked George to write a promotional article about Adventist education that we could include in the special issue of the magazine produced for each General Conference session, or for a theme issue, such as the manuscript he wrote for the October/November 1994 issue commemorating the 150th anniversary of the Great Disappointment: "William Miller and the Rise of Adventism." Other articles have grown out of his book research and varied interests. Occasionally, when I couldn't find anyone to write about a topic I viewed as important, I was able to talk him into tackling it.

The longest and by far the most complex articles George wrote for the *Journal* were a three-part continuing education series on "The Philosophy of Adventist Education," published in an expanded sixty-four-page October/November 2010 theme issue and subsequently translated into French, Spanish, and Portuguese. Almost three years later, the articles continue to function as continuing education study materials. Upon successful completion of a test on each section, North American Division K–12 teachers can earn credit toward denominational recertification. Board chairs and administrators worldwide also use this excellent material to help new teachers and board members understand their responsibilities in Adventist education.

Comprising almost 150 typed pages (with dozens of endnotes in each section, as well as several graphs and charts), plus a test and key for each part, this project was nearly equivalent to writing a book. It eventually stretched over several years. During this time, George was so busy that he wasn't always able to "put it on the front burner" as he'd promised. In fact, the project took so long that the General Conference legal department started threatening to review the contract we'd signed with him to produce the material! When he finally did submit the three manuscripts, it took a number of months to get the material peer reviewed, engage in some back-and-forth with George about the reviewers' recommendations, and then get the manuscripts edited and copy edited. So pressured were we all for time that I found myself having to make arrangements to meet George in a hallway at the General Conference Session in Atlanta to resolve some final questions before the manuscript could go to press!

Because Knight also had to create tests and keys for each of the three sections of the philosophy issue, this dragged out the project even further. Finally, when it was done, he mused, "I'm glad I did it, but I did some kosher swearing in the process"—to which I responded, "I did too!"

George is a professional writer. For me, that means not needing to undertake the sort of massive overhaul of his manuscripts that other articles often require. Knight also has a keen proprietary interest in what comes out under his name. He insists on approving all changes made by the editor, and reviews each manuscript before it goes to press, which is not a problem for us, as it is the *Journal*'s policy to send edited articles back to every author to examine. Probably based on some negative experiences, I'm sure that he suspects that some editors can revise his writing in ways that inadvertently change its meaning or that make it unrecognizable, so he wants to make sure he knows exactly what the final version of each document will look like. Like many an author, he has occasionally gotten a little grumpy about recommendations for revision by peer reviewers, but usually grudgingly admits that they did have a legitimate point and their suggestions strengthened the manuscript.

It was a particularly challenging assignment for me to edit George's lengthy documents on educational philosophy, as I'm certainly not an expert on the subject. But I could identify areas that needed clarification or expansion, and so he and I would go back and forth about the best way to express various ideas accurately (based on his vast study of the subject, which has been compiled into several books), and to ensure that the wording was comprehensible to readers with little background in philosophy (my area of expertise as an editor). Sometimes I'd have to say, "George, that's *still* not clear," and we'd go back over it again. While I don't remember ever having to drag myself through as many revisions of his manuscripts as I have with some authors on occasion, we have had some lively and extended discussions by phone and e-mail in order to arrive at exactly the right way to express a concept.

George's *Journal of Adventist Education* articles often drew their helpful conclusions from research he had done on the early events of Adventist education, which he then applied to modern problems and challenges. Not infrequently, the topics dealt with issues that were quite current. For example, in February 2007, George and I both attended a meeting of the North American Division college and university presidents in Orlando, Florida (he was a presenter, I was an invited guest). In one of the presentations, we heard one of the administrators declare that Adventists needed to focus on Jesus and get rid of all this "apocalyptic emphasis." My mouth fell open, and my eyes were drawn to George, who I found was also looking directly at me and smiling enigmatically. The reason for our reaction? Just a few months before, I had edited George's two-part article "Adventism and the Apocalyptic Vision," to be published in the *Journal of Adventist Education* just a few months later. In the article, he had he argued that "it is Adventism's understanding of being a prophetic people that led generations of its young people to give their lives in obscure mission fields and that led older church members to sacrifice not only their children but also their financial means to fulfill the prophetic imperative.

"It is that vision that has made Adventism a dynamic, worldwide movement. When that vision is lost, Adventism will become merely another somewhat toothless denomination. The losing of the apocalyptic vision and Adventism's place in prophetic history is the greatest threat that Adventism and its educational system face as they enter the 21st century."[2]

Over the years, Knight has enjoyed shocking people through the use of startling and sometimes controversial illustrations and topics. I believe his objective in doing so has been to catch his readers' attention and to get them to think. Several book titles come to mind: *The Fat Lady and the Kingdom; Myths in Adventism; I Used to Be Perfect: A Study of Sin and Salvation; Organizing to Beat the Devil; The Apocalyptic Vision and the Neutering of Adventism; The Pharisee's Guide to Perfect Holiness;* and *Angry Saints.*

Decades after it was written, one of those shocking illustrations is still indelibly fixed in my memory. It appeared in George's 1990 book *My Gripe With God* (updated as his 2008 book *The Cross of Christ: God's Work for Us*). In vivid detail, he described how, following a particularly moving church service, he felt inspired to lure his beloved cockapoo, Scotty, to the basement. Putting his hands on the dog's head, he confessed his sins and then slit the dog's throat in order to "catch the vividness of what the Old Testament sacrificial service must have meant to Adam and Eve and to those subsequent Israelites who maintained sensitivity to the meaning of the sacrificial system." He went on to graphically describe his devastation and nausea at seeing the dog's "arteries pumping out his remaining blood—every throb thundering in my ears the message that 'the wages of sin is death.' " At the end of the illustration, thankfully, George added, *"I hope you realize that the above story is completely fictitious"!*[3]

George's most memorable contribution to the *Journal of Adventist Education* fits the "controversial" classification very well. The article was based on his presentation at an Adventist Philosophy of Education Seminar at Andrews University in 2001. Each seminar presentation subsequently garnered lavish praise when published in the *Journal of Research on Christian Education.* This lured me into complacency about the potential impact of George's presentation on a broader group of readers. The article, "Adolf Hitler and Ellen White 'Agree' on the Purposes of Adventist Education," appeared in the October/November 2002 issue and was subsequently posted with permission on the *Adventist Review* Web site. There it generated numerous impassioned e-mails as well as a few demands that it be removed, mostly from people who appeared to be reacting to the title rather than the content. In addition to the *Adventist Review* responses, a flurry of outraged letters and e-mails also arrived in my office. One letter writer accused the article of being "nothing but [an] apology [for] the Nazi theories." Another claimed it had "caused significant damage and embarrassment." One person contacted the director of education to demand that we print a retraction. Belatedly, I recognized that we probably should have at least refrained from featuring the title on the cover of the *Journal*. One teacher declared that she had to turn the issue face-down on her desk when conducting parent-teacher conferences.

The point of the article (apparently missed by many readers) was that educators need to look at the overall philosophy of an author, not just excerpts from what he or she says in order to determine whether the underlying principles agree with a biblical worldview, and whether the author's philosophy deserves to be implemented in the Adventist classroom.

The article did generate several positive critiques—one writer described it as a "great article" and said it would be used in crafting his conference's mission statement. And several people who discovered that it had been removed from the *Adventist Review* Web site contacted my office to request a paper copy.

The letters' allegations stimulated lengthy discussions between George and me regarding how to respond. The *Journal* declined to issue a retraction, but we did print three pages of letters/e-mails in the Summer 2003 issue, in which Knight, too, weighed in, citing his astonishment that readers would accuse him of "praising Hitler," when the article contained statements like this one comparing the Adventist emphasis on principles of health with Hitler's praise of clean living: "Hitler . . . valued physical health because it made better soldiers, better killers. For him, character meant mindless obedience so that any order would be carried out, even to the cold-blooded murder of innocent men, women, and children." George cited as the source of his inspiration for the seminar presentation his Jewish doctoral advisor, Joshua Weinstein, who had been born in Jerusalem in the 1920s and had been a freedom fighter in the Israeli liberation movement in the 1940s. Weinstein had helped him to see that even good educational ideas can be put to diabolical ends—that it is philosophy that makes the difference and not mere words.

George responded to a reader who "deplored" his use of an "attention ploy" *that this was the point*—that two people with such different philosophies as Hitler and Ellen White could use the same words and even the same ideas provides an absolutely crucial lesson we need to understand.

As George and I worked to assemble a "Letters to the Editor" column, two things contributed a little levity to the uproar over the article: (1) his colleagues at Andrews named him "Teacher of the Year" and (2) I revealed to him that we'd printed the article in part because the *Journal* Advisory Board recommended that the editor publish "more controversial material" (a suggestion they didn't reiterate after the fallout from this article!). I appreciated the fact that Knight took the reactions of the writers seriously and responded to them respectfully, even when he needed to forcefully debunk the allegations. But his *Journal* articles since then have generally employed slightly tamer illustrations.

In the decades since 1980, George Knight has consistently been one of several persons I regard as most influential in shaping the direction of the *Journal of Adventist Education.* His outspoken support for and contributions to the integration of faith and learning have made a permanent and positive impact on Adventist education, as well as on the content of the *Journal.* He has always given generously of his time to answer questions, suggest topics and themes, and to peer review articles. In addition, he's prayed with me and encouraged me when I've been discouraged. George's books continue to inspire and guide my Christian walk.

I feel humbled and honored by his enthusiastic endorsement of the *Journal* because the affirmations come from an accomplished writer and widely respected educational philosopher. It's impossible for me to fully describe how much I have appreciated his personal support and his contributions to the *Journal* and the church over many decades. His friendship is deeply valued, and I wish him well as he "semiretires."

A few months ago, while considering what I might to do keep busy after I officially retire later this year, I offered to help George with research for or editing of his future manuscripts, and he implied that he might take me up on that. More recently, he told me that he plans to cut his writing to a minimum, but if he "repents" of that decision (as he implied that he might), then perhaps there'll be yet another project on which we'll collaborate. If so, I would regard it as a great honor to work with him again.

## Endnotes

1. George R. Knight, *The Pharisee's Guide to Perfect Holiness* (Nampa, Idaho: Pacific Press®, 1992), 131.

2. George R. Knight, "Adventism and the Apocalyptic Vision," pt. 1, *Journal of Adventist Education* (April–May 2007): 8.

3. George R. Knight, "The Bible's Most Disgusting Teaching," in *The Cross of Christ* (Hagerstown, Md.: Review and Herald®, 2008), 44, 45.

# Chapter 4

# George R. Knight as a Teacher

Jerry A. Moon

I n one of his trademark exaggerations, George Knight quipped almost apologetically, "I was basically a writer, and teaching was a job to support my 'habit.'"[1] The wisecrack has a kernel of truth: the size of the Adventist book market means that Knight has always earned more from his teaching than from his writing.[2] But as much as he loves writing, he is also passionate about teaching. He has given thirty-seven years of his salaried life to teaching, plus another eight years after retirement, for contract pay or on a completely volunteer basis.

The above quotation, however, does suggest several of Knight's characteristics: (1) He has a lively sense of humor. (2) He loves words and wordplay; note, for example, the irony of the word *habit*. (3) As a teacher and public speaker, he is never tedious, boring, or bland. He always has something fresh to present. (4) While his penchant for being deliberately provocative makes him a fascinating lecturer in the classroom, it makes him a lightning rod for controversy out in the churches. Listeners who do not know him well can easily miss significant nuances in his humor, vocabulary, or figures of speech. Especially in translation, crucial distinctions can be lost or distorted. (5) Finally, George has spent many thousands of hours researching the primary sources of Adventist history. That doesn't mean he is always right! But because he is a formidable logician with a prodigious memory, even those who disagree with him cannot easily dismiss him.

Had Knight not recorded the fruits of his teaching in a plethora of publications, he might have been legendary among his students, but little known out of school. But forty-plus years of distinguished teaching and publishing have made him a magisterial figure in Seventh-day Adventist educational philosophy, church history, and historical theology. He has taught extension courses for Andrews University all over North America, and in other Adventist colleges and seminaries literally from Australia to Zimbabwe. For many years, he spent as much as one-third of his teaching load each year teaching in remote places where pastors did not have access to an Adventist seminary. George actively sought these opportunities for the exposure they gave him to the world church and the wide diversity of Adventism. Locations were selected at his discretion and by careful planning he could combine multiple places in one trip. Thousands of pastors and teachers took his classes. Thus, his teaching has exerted a massive influence on the thought leaders of Adventism, while his books and articles have shaped the disciplines of educational philosophy and the history of Adventist thought, lifestyle, and theology.[3]

During his first ten years at Andrews University, 1976–1985, Knight taught in the School of Education, published two books on a Christian philosophy of education (both of which are still in print in their fourth editions),[4] and advanced to professor of Educational Foundations. Besides teaching and writing, he compiled a comprehensive list of the most important scholarly literature in his field and by a rigorous regimen of reading—six and more hours a day for most of the decade— he laid the foundation for his subsequent teaching and writing.[5] In 1985, he published *Myths in Adventism,* his first book on Adventist history, and moved across campus from the Andrews University School of Education to the Church History Department of the seminary, where he taught Development of Seventh-day Adventist Theology, Development of Seventh-day Adventist Lifestyle, History of Religious Liberty, several doctoral seminars, and a variety of other courses.

The following sketches of Knight in the classroom came from courses I took during 1987 through 1989. His syllabi were simple, three or four pages typewritten, but rigorous. He typically required the reading of three or four textbooks, a major term paper, and essay examinations. Wise students scheduled their homework for the entire term and began immediately.

Students of today, accustomed to classrooms wired for Internet and lectures presented in PowerPoint, might be surprised to see Knight walk in with a sheaf of yellow paper covered with handwritten notes. But if anyone feared he would be dull or tedious, he quickly laid those fears to rest. He could read his manuscript with as much zest and energy as an actor declaiming to a packed house.

Knight's persona in the classroom was confident, exuberant, and unsympathetic to slackers. His keen mind, vast knowledge, and perfect confidence made him a fearsome and fascinating figure. For example, early in one term, George called out by name, from a large class, a new doctoral student, by a simple, direct question: "When was Ellen White born?" Momentarily frozen, the student wondered whether Knight wanted the date generally accepted by historical scholars, or the account of two competing dates, one erroneously entered in the Harmon family Bible, and the other an engraver's error on her twin sister's tombstone. While he hesitated, George rolled on. "What? You a doctoral student and don't know when Ellen White was born?" Such incidents both intimidated the hapless victim and entertained the onlookers.

Note-taking from Knight was a challenge. Other lecturers, speaking from an outline, would repeat themselves several times on each major point, making it easier to keep up with the main ideas. But Knight's manuscript read like one of his books—rapid fire, varied vocabulary, and very little repetition. To take good notes, one had to work fast and stay focused.

Knight did not appreciate interruptions. He told students to either come on time or don't come at all. He refused to take record of attendance. Only boring teachers or easy teachers took record of attendance, and he would be neither. But if you thought you could pass without attending class, good luck.

In 2003, Knight was voted the "first Seminary faculty recipient of the Daniel Augsburger Excellence in Teaching Award and 'Teacher of the Year.' "[6] In 2006, he received Andrews University's thirty-year service award. The tribute called him "a great teacher, a riveting lecturer, a rigorous but absolutely fair dissertation advisor, a scholar whose publication productivity outstripped the rest of the department combined, and a wonderful colleague who is generous with his mentoring time and expertise." It also noted that "his students hold influential positions all over the world."[7]

A major aspect of Knight's teaching was his mentoring of doctoral students. Some professors were known to take a month, three months, or, in rare cases, even a year to get a dissertation chapter read and returned to the student. George saw such delays as dereliction of duty, a moral and ethical sin. Holding himself responsible for guarding students' time, tuition, and life span, he aimed for a turnaround time of one week. If the manuscript was too bad to correct all at once, he would read and mark eight pages and return the chapter to the student, saying, "I've read these first eight pages. You can do better. I've corrected your punctuation and spelling and given you some ideas; redo these eight pages. We will stay on these pages until they are right."[8] Thus he kept students moving and on task. He conducted a doctoral-level course in research and writing for which he received no remuneration except the satisfaction of seeing his students succeed. He also cared about his students' personal lives. One day he met me coming out of the library. "What's the matter, Jerry?" he boomed. "Nothing looks much worse than a doctoral student turning green from too many hours in the library!" His prescription followed immediately: "Go out on a hill overlooking the lake, spread your poncho on the grass, lie down, and spend an hour or two watching the clouds go by."

A dissertation defense with Knight was always memorable. My first such observation came at a classmate's defense, shortly after Dr. Knight had consented to be my advisor. Six faculty members were involved: three from the student's dissertation committee (the advisor and two other readers); a fourth reader from the Andrews faculty; an external examiner from another university; and the director of the PhD and ThD programs presiding. In this case, Knight was the fourth reader. I learned later that the dissertation committee had tried to persuade the candidate that the dissertation was not ready for defense. But the student was adamant, insisting there was no need for further revisions. At length the dissertation committee broke the stalemate by authorizing the defense. The defense seemed to be going smoothly until Dr. Knight had his turn at questioning the student. In a few minutes, he dismantled the dissertation, exposed its flawed methodology, and left the others to pick up the pieces. The final verdict was "pass with major revisions," namely the complete rewriting of one of the chapters. I left that room on the third floor of the library and followed George to the stairs. "I'm so glad you are going to be my advisor," I told him. "I trust that in my dissertation we will get all these defects removed *before* the defense."

All of George's doctoral students can tell stories of his thorough mentoring during the doctoral program and continued mentoring for years to come. As a high-profile scholar, Knight received frequent invitations to write an encyclopedia article, a book review, or other scholarly writing. Many such invitations he would pass on to one of his students. The most memorable such referral that happened to me came in the fall of 2000. I still remember the room where Knight met with Denis Fortin and me and explained his predicament. He was planning to retire in a few years and his "yet to be written" book list included over sixty titles, one of which was a proposed *Ellen G. White Encyclopedia*. Since that was to be written by many authors and he would be only the editor, he thought it could be delegated, and wondered if Denis and I would be interested in co-editing it. Our eager acceptance set the research agenda for both of us for more than a decade.[9]

Knight has characterized his stance within Adventism as a "radical conservative." He considers himself a "conservative" in terms of his loyalty to historical truth and values, but "radical" in that he uses historical truth to assertively prod the church and its educational system toward what he sees as needed change. When he discovered that the Adventist "past" could be retold in ways that would influence the church's "present" and "future," he began to use Adventist history strategically as a tool to change the church. For example, in the mid-1980s, when the church was rocked with controversy over the doctrine of the sanctuary, the role of Ellen White, and a financial scandal, George brought out *Myths in Adventism*, which quickly became an Adventist bestseller.[10] While some considered it revisionist, not a few thanked Knight that his historical perspective and good sense had helped to stabilize their faith through the crisis.

People have been trying ever since to figure out where Knight belongs on the spectrum of Adventist thought. While he writes on many conservative topics, he gives them titles such as *If I Were the Devil*,[11] *My Gripe With God*,[12] and "The Infinite Hitler."[13] His obvious relish for the role of intellectual provocateur has led some conservatives to question his motivations. But for everyone who finds George too far to the left, there are others who find him too far to the right. For example, a certain Adventist college invited him to present a Week of Spiritual Emphasis. He started off with the prophecy of Daniel 2 and announced his intention to preach on Daniel 7, 8, 9, and Revelation 12 and 13 during the rest of the week. Some of the faculty took him aside after the first sermon. "You can't preach that here," they urged. "We don't believe that anymore." He retorted, "You should have thought of that before you invited me. I believe it and I'm going to preach it."[14]

His book *The Apocalyptic Vision and the Neutering of Adventism* (2008) is a protest against the tendency to downplay Adventist prophetic interpretation.[15] The book was prompted by a treasured acquaintance who appeared to be wavering on the belief that Adventism is, in any transcending way, unique. George labored to change his mind, and when he didn't immediately succeed, he went home and wrote *The Neutering of Adventism*. Thus, his teaching and writing exemplify another of his adages, that when you are being shot at from both sides, you are probably striking the right balance between the two extremes. He is a strong advocate for a centrist Adventism that has points of agreement with both the "left" and the "right," but can also be critical of both the left and the right. The only way to avoid controversy, in George's way of thinking, is to never say anything "meaningful," that is, change-producing.[16]

But George can weather storms of criticism more easily than he could stand being irrelevant. Perhaps that is one reason he feels such a strong attachment for Ellen White, whom he has spent so much of his life studying. She once began a controversial speech by saying, "I know that which I now speak will bring me into conflict. This I do not covet, for the conflict has seemed to be continuous of late years; but I do not mean to live a coward or die a coward, leaving my work undone."[17] Knight has this in common with Ellen White: he, too, refuses to live or die a "coward," and in his "retirement" he still works twelve-hour days determined not to leave his "work undone."

### Endnotes

1. George R. Knight, "Dissertation Advising" (presentation, Andrews University, March 29, 2013); my notes, 2.

2. In the interest of full disclosure, I need to acknowledge multiple debts to Dr. Knight. First, he was my PhD dissertation advisor. Then, when my intended dissertation topic did not prove to be workable, he suggested a prime subject that he himself had intended to write on (W. C. White). He spent hundreds of hours coaching and constructively criticizing my efforts at scholarly writing. Both before and after graduation, he referred me to people with publication opportunities, mentored me, and gave me fatherly counsel. (Some of which I ignored, to my regret.) For all these reasons, this article makes no claim to objectivity, though I have tried to write as honestly as I can.

3. Knight also addressed nondenominational groups of Christian educators, such as the Wisconsin Association of Non-Public Schools. Such presentations dealt with such perennial topics as redemptive discipline and teaching moral values, but a surprising number were on specifically Adventist topics, such as "Seventh-day Adventist Education: An Historical Perspective" (presentation to American Educational Research Association, Chicago, Ill., April 3, 1985). George R. Knight, "Vita," March 2012, 33–37

(section "Scholarly and/or Professional Papers Presented").

4. George R. Knight, *Philosophy and Education: An Introduction in Christian Perspective* (Berrien Springs, Mich.: Andrews University Press, 1980; 2nd ed. 1989; 3rd ed. 1998; 4th ed. 2006). Knight, *Issues and Alternatives in Educational Philosophy* (Berrien Springs, Mich.: Andrews University Press, 1982; 2nd ed. 1989; 3rd ed. 1998; 4th ed. 2008).

5. As told to me by George R. Knight.

6. John K. McVay, dean of the seminary, Andrews University, March 9, 2003.

7. Thirty-year service award tribute to George R. Knight, by Daniel Agnetta, director of Human Resources, Andrews University, 2006.

8. Knight, "Dissertation Advising" (presentation, Andrews University, March 29, 2013); my notes, 4. For similar material, see George Knight, "The Doctoral Student's Mentor" (dissertation advising seminar, Andrews University, 2007).

9. Denis Fortin and Jerry Moon, eds., *Ellen G. White Encyclopedia* (Hagerstown, Md.: Review and Herald®, 2014) includes some 1,200 articles by about 180 authors, many of them experts in the topics they wrote on.

10. George R. Knight, *Myths in Adventism: An Interpretive Study of Ellen White, Education, and Related Issues* (Washington, D.C.: Review and Herald®, 1985).

11. George R. Knight, *If I Were the Devil* (Hagerstown, Md.: Review and Herald®, 2007).

12. George R. Knight, *My Gripe With God: A Study in Divine Justice and the Problem of the Cross* (Washington, D.C.: Review and Herald®, 1990).

13. "The Infinite Hitler," *Signs of the Times,* July 1997, 10–13. This article on the biblical doctrine of hell won an Award of Merit (June 1998) from the Associated Church Press. Knight, "Vita," March 2013, 4 (section "Academic Honors and Awards").

14. As told to me by George R. Knight.

15. George R. Knight, *The Apocalyptic Vision and the Neutering of Adventism* (Hagerstown, Md.: Review and Herald®, 2008; rev. ed. 2009).

16. George R. Knight, "The Doctoral Student's Mentor" (dissertation advising seminar, Andrews University, 2007), 1.

17. Ellen G. White, *The Southern Work* (Washington, D.C.: Review and Herald®, 1966), 9–11. White read the speech on March 21, 1891, to thirty denominational leaders just before a General Conference session in Battle Creek, Michigan.

# Chapter 5

# George Knight as a Historian

Brian E. Strayer

lthough most professional historians enter academia through the "front door" with BA, MA, or PhD degrees in history, George Knight came through the "back door" with a BA in religion, MA and MDiv degrees in theology and Christian philosophy, and an EdD degree in the history and philosophy of education. As the American educator John Dewey would say, George has "learned by doing" how to write Adventist history. By all accounts, he has done it very well.

In fact, the popularity of his books among Adventists has enabled him to recycle many of his monographs on church history. A quarter century after *From 1888 to Apostasy* was published in 1987, it reappeared in 2011 as *A. T. Jones: Point Man for Adventism's Charismatic Frontier*. *Millennial Fever and the End of the World* (1993) returned seventeen years later as *William Miller and the Rise of Adventism* (2010). His popular *Anticipating the Advent* (1993) was repackaged only six years later as *A Brief History of Seventh-day Adventists* (1999), while *Organizing to Beat the Devil* (2001) was resurrected five years later as *Organizing for Mission and*

*Growth* (2006).[1] In each case, new covers and minor revisions to the text enabled the Review and Herald® Publishing Association or Pacific Press® Publishing Association (only a handful of George's books have been published by Pacific Press®)[2] to sell them to new readers in Knight's growing group of admirers.

Certain elements that characterize Knight's style account for the growing popularity of his historical works among Adventist readers. Reviewers (including church officials, pastors, academics, and historians) agree that his books are "clear and readable," offering "fascinating insights" and "interesting historical details" for the average layperson who typically avoids historical books.[3] Adventist scholars admire his penchant for treating controversial issues (the Shut Door, the 1888 General Conference, reorganization in 1901, Ellen White's inspiration, etc.) in an "open, honest, unemotional" manner while avoiding "obvious ideological biases." Instead, Knight occupies the "middle ground" between "harsh criticism" and "defensive apology" in his writing. In addition, his books, which usually correct misunderstandings about the past (*Myths in Adventism*), highlight lessons to be learned from the pioneers (*Joseph Bates, A. T. Jones*), analyze formative eras in Adventist history (*Millennial Fever, Development of Adventist Church Structure*), advance our understanding of prophetic interpretation (his four-volume set on Ellen White), and are based on scholarly research in primary and secondary sources related to Millerism and Seventh-day Adventism.[4]

Among other qualities, readers admire Knight's narrative and biographical (but not hagiographic) approach to history. His interpretation of the Adventist past focuses on key pioneers (*Early Adventist Educators, A. T. Jones, Millennial Fever*, the *Ellen White* set, *Joseph Bates*) without making heroes of them or whitewashing their mistakes and idiosyncrasies. Instead, he earns high marks for correcting erroneous ideas in a balanced manner and for covering broad historical periods succinctly and insightfully. In addition, readers applaud his method of making the past relevant by highlighting key issues (congregationalism, fanaticism, top-heavy bureaucracy, materialism, etc.) that the church still faces today.[5]

However, the fact that all of Knight's books have been published by Adventist presses makes him "a very big fish in a rather small pond." Outside Adventist circles, his books are largely irrelevant to Christians of other faiths and virtually unknown to secular historians. The one exception, *Millennial Fever*, was reviewed in 1995 by two eminent scholars. In the *American Historical Review*, David L. Rowe (Middle Tennessee State University) disapproved of his title ("fever" was "a sign of pathology") and his "devotional tone" (ardent dedication to Adventism) but praised the book for bridging the chasm between older, biased treatments such as Clara Endicott Sears's *Days of Delusion* (1924), Adventist apologetics such as F. D. Nichols's *Midnight Cry* (1944), and recent scholarly histories of the movement by Clyde Hewitt, David Rowe, Michael Barkun, Ruth Doan, and an edited work by Ron Numbers and Jonathan Butler.[6] *Millennial Fever,* he asserted, testified not only to its author's ability to synthesize huge amounts of material, analyze Millerism from a national perspective, and consider even-handedly the radical and fanatical roots of Sabbatarian Adventism, but it also reflected "a mark of a mature denomination, secure in its faith," capable of accurately interpreting its past.[7] Hopefully, this commendation will convince Knight (and other Adventist historians) that publishing their work in secular journals and with university presses is truly a form of academic witnessing.

In the *Journal of American History,* Michael Barkun (Syracuse University) agreed with Rowe that Knight "is fully conversant with the new literature and uses it to good effect"; that his narrative "is clear, accessible, and abundantly documented"; and that his book presents "a clear, reliable account of an important religious movement." Nonetheless, Barkun faulted Knight for certain "defects of omission": he provides "little in the way of interpretive position" and does "little to resolve [scholars'] sometimes conflicting views." Consequently, while the book was "rich" in the "what" (names, dates, events), it fell far short in providing the "why" (analysis of cause and effect factors).[8]

Even within Adventist circles, some scholars who praise Knight for balanced treatment of controversial issues have prodded him to go deeper and broader in his research and interpretation of the past. Although *Myths in Adventism* (1985) examined nineteen misunderstandings related to Ellen White and Adventist education, Steve Daily (then chaplain at La Sierra University) felt that it failed to address White's own inconsistencies, the development of her thought over time, and the "mega-myth" that studying her writings "frees us from the continuing responsibility of doing creative moral thinking."[9] In his review of *From 1888 to Apostasy: The Case of A. T. Jones,* Ben McArthur (History chair at Southern Adventist University) faulted Knight for not addressing the political role of Ellen White within the denomination or explaining how bureaucratic organizations dealt with nonconformity in order to understand how someone like Jones, with his "unconventional and abrasive ways," could have become so prominent in the first place.[10]

Frederick Hoyt (La Sierra University) suggested that the answer to Jones's idiosyncrasies within Adventism lay buried in his childhood, youth, and young manhood, but since Knight did not examine the relevant sources for his pre-Adventist years (school, army, land, court, and genealogical records), his biography was "seriously flawed." A quarter century later when the book was republished as *A. T. Jones: Point Man for Adventism's Charismatic Frontier* (2011), this crucial part of Jones's life had still not been analyzed. Hopefully in the book's third reincarnation, it will be.[11]

Three Adventist historians also reviewed *Millennial Fever and the End of the World* (1993). Brian Strayer (Andrews University), who praised the author for his thorough research (the book has 912 endnotes), expressed disappointment that it had no bibliography (a common characteristic of his books). Although Knight had admirably explained the post-1844 relationship between Millerism and Shakerism, he had not done the same for Millerism and Spiritualism.[12] Likewise, Doug Morgan (Washington Adventist University) faulted Knight for not referencing Nathan Hatch, George Marsden, and Mark Noll in his discussion of Common Sense Realism and the individualization of conscience in Antebellum America to show how Millerism tapped into the intellectual and spiritual currents of that era.[13] Finally, Ben McArthur (Southern Adventist University), who considered *Millennial Fever* the most complete Millerite history yet written, praised Knight for focusing on the inner dynamics of the movement, seeing Millerism as "a radical movement," and addressing unapologetically both believers and critical audiences.[14]

*Ellen White's World* (1998)—the third volume in a set focusing on White's life and writings[15]—provides a contextual study of some of the key individuals, issues, reforms, and events that occurred between 1827 and 1915. However, although Knight does a credible job of surveying the religious, social, cultural, and intellectual landscape of nineteenth-century America, one reviewer regretted that he omitted the political influences of the time (except for the Anti-Slavery movement). He also decried the absence of endnotes and a bibliography for "the serious student of history" (a frequent litany voiced by scholars).[16]

A glance at the tables of contents for Knight's historical works reveals his predilection for the nineteenth over the twentieth century in the history of the Adventist church. Indeed, he consistently devotes more pages to the Millerite movement and to the events and personalities surrounding the 1888 General Conference than he does to any other single event in the church's past. In *A Brief History of Seventh-day*

*Adventists* (1999), he devotes 110 pages to sixty years (1840–1900) in the nineteenth century (71 percent) but only forty-six pages to the entire twentieth century (29 percent). In so doing, he positions himself squarely within the camp of previous church historians (Loughborough, Nichol, Maxwell, and Moon among them) who focused their research primarily on the nineteenth century. What the twenty-first century Adventist Church needs are historians who will help it understand the issues, events, and trends of the twentieth century.[17]

Finally, Knight's latest biography, *Joseph Bates: The Real Founder of Seventh-day Adventism* (2004)—the second volume in the Review and Herald's Adventist Pioneer Series of which he is the editor—has garnered some criticism from at least one historian. Frederick Hoyt (La Sierra University), although praising Knight's thorough research and balanced treatment of Bates, strongly disagreed with the subtitle, asserting that no Adventist pioneer ever attributed such high praise to Bates.[18]

Although readers and reviewers alike applaud Knight for his provocative, insightful, and fascinating historical narratives, it is difficult to place him in a specific school of interpretation. While he has written about the parallels between Marxism and Adventism, George is *not* a neo-Marxist or Socialist historian.[19] Likewise, even though his narrative style, emphasis on biographies, and devotional tone resembles predecessors like J. N. Loughborough, F. D. Nichol, and C. Mervyn Maxwell, Knight is not an apologetic historian who whitewashes the past as they often did. Nor is he in the camp of the Whigs who present heroes who can do no wrong; his biographies of Ellen White, Joseph Bates, and A. T. Jones portray the pioneers "warts and all" as "crusty old saints" whose failures can teach us lessons today. Despite his frequent criticisms of the pioneers' mistakes, neither can Knight be classified with those who attack the church and its teachings (D. M. Canright, Walter Rea, Dale Ratzlaff). Perhaps he should be considered a Revisionist Utilitarian Historian, for while Knight attacks Adventist myths, he also seeks to apply past lessons to the present. In a paper presented at a Seminary Scholarship Symposium in 2009, he challenged historians to share "a usable past" with the Adventist laity.[20]

Like the title of Otto Bettmann's *The Good Old Days—They Were Terrible!* that became a model for his book *The World of Ellen White* (1998), Knight portrays the Adventist past as full of complexities, contradictions, and challenges.[21] Indeed, if there is a golden thread that ties his historical writings together, it might be his perennial focus on watershed events that changed the trajectory of Adventism over the past 150 years. He likes to sprinkle such words as "transformation," "dynamic," and "crisis" in his articles and books.[22] Some of his favorite turning points in the Adventist past include the impact of faith healing,[23] fanaticism among the Millerites,[24] debates about organization and reorganization,[25] conflicts at the 1888 General Conference,[26] and controversy concerning the publication of *Questions on Doctrine* in 1957.[27]

In addition to his penchant for controversy, Knight's provocative style flavors his historical narratives, making them more palatable—and salable—to Adventist readers. Rather than beginning with a narrative hook or a nifty quotation, he prefers to surprise readers with shocking statements. In *Early Adventist Educators* (1983), he calls Ellen White's 1872 testimony "one of the most unbalanced statements" she ever made; indeed, he asserts, she "did not understand the full implications" of it herself at the time.[28] In *Myths in Adventism* (1985), he confesses that "some readers will probably label me a hopeless conservative, while others will undoubtedly believe that I am a wild-eyed liberal of the most dangerous proportions. I trust that I am neither."[29] He declares that "*Questions on Doctrine* easily qualifies as the most divisive book in Seventh-day Adventist history."[30] Doubtless many Adventist pastors gasped when they read Knight's assertion that God is a socialist;[31] he also declared that "most of the founders of Seventh-day Adventism would not be able to join the church today if they had to agree to the denomination's '27 Fundamental Beliefs.' "[32] Until George enlightened them, some academics may not have realized that the individuals who contributed the four "pillar doctrines" (Sabbath, Second Advent, sanctuary, and state of the dead) never joined the Sabbatarian Adventist movement.[33] Finally, after reminding readers that in the church's history reorganization has always furthered mission goals, Knight raised the provocative question, "Will Adventism in the twenty-first century gain its identity from its structures (and institutions) or from its mission?"[34]

While secular historians have expressed discomfort at Knight's ardent tone and some Adventist scholars find his provocative statements disturbing, his sometimes informal style has wide appeal among devoted lay readers. His scholarly biography of Joseph Bates, for example, is sprinkled with catchy expressions or plays on words such as "the Connexion Connection," "the real bomb was yet to be dropped," and "gathering in the who's who of Sabbatarian Adventism," phrases most scholars would avoid.[35] Yet it is the folksy prose and down-home mannerisms of this "gentle Jeremiah" that endear him to Adventist congregations, camp meetings, and conventions across America. Like J. N. Loughborough in the nineteenth century and C. Mervyn Maxwell in the twentieth, George is passionate about winning converts to Adventist history. Indeed, he is one of only a handful of church historians active on the camp meeting circuit today. Yet he continually tries to recruit others to assist him in sharing lessons from the past with Adventist laity.[36]

In fact, George deserves the credit for my sharing Adventist history in scholarly and lay circles today. Shortly after I arrived at Andrews University in 1983, he encouraged me to join the Speakers Bureau and take the Adventist heritage to churches and schools throughout the Lake Union. Thirty years (and scores of presentations) later, I'm still active on this speaking circuit. Then in the late-1980s, when I was researching the history of tithing in the church and Adventists' changing attitudes toward TV and movies, he invited me to share my findings with his doctoral students in his Adventist Lifestyles course at the seminary. Helpful feedback from George and his students led me to revise both papers, which were subsequently published in *Spectrum* and *Dialogue* respectively.

Then as the sesquicentennial of 1844 approached, I began receiving invitations to speak at camp meetings (Saskatchewan-Manitoba, Oklahoma, and Potomac Conferences) where I was certain no church official knew me. Much later, George confessed that he had dropped my name into the hat because he was receiving far more camp meeting invitations than he could accept and he felt that I was ready to assist him. The experience of sharing the Adventist heritage with congregations eager to hear it has been rewarding, especially when I have been invited to speak for local church centennials and sesquicentennials (the latter in Jackson, Michigan in 1999 and the New York Conference in 2012).

But the greatest honor George bestowed on me came in 2009 when he asked me to write the biography of J. N. Loughborough for the Adventist Pioneer Series published by the Review and Herald®. "I want a historian to tackle the life story of our church's first official historian," he told me with a smile. To his credit, George approved at least two-thirds of my requests to add more contextual detail, even when the original manuscript topped five hundred pages. Hopefully, this biography of "The Last of the Adventist Pioneers" will provide Adventist scholars and lay readers with fresh insights into the Adventist past as important as those George has shared with us in his biographies of Joseph Bates and A. T. Jones.

In conclusion, George Knight has bequeathed a staggering legacy to Adventist scholars, church leaders, and lay readers. His historical books, articles, reviews, introductory essays (for the volumes in the Adventist Classics Library[37]), and papers (which have been translated into twenty-five languages so far) demonstrate that solid research in primary and secondary sources can generate both scholarly and devotional interpretations of the past relevant to current problems faced by our church. In addition, his teaching in the Church History Department of the Theological Seminary at Andrews University (where he chaired more than a dozen doctoral dissertations on aspects of Adventist history) has insured that the future dissemination of our church's history is in the capable hands of scholars he has trained.

## Endnotes

1. Likewise, his *The Pharisee's Guide to Perfect Holiness* (1992) was republished as *Sin and Salvation* (2008), and *I Used to Be Perfect: An Ex-Idealist Looks at Law, Sin, and Grace* (1994) was recycled as *I Used to Be Perfect: A Study of Sin and Salvation* (2001).

2. See the bibliography at the back of this book.

3. Warren Johns, *Ministry* 56 (December 1983): 32; David Bryce, *South Pacific Record* 93 (August 20, 1988): 5; Steve Daily, *Spectrum* 18, no. 2 (1987): 58, 59.

4. Ben McArthur, *Andrews University Seminary Studies* 26 (Summer 1988): 187–190; Thomas Geraty, *Journal of Adventist Education* 50 (April–May 1988): 30; Brian Strayer, *Andrews University Seminary Studies* 32 (Autumn 1994): 281–283; Paul Fisher, *Ministry* (October 1994): 57; Nancy Vyhmeister, *Dialogue* 14, no. 2 (2002): 28, 29; and Robert Wearner, *Adventist Review*, December 23, 2004, 29.

5. Frederick Hoyt, *Spectrum* 19, no. 3 (1989): 58–60; Paul Fisher, *Ministry* (October 1994): 57; Doug Morgan, *Church History* 64 (June 1995): 308–310; Howard Krug, *Andrews University Seminary Studies* 37 (1999): 321, 322; and Steve Daily, *Adventist Today* 9 (January–February 2001): 23.

6. Clyde E. Hewitt, *Midnight and Morning* (1983); David L. Rowe, *Thunder and Trumpets: Millerites and Dissenting Religion in Upstate New York, 1800–1850* (1985); Michael Barkun, *Crucible of the Millennium: The Burned-Over District of New York in the 1840s* (1986); Ruth Alden Doan, *The Miller Heresy, Millennialism, and American Culture* (1987); and Ronald L. Numbers and Jonathan M. Butler, eds., *The Disappointed: Millerism and Millenarianism in the Nineteenth Century* (1987).

7. David L. Rowe, *American Historical Review* 100 (June 1995): 946.

8. Michael Barkun, *Journal of American History* 82, no. 1 (June 1995): 228, 229.

9. Steve Daily, *Spectrum* 18, no. 2 (1987): 59.

10. Ben McArthur, *Andrews University Seminary Studies* 26 (Summer 1988): 187–190.

11. Frederick Hoyt, *Spectrum* 19, no. 3 (1989): 58–60.

12. Brian E. Strayer, *Andrews University Seminary Studies* 32 (Autumn 1994): 281–283.

13. Doug Morgan, *Church History* 64 (June 1, 1995): 309.

14. Ben McArthur, *Reviews in American History* 24, no. 3 (September 1996): 377, 379.

15. The other volumes are *Meeting Ellen White* (1996), *Reading Ellen White* (1997), and *Walking With Ellen White* (1999).

16. Howard Krug, *Andrews University Seminary Studies* 37 (1999): 321.

17. Steve Daily, *Adventist Today* 9 (January–February 2001): 23.

18. Frederick Hoyt, *Andrews University Seminary Studies* 43 (Autumn 2005): 355–358.

19. "Challenging the Continuity of History," *Ministry* (December 1992): 8–11.

20. "Seventh-day Adventist History and the Search for a Usable Past: One Man's Journey," Annual Seminary Scholarship Symposium, Andrews University, February 5, 2009.

21. The other model Knight followed for *Ellen White's World* was Gary Land's *The World of Ellen White* (1987).

22. For example, "The Transformation of Education," in Gary Land, ed., *The World of Ellen White* (1987); "dynamic" is a favorite buzzword in his *Search for Identity* (2000).

23. "Adventist Faith Healing in the 1890s," *Adventist Heritage* 13, no. 2 (Summer 1990): 3–15.

24. "William Miller and the Rise of Adventism," *Journal of Adventist Education* 57 (October–November 1994): 10–13; *Millennial Fever and the End of the World* (1993).

25. "Early Seventh-day Adventists and Ordination, 1844–1863," in Nancy Vyhmeister, ed., *Women in Ministry* (1998): 101–14; *Organizing to Beat the Devil* (2001); *A Brief History of Seventh-day Adventists* (1999).

26. *From 1888 to Apostasy* (1987); *A. T. Jones* (2011); *A Brief History of Seventh-day Adventists* (1999).

27. "Historical and Theological Introduction to the Annotated Edition," in *Seventh-day Adventists Answer Questions on Doctrine* (Berrien Springs, Mich.: Andrews University Press, 2003), xiii–xxvi.

28. *Early Adventist Educators*, 27, 29.

29. *Myths in Adventism*, 12.

30. "Historical and Theological Introduction to the Annotated Edition," xiii.

31. "Challenging the Continuity of History," *Ministry* (December 1992): 9.

32. *A Search for Identity: The Development of Seventh-day Adventist Beliefs* (2000), 17. At the time of this writing (2012), the church teaches twenty-eight fundamental beliefs.

33. *Search for Identity*, 86.

34. *Organizing to Beat the Devil: The Development of Adventist Church Structure* (2001), 8.

35. *Joseph Bates: The Real Founder of Seventh-day Adventism* (2004), 38, 45, 174.

36. Other professionally trained historians who speak at local churches, schools, and camp meetings include Jerry Moon, Alberto Timm, Merlin Burt, Brian Strayer, and Michael Campbell. Perhaps to perpetuate Knight's legacy, a list of church scholars willing to share the Adventist heritage at camp meetings and conventions could be compiled and shared with conference, union, division, and General Conference leaders. This group of speakers could be called "Knights of the Adventist Heritage" or "The George Knight League" (after the Loughborough League a half century ago).

37. In 2012, titles in the Adventist Classics Library included James White's *Life Incidents*, Joseph Bates's *Autobiography*, Sylvester Bliss's *Memoirs of William Miller*, *Seventh-day Adventists Answer Questions on Doctrine: Annotated Edition*, *Earliest Seventh-day Adventist Periodicals*, and *Historical Sketches of the Foreign Missions of the Seventh-day Adventists*.

## Chapter 6

# George Knight and the Art of Biography

Gilbert M. Valentine

George Knight has done more to foster the development of the genre of scholarly biographical study in the Adventist community than any other scholar or writer. He has achieved this not only by producing two groundbreaking biographical studies himself but by encouraging and nurturing the development of serious biographical study on the part of his students and by numerous other authors interested in helping the church better understand its past. Perhaps equally important, however, is his achievement in making such serious studies accessible to the wider Adventist Church beyond the confines of just the academic community. Furthermore, he has been remarkably successful in persuading leading church publishers to invest substantial means to ensure that critical scholarly biography continues to inform and shape a more accurate understanding of Adventist history for future generations.

Biography as a literary genre has long been valued for its role in providing not only inspiration but also insight on the ultimate question of how to live. Its enduring value has been particularly prized for its ethical instruction. Thus, *Plutarch's*

*Lives,* for example, has been essential required reading for generations for anyone who wanted to be considered educated in the classical sense. Alban Butler's *Lives of the Saints* has performed a similar function in the Catholic community.[1] In the Adventist community, popular devotional biography in the style of the *Lives of the Saints* has long been a staple of the Adventist press and has played its role in nurturing piety in the community and encouraging an understanding of and an appreciation for the heritage that has been passed on to each new generation. But the limitations and distortions of simple idealized and romanticized stories of faith have their limits. The inadequacy of hagiography has become ever more apparent as new generations of educated Adventists have been equipped with the tools of critical scholarship in a wide range of disciplines and have been taught to question and to think for themselves. The information age, with its emphasis on freedom of information and transparency in government, and producing a huge array of documentary materials, which have become more widely and readily available, has raised questions about the adequacy of the traditional hagiography. As George began to teach at Andrews University in late 1976, he became acutely aware of these developing trends. They only reinforced his awareness of the need for more serious biography and that this approach to understanding history provided valuable insights.

The development of critical scholarly biography in the Adventist community, however, did not begin with George. It began with Richard Schwarz's study of John Harvey Kellogg published by Southern Publishing in Tennessee in 1970, followed by Godfrey Anderson's 1972 study of Joseph Bates, then by John T. Robertson's scholarly assessment of A. G. Daniells's early years of ministry published in 1977 and Eugene Durand's study of the life and work of longtime *Review* editor Uriah Smith published in 1980. Each of these studies grew out of work undertaken by scholars in an academic setting where the stringent requirements of historical method were required for the earning of academic awards. Other more popular biographical studies, but still with a more scholarly basis, also appeared in the 1970s, including two works by Emmett K. Vandevere, one on General Conference president George I. Butler, and one on the presidents of Andrews University.[2]

Knight's own interest in the value of the biographical perspective on history developed out of his doctoral work at the University of Houston. In 1976, he completed a study of the educational theory of the noted American progressive

educator George S. Counts (1889–1974), although his study integrated little actual biographical perspective.[3] As he took up the challenge of teaching graduate
level classes in Adventist educational history and philosophy in his new appointment at Andrews University, George quickly became aware of the paucity of historical resources available. While Adventists had given study to their general denominational history, the medical work and aspects of their theology, his impression was that they had neglected any serious study of the history of the extensive
educational system that they had developed. What was available was comprised
largely of institutional histories.

After he had first given attention to developing his teaching resources for his
philosophy classes with the publication of his two works on educational philosophy from an Adventist perspective, he turned his attention to filling in some of
the wide gaps in the field of the history of Adventist education. Enthused by his
history classes and his passion for understanding educational and church history
and enticed by his interest in the importance of biography as a window into the
past, a number of his students linked up with him to write their dissertations
under his supervision, each choosing a topic that they could approach from a
biographical perspective. George had developed among his students a reputation
for expecting high standards. The rigor he demanded of himself and his classes
challenged and attracted his students. Allan Lindsay wrote on Goodloe Harper
Bell, Warren Ashworth on E. A. Sutherland, Arnold Reye developed an interest in
Frederick Griggs, and I studied W. W. Prescott.

It was during this period that George took up his own first biographical publishing project in the editing of a multiauthored volume published by Andrews
University Press in 1983, entitled *Early Adventist Educators*. He had solicited the
help of a number of specialists and asked them to each develop a chapter focused
on a significant Adventist educator and written in a biographical sketch format.
His goal was to shed light on the dynamics of the church's early educational struggles and the roles that these particular individuals played. Each of the sketches
explored in some way the tension in Adventism between traditional education
and educational reform and attempted to fill in gaps in present understandings.
Filling in such knowledge gaps soon became a mantra for him. It has become one
of the enduring achievements of his career. His first book was already correcting
misperceptions. Joseph Smoot's chapter on Sidney Brownsberger, for example,
on the basis of new research was able to show Brownsberger in quite a new light.

This educator had often been scapegoated for his alleged failures as Battle Creek College president in the late 1870s. George's book also provided a bibliographic listing of available sources that indicated the paucity of research available at that time.

His own contribution to the volume consisted of three chapters. The first was a brief contextual background chapter in which he outlined the contours of the various educational reform movements, the tensions between them and traditional education, and the developments happening in American education outside the emerging Adventist system. The second was not so much a biographical sketch as it was a contextual introduction to Ellen White's writings on education, emphasizing the developmental nature of her educational ideas against the background of Adventist educational history. The essay quietly challenged the commonly held view of Ellen White that understood her concept of education as having been delivered as a ready-made, divinely designed and delivered package that the church then simply had to implement. George argued that to divorce Ellen White's contribution from its historical context rather than viewing it as a developing set of ideas shaped by the context was in fact a "major flaw" in Adventist thinking. He daringly suggested that the development of Adventist education had been something of an "evolutionary struggle" fraught with trial and error and that the relationship between Ellen White and Adventist educators had been a dynamic one with each side learning from the other in the search for "proper" education.[4]

At the time, I was in the happy situation of serving as George's research assistant on the project and thoroughly enjoyed the task of reviewing chapters, locating resources, and confirming citations used in the articles. I was researching the early chapters of my own work on Prescott at the time and had already become familiar with the various archives relevant to the project. My own research into Prescott's personal interactions with Ellen White had partially supported the need for the corrective to the commonly espoused understanding of Ellen White's role. The to and fro of the dialogue with Ellen White, as educational ideas clarified in the 1890s, could now be easily documented. Ellen White had specifically commented on the mutual benefit of her discussions with Prescott and their learning from each other both in Battle Creek and at the time of his visit with her in Australia. Other doctoral research had also confirmed this perspective and I recall numerous "aha" moments shared with George as the research projects progressed.

Knight's article also clarified and corrected another commonly recited mantra that Ellen White was ahead of her time in the educational views she had espoused and that this was by implication an evidence of her inspiration. George demonstrated clearly that her views were not ahead of the "reforms" or of the ideas of other reformers of her time, although they were in advance of the commonly accepted "educational mentality of their day."[5] I suspect that it was for these more carefully nuanced explanations and enlightening perspectives, rather revolutionary in the early 1980s, that Warren Johns, associate editor, warmly welcomed the book in the columns of *Ministry* magazine as "long overdue." He felt it would "serve to correct many misperceptions long promulgated about our early history."[6]

This was George's first attempt at editing a multiauthored volume. In a conversation in the midst of the project, I recall him vowing to himself that it would be his last. Melding the disparate authors each with their different styles and approaches into a coherent and cohesive whole had its frustrations. Writing his own books was so much easier. It was a vow he did not entirely keep and later spent some time as editor of the *Andrews University Seminary Studies* journal, but his future editorial roles with books were more removed from close textual issues. In future multiauthored projects, he served as the general editor or series editor—a topic others address in this *festchrift*.

Educational history was important to George because he believed passionately that to fully understand the present it was important to understand the past.[7] Present problems, successes, and opportunities were more often than not the result of the past. But beyond this he argued, some of the denomination's most important education documents—those of Ellen White—were written in the late nineteenth and early twentieth centuries against the background of both the general development of Western education and the specific development of Seventh-day Adventist education. To not recognize this was to seriously risk misunderstanding the intent of Ellen White's advice. Probing the roots of Adventist education was, therefore, more than just an enjoyable and informative activity. It was absolutely essential. He believed that biographical study was vital to this process because it provided critically important insights into the dynamics of the struggles over ideas, policies, and practices. Such study gave unique perspectives on the triumphs and failures of the educational enterprise that became Adventist education and the roles that various individuals played and what motivated them—their hopes and ideals—and how they interacted with others. Understanding this context of conflict and how it shaped Adventist education would be enlightening for educators facing the challenge of overseeing and delivering Adventist education in the present context "of a constantly shifting society not in harmony with Biblical Christianity."[8]

Having discovered from his close involvement with his doctoral students in their biographical projects the richness of insights into denominational history possible from such study, George soon launched into a full scale project of his own—a scholarly biography of the enigmatic and highly controversial figure of Alonzo T. Jones.[9] One of the most influential voices in Adventism in the 1890s, a central figure in the soteriological debates in the church, an editor at various times of the church's leading publications, and a favorite of Ellen White, Jones had left the church during the Kellogg crisis in 1906 and thereafter became a vocal critic. It was a brave choice of subject for George. Neither Adventist nor non-Adventist authors had previously written on Jones. It was all virgin territory. Jones was a challenging subject at any time but more so in the lead up to 1988 as the church became absorbed in much anticipated centennial reflections on the implications and the meaning of the celebrated 1888 Minneapolis General Conference Session. This historic session had had an enormous impact on Adventist theology, polarizing theological opinion and positions in the church for decades. It continued to do so a century later as various parties adopted different interpretations of what were the central ideas debated at that time. The relationship between A. T. Jones, his preaching, and Ellen White was crucial to this debate.

George is not a biographer in the tradition of a Ron Chernow on George Washington and Alexander Hamilton, or a Jon Meacham on Thomas Jefferson, with the resources and time to undertake massive comprehensive analysis and a publisher and a market to sustain the cost. The realities of resources and markets necessitated a more limited endeavor. Nevertheless, his biographical approach to the study of Jones was the same—he simply wanted to understand the man. He was also interested in arriving at a clear and accurate grasp of Jones's distinctive contribution to Adventism and Adventist theology. Thus, the volume contains several chapters that take detours into key theological issues with a focus on the history of Adventist theology. George justified this on the basis that the issues were matters that Jones was closely connected with and had continued to be focal points of Adventist discussion ever since. The central question for the study, however, was to seek to understand how Jones could spend more than thirty years of his life in nurturing and promoting a religious movement, only to then turn on it and spend his last decade viciously attacking it, along with his former colleagues and friends. What had happened? Knight's research led him to perceive the man as being basically flawed from the start, "aberrant from beginning to end," as he would later reply to a critical reviewer. Jones, in George's assessment, never succeeded in overcoming a basic character flaw of egotism exacerbated by a mind-set conditioned to see only black and white. His rigidity inclined him to run to extremes. These attributes, according to George, manifested themselves all through Jones's ministry in harshness, a readiness to judge others, a failure to manifest Christian courtesy, and a cocksure certainty that he was always absolutely right. He was not without the ability to exercise pastoral care, and his oratory in the pulpit could be spellbinding. The latter qualities served to compensate for and moderate his negative characteristics. But in George's view, Jones's inability to internalize the gospel and allow it to transform his character flaws finally led to his undoing when the church and Ellen White in the years following 1901 failed to do and say what he thought they should.

The book made an enormous contribution in introducing vital and perceptive new insights into the background and the political dynamics of the 1888 conference, and it set the record straight on many disputed historical issues. It gained a wide readership and was promoted heavily during the centennial reflections. George, himself, used the Jones study to springboard into deeper research about the conference and its implications for modern Adventism that has resulted in several other exceedingly helpful volumes on the event itself and on the theological and ecclesiological issues that flowed from it. Woody Whidden reviews these in another chapter. But the Jones book also produced a storm of vigorous responses of disagreement over the assessment that Knight had made of Jones himself.

George sent me an autographed copy in October 1987 when I was serving as president of Pakistan Adventist Seminary in the interior of Punjab province. I devoured the book with enormous appreciation for the research effort that undergirded it, and for its "warts and all" approach. This was certainly not hagiography. And I delighted at the spicy, highly readable style. At the same time, I wondered at his frequent use of military and warfare metaphors and the sense conveyed even in Jones's early period of ministry that those whom he disagreed with were portrayed as his "enemies." While such terminology makes for good reading, had George overdone it, and did it convey a sense of extreme un-Christian hostility that may have unfairly skewed the picture of Jones? I noted this in my letter of thanks to

George. It was only afterwards that I learned that others had also critiqued the study from this perspective. Historian Fred Hoyt of La Sierra University, who highly valued the overall study, also questioned whether Knight had overdrawn the metaphors.[10]

The theological right in the church objected fiercely to George's reading of A. T. Jones. They violently disagreed with Knight's basic thesis and faulted the whole methodology of reading into the Jones pre-1897 period the extremism and harshness that, as they viewed it, became uncontrolled only in his later years. This critique appeared to be theologically motivated. The critics viewed the volume as an attempt to discredit Jones, making far too big an issue of the man's alleged failings, and that in the process it had discredited "the precious message" that he had preached in 1888. So troubling did the right find George's interpretation of Jones that they went to the trouble of producing a forty-three-page, book-length review of the biography, *A. T. Jones: The Man and the Message*. Calling George's account nothing more than "a chamber of horrors," the review complained that in "chapter after tedious chapter," it was as if Knight was "conducting an odoriferous post-mortem. Long before one gets to the end of the book he already knows the patient has died." Those on the right, however, had no alternative explanation for Jones's turnabout other than perhaps to blame God. "There may lurk in the shadow some profound providential reason for Jones' failure that we do not yet understand."[11]

From the left, George's take on Jones also received heavy criticism. His reading of Jones did not give due weight to contextual factors and seemed to portray an immaculate Ellen White who could do no wrong and whose messages were always the epitome of clarity. Denis Hokama could not find in the biography "a single incident" where George had conceded "that Ellen White's counsel may have been in any way flawed such that Jones would have had sufficient reason to wonder." Any inconsistencies or mistakes "existed only in Jones' unsanctified imagination."[12] Jones was always the one at fault. The critique took issue with several specific interpretations, to which George had the opportunity to respond to in justifying his reading.[13] But for whatever reason, he did not address the central critique. Other reviewers saw the absence of any discussion of the first twenty-four years of Jones's life as a major flaw in the book if it was claiming to be a serious biography. Whether this omission was because there was simply a lack of material to fill in the picture or there was not enough space to discuss it or whether George had lacked the resources to research this background is not clear, but it remains a major gap in the understanding of Jones's life. As Hoyt pointed out, "some clue to Jones' problems as an Adventist leader almost certainly lie hidden in the first 24 years of his life."[14] What impact did genetics and environment have on his character, intelligence, and personality that surely must have been largely fixed during this period? Other reviewers noted questions the book did not address, such as the way a bureaucratic organization deals with nonconformity or a study of the political role Ellen White played and how this may or may not have contributed to the controversies.[15]

In 2011, George revised and reissued his study on Jones as part of his new Pioneer series published by the Review and Herald® and reported that he had made changes in every chapter. He added a chapter on Jones and faith healing, rewrote the chapter on the meaning of Minneapolis, modified the discussion of Jones's views on Christology, and updated the discussion of Jones's post-1901 bitter years. But there was still no discussion of Jones's family background, the first twenty-four years of his life, nor any alteration of his basic reading of Jones or response to Hokama's observation concerning the faultless Ellen White. It will take a large commitment to research and scholarship and probably the discovery of significant quantities of new material to produce any worthwhile reassessment of Jones who, in spite of Knight's insightful study, still remains somewhat of an enigma.

The publication of George's Jones biography had a powerful motivational effect on my own career as a writer. Before I left Andrews in 1982, he had encouraged me to turn my study of Prescott into a book for a wider readership. But the challenge of getting my post-doctorate world back together in a busy pastorate in Sydney, followed not long afterwards by a missionary assignment to Pakistan, did not allow any time for writing, and my dissertation continued to gather dust. The arrival of George's work on Jones in 1987 finally prompted me to action. I could visualize an end product and a popular style of writing that was nevertheless rooted in rigorous scholarship. Repeatedly, George encouraged me—indeed challenged me—to follow his example. Thus, in spite of a pressured administrative schedule, I developed a pattern of rising early with the maulvi's regular 3:00 or 4:00 A.M. call to prayer from the mosque just over our mission compound wall and spent the first two or three hours of the day developing the manuscript for a popular version of my biography on Prescott. Knight provided encouraging feedback for me on the first chapters. Then, when I was done, he served as a go-between for me with Bob Firth and the press at Andrews. The book was published in 1992 as *The Shaping of Adventism: The Case of W. W. Prescott,* a title that followed a rubric George had used for his Jones volume. At that stage in church life, some considered the Prescott volume too *avant garde* for the church's regular press to handle, although George and I were both delighted when William Johnsson, editor of the *Adventist Review,* came out with a very positive review of the book in his column "Best From the Press in '92."[16] I have George to thank for modeling the way for me with his study on Jones, for mentoring me, and for introducing me to the joy and fulfillment of writing a biography.

His biography of Jones had other powerful spin-off effects. Doug Morgan relates that it was in the pages of the Jones book that he encountered the name of Lewis C. Sheafe, the noted African American whose uncomfortable experience as an Adventist preacher had a powerful influence in shaping race relations in the Adventist Church. The encounter led Doug to develop a richly documented scholarly biography of Sheafe's life and his role in the church. It has also recently been published in the Pioneer series that George has persuaded the church to undertake.

George continued to wax passionate about the huge value of such biographical studies as a way of getting to a much more complete and accurate picture of the often hidden inner processes of developments that had taken place in the church. He valued the way that such studies enabled a peeling back of the varnished layers of the public relations version of church decisions and development. And he continued to attract students who wanted to explore the lives of other noted church leaders. Jerry Moon's study of W. C. White was an example, as was Paul Evan's study of M. L. Andreasen. Then, in 2002, he persuaded the acquisition editors and the management of the Review and Herald® to undertake the publishing of a series of serious scholarly biographies on church pioneers. The series would be well documented and tell the stories, "warts and all," not in travel brochure mode, but just as things happened for good or ill. It was a brave commitment for the church to take on and is indicative of the maturing of the intellectual climate in the church over such things that had followed the publication of George's work on Jones.

The Pioneer series began in 2003 with the publication of Gerald Wheeler's fresh assessment of James White as an innovative leader. The frank discussion of the marital difficulties between Ellen and James caught the attention of many readers and indicated the strength of the new commitment to openness, the need to educate church members about the reality of the past, and the fact that such openness strengthened confidence in the church rather than weakened it. Knight wrote of the introduction of this new series as "a much needed series" and that it was a project "unprecedented in the denomination's history." Never before had there been such "a concerted effort to systematically treat the lives and contributions of the men and women who have stood at the center of Adventism's development." He was sure that it would not only help church members understand the individuals better but that it would shed much "additional light on the history of the Adventist movement."[17] George had lined up subjects and authors that would extend well into the future. Authors would not be compensated for writing other than through the usual royalty arrangements, but their work was at least being commissioned, and the resultant volumes were very attractively presented. The projected series thus drew in highly qualified historians to undertake the research and writing. It was a breathtaking initiative that required serious financial investment—but it would have enduring value.

The line-up of the subjects selected for study in this series itself speaks to the stature and respect that George has established with church publishing house leaders, the academic community, and church leaders. Of the first seven books published in the series, four are about men who departed from the church, most of whom became quite hostile after their departure. Previously, the church had regarded them as "apostates." Jones, Waggoner, Kellogg, and Sheafe all left the church in this way. The fact that these lives are being studied indicates a willingness on the part of the church to recognize the significance of their contributions in spite of their later disagreements and departures. In the case of the choice of Sheafe for consideration in the series, there is even a subtle recognition, as Doug Morgan points out, that the individual made a contribution to the church even in the act of departure, painful and distressing as such a departure could be. The fact that the church's leading publishing house was also now willing to publish the Prescott biography as part of the series (as it did in 2005) was also an indication of a growing maturity on the part of the church. It demonstrated its ability to follow the evidence where it led and to consider perspectives other than the highly apologetic gilded versions of church history promulgated by official church writers of earlier generations. Also a measure of the stature and respect in which George is held, it is a tribute to the unique contribution he has been able to make to the enrichment of Adventist history and the strengthening of the Adventist community. This one project alone would appear to set him apart as an author and thinker who will shape the future of Adventist self-understanding for decades to come.

Knight's own contribution to the ongoing pioneer biographical series is a provocative biographical study of Joseph Bates published in 2004 that has caused almost as much surprise and challenge to Adventist thinking as his Jones biography. Rather than seeking to redo the excellent work undertaken by Godfrey Anderson in his study on Bates, George built on that foundation and prepared a thorough analysis of Bates's distinctive theological and intellectual contribution to the Adventist movement. His analysis challenges the current orthodoxies in an astounding way. According to Hoyt, George suggested "nothing less than a revolution in Adventist history," when he concluded that without the theological ideas of Joseph Bates, James and Ellen White as co-founders would have had nothing to build the denomination on.[18] Bates, therefore, was in fact "the real founder of Seventh-day Adventism," a claim George tucked into the subtitle of the book. Bates is its first theologian, its first historian. Introducing the seventh-day Sabbath to the small group of disappointed Millerites, he distinctively linked it with prophetic significance. Furthermore, he developed the central idea that Adventism had a specific place in prophetic history, a concept that came to be explained later as the great controversy theme. Bates was the movement's first missionary theorist and its first missionary as well as its first health reformer, although his role in this latter area was not a major one. All of these key concepts became central to the self-identity of later Sabbatarian Adventism. On the downside, as George bravely pointed out, Bates was also the source of the problematic strand of legalism that arose from his imperfect grasp of salvation by grace and which became so deeply embedded, attaching itself almost inherently to early Adventism's thinking and teaching. Knight argued, however, that the overall benefit that arose out of Bates's welding together of these key theological insights "far overshadowed" the unhealthy impact of his legalism.[19]

Ben McArthur wondered whether the "real founder" interpretation might have been "a marketing department hyperbole," but conceded, nonetheless, that George had a point and that at the very least his study restored Bates to an equal status alongside James and Ellen as founders of the movement. In Hoyt's view, Knight's argument was "nicely developed, adequately documented and convincingly argued."[20] It is clear that the reevaluation of Bates will change and clarify Adventist self-understanding. With his characteristic professional courtesy as an author, George generously acknowledges his indebtedness to a number of his students, two of whom in particular, Merlin Burt and Alberto Timm, through their own doctoral studies, had helped him develop the broader appreciation of the contribution of Bates that he presents in this study. Such acknowledgment was the pattern for the way George thought of the voyage of discovery with his students. They were all learners together.

Knight's students feel a huge indebtedness for his contribution to their intellectual and spiritual development. Even now, his warm and cordial relationship with his doctoral students is remarkable. The shared passion for understanding Adventist history and for the development of the community of faith established bonds of easy friendship that he continued to maintain long years afterwards. Students became friends. In many cases, he continued to be their advocate, paving the way for publishing opportunities, serving as a highly influential reference in support of teaching or research employment opportunities, and willingly providing counsel and advice at other important transition points in their lives. My own experience bears this out.

George's advocacy on my behalf started quite early. As an idealistic graduate student at Andrews at the time of the Glacier View upheaval, I followed the discussions and developments with keen interest. Dr. Ford had been my teacher at Avondale for four years, and his classes for me had been a doorway to a genuine experience of the rich forgiving grace of God in Christ. George and I would occasionally chat together about this in his office as we discussed the progress in my research and the development of affairs in the church. As the fallout from the decisions of Glacier View began to hurt so many, I became distressed at the hostility I perceived in the attitude of church officials to Ford and the injustices in the Glacier View process. I wrote letters to the *Student Movement* at Andrews and to the *Review* editor, Kenneth Wood, objecting to what I perceived as the scandalously one-sided reporting of issues. This correspondence, as I look back on it now, had an edge of indignation and perhaps impertinence to it. It would cause serious problems for me then and long years afterwards. Just the memory of it spiked several employment opportunities.

In the spring of 1981, my research called for me to spend time at the General Conference researching in the archives and in the White Estate vault. George had generously invited me to travel down with him in his car to save expenses for me, and he had written the customary letters of introduction for me to those in charge of the archival collections. Gaining access to the GC archives was no problem. But his introductory letter did not work at the White Estate. We learned on my arrival that Kenneth Wood was also the chair of the White Estate trustees and permission for me to use the White Estate resources was denied. Kenneth Wood summoned me to his office for an interview in an attempt to ascertain my orthodoxy. George, distressed at this development, in his adept and gracious way intervened for me by talking to GC vice president Duncan Eva, who had heard of me through my friendship with his son Wilmore. Elder Eva also served on the Board of Trustees, probably outranked Wood, and was prepared to assure the trustees of my bona fides. Consequently, after several days, I received permission to use the vault materials in my research, although the atmosphere was a little tense at first. In later years, George and I have often laughed about this hiccup to my start into research and his helpful intervention to rescue his suspect "Ford" student from the *Review* editor. I am forever grateful to his intervention on my behalf. As it happened, White family relative Alta Robinson, who also worked at the Estate, felt sympathetic and befriended me. Taking me under her wing, she proved enormously helpful in providing me with resources and valued insights about where to look and the inner dynamics of the estate. Later, she wrote a deeply appreciative letter for the dissertation on Prescott.

The friendship that George and I developed at the time of my work on Prescott continued to deepen through the years, and, as a mentor, he took a keen interest in my broadening research interests. I valued the frank and insightful feedback he provided on ideas for book projects and on the manuscripts themselves. Not only opening his home to me in Berrien Springs, he gave me the use of his car when I visited Andrews for research in the Heritage Room. In turn, he and Bonnie stayed with my family on his teaching or preaching visits to Australia, England, and Thailand. Some of these visits I was delighted to be able to initiate. I treasure the memories of elephant rides and motorcycle excursions across the border into Myanmar. And I will never forget how impressed I was when he held spellbound a chapel audience of nine hundred undergraduate students in Thailand during his extended teaching spell with us in 2004. Fifty percent of the audience was Buddhist, but George's story of his own conversion to Christianity as a young person communicated powerfully across both cultural and language barriers.

More recently, George provided a valued repeat of his 1980s advocacy for me. I had completed the manuscript for my book on *The Prophet and the Presidents* and, after an exhaustive review involving two separate reading committees set up by the Review and Herald®, I had made recommended changes and the manuscript had been accepted. The book had already been through the editing process and was ready for a final copy editing when there came a change of administration. Economic difficulties presented themselves and a different editorial climate set in at the Review and Herald®. I learned that now the book would not be published, even though I had already been paid advanced royalties. Fortunately, Pacific Press® quickly saw potential in the manuscript and agreed to consider it. George took up the cause with his friends at Pacific Press®, urging them to resist whatever pressures might be brought to bear against publishing the manuscript in its present form. Arguing that there was great need for it in the church, he agreed to write a foreword with a strong endorsement, for which I am deeply grateful. I am not sure he would accept all my readings of the evidence discussed in the book, but he valued the fresh approach to examining the political dynamics in the relationship between Ellen White and the executive leadership of the church and the new understanding of Adventist history that this allowed. George was never fearful of a fresh idea. His openness in thinking about the church and its history has for me continued to spark ideas for research and new paths to explore.

Someday a biographer will have the pleasure of setting down for posterity the story of George Knight's life and will endeavor to make an assessment of his contribution to the development of the church community that he loves and has spent so much of his energy and intellect to strengthen and build up. Hopefully, they will have the resources to provide a complete picture of his family heritage and antecedents, his youthful environment, and the influences that shaped him. When they come to assessing the contribution he has made to Adventist Church history and the shaping of its life and thought, there should be material aplenty and they could have no better motivation for the endeavor than that which stimulated George's own biographical work.

## Endnotes

1. One of the most influential works of piety produced within the English Catholic community, together with the Douai version of the Bible. In the opinion of one of his early editors, Donald Attwater, Butler was "as critical a hagiographer as the state of knowledge and available materials of his age

would allow." Michel Walsh, ed., *Butler's Lives of the Saints* (New York: Harper Collins, 1991), vii.

2. Richard W. Schwarz, *John Harvey Kellogg, M. D.* (Nashville, Tenn.: Southern Publishing Association, 1970). Godfrey T. Anderson, *Outrider of the Apocalypse: Life and Times of Joseph Bates* (Mountain View, Calif.: Pacific Press®, 1972). John J. Robinson, *A. G. Daniells: The Making of a General Conference President, 1901* (Mountain View, Calif.: Pacific Press®, 1979). Eugene F. Durand, *Yours in the Blessed Hope, Uriah Smith* (Washington, D.C.: Review and Herald®, 1980). Emmett K. Vandevere, *Rugged Heart: The Story of George I. Butler* (Nashville, Tenn.: Southern Publishing, 1979); *Wisdom Seekers* (Nashvillle, Tenn.: Southern Publishing, 1972).

3. George reported that a more complete biography would probably never be possible because Counts never kept a diary and after his retirement he destroyed most of his correspondence. "An Analysis of the Educational Theory of George S. Counts" (EdD diss., University of Houston, 1976), 13.

4. George R. Knight, *Early Adventist Educators* (Berrien Springs Mich.: Andrews University Press, 1983), 26.

5. Ibid., 8.

6. Warren H. Johns, *Ministry* (December 1983): 32.

7. Knight, "Probing the Roots of Adventist Education: A Report of Recent Research," *Journal of Adventist Education* 46 (February–March 1984): 18, 19, 44.

8. *Early Adventist Educators*, 9.

9. George graciously dedicated the volume to his first four doctoral students, "who were my teachers in the researching and writing of Adventist biography."

10. Frederick Hoyt, "Knight on Jones: Biography Without Hagiography," *Spectrum* 19, no. 3 (Spring 1989): 58–60. Benjamin McArthur, review of *From 1888 to Apostasy: The Case of A. T. Jones*, by George R. Knight, *Andrews University Seminary Studies* 26, no. 2 (1988): 187–190.

11. *A. T. Jones: The Man and the Message*, prepared by The 1888 Message Study Committee, Ohio 1988, 18, 20, 21. Wayne Willey, "Knight Falls on Brother A. T. Jones," *Spectrum* 19, no. 3 (Summer1988): 61.

12. Denis Hokama, "Knight's Darkest Hour: Biography as Indictment," *Adventist Currents*, April 1988, 37–42.

13. George Knight, "A Spark in the Dark," *Adventist Currents*, April 1988, 43.

14. Hoyt, "Knight on Jones."

15. Hokama, "A Fizzle in the Drizzle," 44–45.

16. *Adventist Review*, December 10, 1992, 12.

17. Knight, foreword to *James White: Innovator and Overcomer*, by Gerald Wheeler (Hagerstown, Md.: Review and Herald®, 2003), xi.

18. Frederick Hoyt, review of *Joseph Bates: The Real Founder of Seventh-day Adventism*, by George R. Knight, *Andrews University Seminary Studies* 43, no. 2 (2005): 355–358.

19. Knight, *Joseph Bates: The Real Founder of Seventh-day Adventism* (Washington D.C.: Review and Herald®, 2004), 212.

20. Ibid. Benjamin McArthur, "Early Adventism's Leon Trotsky," *Spectrum* 33, no. 2 (Spring 2005): 70–72.

# Chapter 7

# Coming to Terms With the Millerites

Gary Land

P rior to the publication of George R. Knight's *Millennial Fever* in 1993,[1] Millerite historiography had gone through three basic phases.[2] The first phase extended from the mid-1850s to the early twentieth century. Two works by Millerite participants shaped the discussion. First, Sylvester Bliss's *Memoirs of William Miller* presented Miller, often in his own words, as a pious and intelligent man who sought genuine religious revival and opposed fanaticism.[3] Furthermore, he held much in common with his theological critics. Second, Isaac Wellcome's *History of the Second Advent Message*[4] sought to dispel misrepresentation of his movement by emphasizing its positive religious results, pointing out the theological problems of his critics, and noting the reproach brought on the movement by its bigots and fanatics. Most importantly, Wellcome placed Miller and his movement within the context of the growing premillennialism that began taking hold of a significant sector of American Protestantism during and after the mid-nineteenth century. Bliss and Wellcome obviously wanted to present a positive view of Miller, his theology, and the movement that he had sparked but which had experienced ignominious failure when Jesus did not come in either 1843 or 1844 as the Millerites had predicted.

Clara Endicott Sears prompted a new period in Millerite historiography in the 1920s with her *Days of Delusion*.[5] Sears gathered many stories of the movement's alleged craziness. She described the Millerite movement as a "strange bit of history," offering accounts of its participants giving up their property as October 22, 1844, approached, putting on white ascension robes, and meeting in graveyards as they awaited the return of their Lord. It did not matter that Sears's stories often rested on questionable contemporary newspaper accounts and supposed witnesses who were very young or not even born by 1844. Nonetheless, she shaped the popular understanding of the Millerite movement from the 1920s to the 1960s, with her stories of the movement's apparent foolishness, many of which appeared in the college textbooks of the period as authors sought a bit of comic relief in a genre often criticized as boring.

Twenty years after Sears's book appeared, Francis Nichol, a Seventh-day Adventist writer and editor, published *The Midnight Cry*,[6] a strong defense of the Millerites from which his denomination had emerged. By critically examining contemporary sources, he sought to demonstrate that many of the stories recounted by Sears had little basis in fact and were repeated from newspaper to newspaper, often picking up new elements in the process. Thus, like a defense lawyer, he dispelled stories of Millerite insanity and ascension robes as having little basis in fact. Although his book received good reviews in historical journals and influenced some historians of American social and religious history, it made little impact on the public perception that the movement was made up of fanatics who lay outside the mainstream of American history. Defenders such as Nichol did not want their church to be historically linked to a movement whose wildness could not be tamed, and thus they sought any evidence they could find to contradict such an image. This second period of Millerite historiography thus was characterized by argument between polemicists who emphasized its fanaticism and apologists who largely denied the alleged extreme behavior.

Most of the writing about the Millerites during the first half of the twentieth century appeared from the pens of people outside of the academic profession of history who also had agendas that prevented them from viewing the movement objectively. One exception was Everett N. Dick, the first Seventh-day Adventist to achieve a PhD in history. He wrote his 1930 dissertation on the Millerites as a part of American social history, arguing that they borrowed techniques from the reform and revival movements popular in their day, examined the social and denominational characteristics of its participants, and noted the elements of fanaticism that appeared among them.[7] Dick's was a serious work of social history that sought to view the Millerites objectively without an agenda that lay outside historical understanding. Unfortunately, when he attempted to publish his work, Seventh-day Adventist leaders preferred an apologetic work such as the one Nichol eventually wrote. They prevented Dick from putting his research into print.

Nonetheless, his approach gradually took over historical scholarship, although there is little evidence that his work had much direct influence. During the 1950s and 1960s, historians began to broaden their interest beyond government, politics, and wars to write intellectual and social history. It gradually began to include accounts of the Millerites that ushered in a third period of Millerite historiography. First appearing in scholarly articles and relatively short accounts in books that had broader subjects, by the 1980s the Millerites began receiving book-length attention, several from historians not connected with a church that had descended from the movement. David Rowe, who had grown up in Upstate New York where the Millerites had been active, wrote a dissertation on the movement that was eventually published as *Thunder and Trumpets*.[8] This was followed by Clyde E. Hewitt, an Advent Christian, whose *Midnight and Morning*[9] he largely based on secondary sources such as Dick's dissertation, but the work presented a balanced account of the Millerites. Ronald L. Numbers and Jonathan Butler, who came from Seventh-day Adventist backgrounds, then edited a collection of essays, *The Disappointed*, largely written by scholars who had no connection with the church.[10] All of these works emphasized the similarities rather than the differences between Millerism and its contemporary American culture. This theme received further development by Michael Barkun's *Crucible of the Millennium*,[11] which argued that economic and environmental disturbances had contributed to the rise of Millenarianism, and Ruth Alden Doan's *The Miller Heresy*,[12] which attempted to explain why a movement that held so much in common with the rest of American society still received heavy criticism. She concluded that it was Miller's strong supernaturalism that most distinguished it from the mainstream and that aroused criticism. Thus, as the 150th anniversary of the "Great Disappointment" approached, scholars interpreted Millerism, not as an aberration, but as a largely integral element of nineteenth-century American culture.

As the title suggests, Knight's *Millennial Fever* saw the Millerite movement as something more than a typical American religious revival. To be sure, he accepted the arguments of recent historians that the Millerites held much in common with American society. Premillennialism, while a minority position within American Christianity in the first half of the nineteenth century, was not unique to Millerism. Furthermore, Miller reflected much of the revivalist Christianity of his day with his restorationist, rationalist, and literalist approach to Scripture. His linking of prophecy and history met the felt needs of his audience, making him, according to Knight, perhaps the most successful revival preacher of the last phase of the Second Great Awakening. Joshua V. Himes, a Christian Connexion minister, became Miller's publicist in 1839 and turned his regional upper New York and New England revival efforts into a movement that swept through the Northeast, reaching as far south as Maryland, and penetrating the states west of the Appalachian Mountains. The movement's expansion took place through methods used by both reform and religious groups: public speaking, periodicals, tracts, books, camp meetings, and conferences. Thus, much of the Millerite movement appeared familiar to the American public.

But, in Knight's view, it did not take long for the Millerites to become increasingly radical. Beginning about 1842, they increasingly focused on the time of Jesus' coming and consequently faced growing resistance from the mainstream churches. Finally, in July 1843, Charles Fitch called on the Millerites to "Come Out of Babylon," which encouraged an already festering separatist tendency. When Jesus had not returned by the spring of 1843, the "First Disappointment," the movement entered a period of uncertainty, which many called the "Tarrying Time." New ideas began to crop up that further separated Millerism from its surrounding culture, among which was the annihilationist doctrine promoted by George Storrs, which denied that humans had immortal souls and that the dead would "sleep" in death until the resurrection. Even more significant for the time was S. S. Snow's teaching that the Second Coming would take place on October 22, 1844, the Day of Atonement, a belief that went through the movement like wildfire and, after initial opposition, was accepted by the leaders in early October. When Jesus again did not return, the "Great Disappointment," the movement was bewildered and disoriented, soon fracturing into a number of sects.

Knight noted that fanatical elements began to appear as early as 1843 with John Starkweather's views of personal sanctification that at first included such manifestations as the loss of bodily strength and later expanded to "gifts" that supposedly enabled believers to walk on water and even stop locomotives through the power of their wills.[13] George commented that "though fanaticism in pre-October 1844 Adventism was present, it did not involve a major part of the movement. . . . During the tarrying time, the fanatical elements smoldered, but, unfortunately, they would achieve greater prominence in late 1844 and 1845."[14]

Theologically, the most significant division in the movement after the "Great Disappointment," revolved around the significance of October 22, 1844, with leaders such as Miller and Himes moving away from seeing any importance in the date while Apollos Hale and Joseph Turner reinterpreted it as the time when the door to salvation was shut to anyone who had not accepted the Millerite teaching. While the "shut-door" was a doctrine with no explicit behavioral implications, related movements, what Knight called the "Radical Fringe," emerged, advocating such views as the abandoning of all work, acting as children by crawling on one's knees, engaging in "holy kissing," practicing "spiritual wifery," and becoming Shakers. Other radicals adopted doctrinal innovations, including the seventh-day Sabbath and the pre-Advent judgment, both of which had Millerite antecedents.

The Albany Conference of March 1845, called by Himes, sought to separate moderate from radical Adventists and ultimately laid the foundation for the later organization of four groups: the Evangelical Adventists, the Advent Christians, the Life and Union Adventists, and the "Age-to-Come Adventists," known formally as the Church of God of the Abrahamic Faith.

Meanwhile, Knight stated, the sabbatarian Adventists "began in the midst of a segment of Adventism up to its armpits in fanaticism by 1845."[15] Unlike previous Adventist writers such as Nichol, who minimized the element of fanaticism in the Millerite movement and denied its continuance in sabbatarian Adventism, George recognized his denomination's origins in fanatical Adventism and described its subsequent development as a "disentanglement." James and Ellen White, Joseph Bates, and other sabbatarians, for instance, accepted the shut-door doctrine. Knight wrote that "even a casual reading of Ellen (Harmon) White's earliest writings repeatedly indicates that both her and her husband's work took place in the midst of fanatical elements as they struggled to bring some rational order out of the chaotic situation of shut-door Adventism between 1845 through 1849."[16] Gradually, this disentanglement took place through doctrinal developments such as that of the sanctuary, the investigative judgment, and the role of the

Sabbath in prophecy, the group's self-understanding as bearers of the "third angel's message" of Revelation 14, and the publication of papers beginning in 1849 that led ultimately to the organization of the Seventh-day Adventist Church in 1863.

Of the major sects that emerged from the Millerite movement, Seventh-day Adventists have been the most successful. Knight explained this success as rising out of both external and internal factors. The external elements are those identified by recent historical studies, including Millerism's commonalities with American revivalism and more generally with evangelical Christianity, and environmental factors such as natural disasters and wars that encourage apocalyptic thinking. Internal reasons, according to Knight, include Adventism's rationalism, distinctive doctrinal positions that lead to a strong commitment to a cause, the denomination's organizational structure, and a sense of prophetic mission and of urgency. Knight, who was strongly influenced by the concept of a "usable past," closed his book on a cautionary note, however, observing that it is difficult to keep alive a prophetic hope for more than 150 years, that some in the church seek to downplay its doctrinal distinctives, and, finally, that the church tends to overinstitutionalize. He concluded his book with a warning that Seventh-day Adventists must not give up their self-understanding as a people of prophecy. "To deny its prophetic heritage," he wrote, "is a certain way to kill its 'millennial fever.' "

His achievement in *Millennial Fever* was to bring together two conflicting views of Millerism. On the one hand, apologists going back to Bliss and Wellcome and extending to Nichol, had sought to "tame" the movement by minimizing and often denying its fanatical elements. Professional historians, while not functioning as apologists for the movement, increasingly regarded it as holding much in common with the American culture of the period but puzzled over why mainstream religion rejected it. On the other hand, Sears and writers who followed her regarded Millerism as essentially fanatical and enthusiastically recounted stories of extreme and wild behavior. Knight accepted the commonalities that Millerism shared with nineteenth-century American culture but accepted that at the same time fanaticism began developing as early as 1843 and flourished after the Great Disappointment. Ultimately, he recognized that a full and accurate view of Millerism realizes that it cannot be "tamed," that its fanatical elements as well as its commonalities must be accepted but then analyzed to understand how the sabbatarians and other groups "disentangled" themselves from the post-Disappointment mess it had become. While I am sure Knight would not regard his book as the last word on the Millerite movement, his discussion of the disentanglement process leaves much to explore.

Reviewers responded favorably to his work. Writing in the *Journal of American History*, Michael Barkun stated that "Knight is fairly conversant with the new literature and uses it to good effect. His narrative is clear, accessible, and abundantly documented. . . . Knight provides as clear and complete a picture as we are likely to get, especially in his treatment of the years after the Great Disappointment." Barkun's only significant criticism was that George provided "little in the way of an interpretive position," focusing mostly on the "what" and little on the "why." David L. Rowe's review in the *American Historical Review* emphasized what he called the "devotional" aspect of the book, saying that Knight conveyed the idea that Adventist "history has meaning that informs their [the Adventist's] mission to the present. This devotionalism is a mark of a mature denomination, secure in its faith. . . . Knight does not buy devotion with the price of historical accuracy or objectivity. It is not only genuine history but also one that is comprehensive and useful." Neither Barkun or Rowe had any connection with the Seventh-day Adventist Church, but Douglas Morgan, an Adventist historian writing for *Church History*, noted that Knight's achievement lay in synthesis and analysis rather than original research. He further commented that George's focus on a "combination of Biblicist rationalism and warm evangelical piety surely brings the reader to the heart of Millerite Adventism." Brian E. Strayer, also an Adventist historian, wrote in *Andrews University Seminary Studies* that *Millennial Fever* was "the first truly comprehensive scholarly survey of Millerism." Knight, according to Strayer, "analyzes nearly every known Millerite idea and leader—irrespective of gender, race, religion, religious background, or mentality." Finally, in a retrospective essay on Millerite historiography that appeared in *Reviews in American History*, another Adventist historian, Benjamin McArthur, stated that Knight "refocuses on the people and message of the movement itself" and "has no compunction about admitting that Adventism arose amidst a fever of enthusiasm."[17]

In addition to *Millennial Fever*, Knight has made other contributions to Millerite scholarship. The year following *Millennial Fever*, Knight published *1844 and the Rise of Sabbatarian Adventism*. This volume complemented the narrative history by providing primary documents and included such items as Josiah Litch's history of the emergence of the Millerite movement, several letters of William Miller and other leaders in the movement, and O. R. L. Crosier's *The*

*Law of Moses.* Not only did this volume make available otherwise hard-to-find documents for both scholars and general readers, in his introductions to each section of the book, Knight often provided something akin to a reader's guide to help in understanding these sometimes archaic documents. For example, regarding the "Advent Herald" article that "provides us with the first 'official' perspective on the Millerite experience after the October 22 date," George wrote that "it provides data on the disruptive behavior of some opposers to the Advent doctrine as the day approached. But of special interest is the remark near the bottom of the third column of page 93 that the Adventist leaders still regarded the seventh-month movement with its October 22 date as 'the true midnight cry.' Beyond that fact, the closing paragraph repeated the oft expressed belief that the believers would experience only a 'little delay' before the Advent."[18] Such comments were potentially helpful to nonacademic readers.

Knight's biography of Joseph Bates, published in 2004, offered him the opportunity to explore in greater detail the role of a particular individual in the Millerite movement. He argued that Bates's chairmanship of the May 1842 Millerite conference changed the nature of the movement in three ways: First, it led the movement to strongly affirm that Jesus would return in 1843, thereby committing itself to a timeline; second, the movement adopted camp meetings as a means to promote its message; and third, it introduced the prophetic chart that Bates and others would use to attract attention. Knight also described Bates's venture into Maryland, one of the few Millerite excursions into the South, and, most significantly, his developing understanding of the three angels' messages of Revelation 14. He observed, "The message of the three angels would be absolutely central to the Sabbatarian theology that Bates developed in 1846 and 1847. He would build on Millerite understandings, but he would also transcend them in giving them a sequential emphasis not found in Millerite discussions and in stressing the third message, especially as it related to Revelation 14:12." This focus on the thought of a single individual significantly clarified the theological development of sabbatarianism as it emerged from the Millerite movement.[19]

Knight also contributed to Millerite studies in less direct ways. While he was serving as the director of Andrews University Press, I suggested to him the possibility of publishing Everett Dick's manuscript on the Millerite movement, which by this point was itself a significant document in the development of Millerite historiography. He agreed that it was a good idea and supported me in my effort to prepare this volume for publication, which took place in 1994.[20] Through his editorship of the Adventist Classic Library, George also oversaw the reprinting of Bates's autobiography, Bliss's *Memoirs of William Miller,* and Isaac Wellcome's history of the Advent movement, each with an introduction that placed the work in its historical context and provided analysis and interpretation. The publication of these primary sources made available to contemporary readers and researchers works otherwise often difficult to find.[21]

In retrospect, George Knight's research, writing, and editing represents Seventh-day Adventism's coming to terms with the full dimension of its Millerite past. No longer needing to downplay or deny the less favorable parts of that past, hopefully future Adventist scholars will expand our knowledge and understanding on the baseline that Knight has established.

George Knight has made many contributions to Adventism beyond his work in history. Although he earned a degree in educational philosophy, he expanded his interests to theology, biblical commentary, and Christian spirituality, among other subjects. He told me once that he "read himself" into these areas beyond his original specialty. In other words, he educated himself in a variety of fields, but unlike some autodidacts, he achieved both respect and influence for his work, as this present volume attests.

Knight also contributed significantly to the church through his chairmanship (I don't recall his exact title) of the Andrews University Press Board, on which I worked with him for a number of years. Through his leadership, he transformed the press from a largely house publisher for Andrews University professors to the Seventh-day Adventist Church's major scholarly outlet. In the process, he instated more rigorous peer review policies and expanded both the subjects and the authors published by the press.

Finally, on a more personal note, in the early 1990s, a young man from the Church of God of the Abrahamic Faith contacted some of us about the possibility of starting a historical association that represented all of the churches with Millerite origins. George, Brian Strayer, and I met with this individual, whose name I do not recall, at Aurora College. I remember that George was very enthusiastic in his support of this interdenominational effort. Rather than seeing Adventist history as confined to Seventh-day Adventism, he believed that a broader understanding was much needed. I was impressed with his openness to alternative understandings of the Adventist experience. Unfortunately, nothing came of this meeting beyond a one-issue newsletter, but perhaps in the future someone will find both the energy and time to pursue a similar effort with the openness displayed by George.

## Endnotes

1. George R. Knight, *Millennial Fever and the End of the World* (Boise, Idaho: Pacific Press®, 1993); reprinted as *William Miller and the Rise of Adventism* (Nampa, Idaho: Pacific Press®, 2010). Knight had previously written several articles and books that touched on the Millerite movement, but *Millennial Fever* was his major work on the subject.

2. The following historiographical discussion is drawn from "The Historians and the Millerites: An Historiographical Essay," in Everett N. Dick, *William Miller and the Advent Crisis, 1831-1844*, ed. Gary Land (Berrien Springs, Mich.: Andrews University Press, 1994), xiii–xxviii; also published as "The Historians and the Millerites: An Historiographical Essay," *Andrews University Seminary Studies* 32 (Autumn 1994): 227–246.

3. Sylvester Bliss, *Memoirs of William Miller Generally Known as a Lecturer on the Prophecies and the Second Coming of Christ* (Boston, Mass.: Joshua V. Himes, 1853).

4. Isaac C. Wellcome, *History of the Second Advent Message and Mission, Doctrine and People* (Yarmouth, Maine: author, 1874).

5. Clara Endicott Sears, *Days of Delusion: A Strange Bit of History* (Boston, Mass.: Houghton Mifflin, 1924).

6. Francis Nichol, *The Midnight Cry* (Washington, D.C.: Review and Herald®, 1947).

7. See Dick, *William Miller and the Advent Crisis.*

8. David L. Rowe, *Thunder and Trumpets: Millerites and Dissenting Religion in Upstate New York, 1800-1850* (Chico, Calif.: Scholars Press, 1985).

9. Clyde E. Hewitt, *Midnight and Morning* (Charlotte, N.C.: Venture Books, 1983).

10. Ronald L. Numbers and Jonathan M. Butler, eds., *The Disappointed: Millerism and Millenarianism in the Nineteenth Century* (Bloomington, Ind.: Indiana University Press, 1987).

11. Michael Barkun, *Crucible of the Millennium: The Burned-Over District of New York in the 1840s* (Syracuse, N.Y.: Syracuse University Press, 1986).

12. Ruth Alden Doan, *The Miller Heresy, Millennialism, and American Culture* (Philadelphia: Temple University Press, 1987).

13. Knight, *Millennial Fever*, 174, 175.

14. Ibid.,177.

15. Ibid., 295.

16. Ibid., 296.

17. Michael Barkun, *Journal of American History* 82 (June 1995): 228, 229; David L. Rowe, *American Historical Review* 100 (June 1995): 946; Douglas Morgan, *Church History* 64 (June 1995): 308–310; Brian E. Strayer, *Andrews University Seminary Studies* 32 (Autumn 1994): 281–283; Benjamin McArthur, "Millennial Fevers," *Reviews in American History* 24 (September 1996): 369–382.

18. George R. Knight, comp. and ed., *1844 and the Rise of Sabbatarian Adventism* (Hagerstown, Md.: Review and Herald®, 1994), 121.

19. George R. Knight, *Joseph Bates: The Real Founder of Seventh-day Adventism*, Pioneer Biography

Series (Hagerstown, Md.: Review and Herald®, 2004), 61–64, 67, 68.

20. Dick, *Willliam Miller and the Advent Crisis.*

21. Joseph Bates, *The Autobiography of Elder Joseph Bates,* introduction by Gary Land, Adventist Classic Library (Berrien Springs, Mich.: Andrews University Press, 2004); Sylvester Bliss, *Memoirs of William Miller Generally Known as a Lecturer on the Prophecies and the Second Coming of Christ,* introduction by Merlin D. Burt, Adventist Classic Library (Berrien Springs, Mich.: Andrews University Press, 2005); Isaac C. Wellcome, *History of the Second Advent Message and Mission, Doctrine and People,* introduction by Gary Land, Adventist Classic Library (Berrien Springs, Mich.: Andrews University Press, 2008).

# Chapter 8

# Fresh Perspectives on Developments in Early Adventist Theology

Paul M. Evans

t was in analyzing Adventist theological developments of the late nineteenth century that George Knight's genius for getting to the core of an issue perhaps first came to be widely noticed. His apparent knack for creating enemies on both sides of the various theological controversies was, and continues to be, a necessary by-product of his incisive thinking and writing. The theological issues that would come to dominate Adventism for more than a century were to a great degree born in the doctrinal conflict surrounding the 1888 General Conference Session. As another chapter will discuss Knight's substantial treatment of this period and its related issues, we will here confine ourselves to his contributions toward an Adventist self-understanding in some less obvious areas of theological development. While Knight's spotlight has shone brightly on the developments surrounding the Minneapolis session, his analyses of issues seemingly less connected to the great issues of salvation and righteousness by faith have nonetheless also served to promote fresh understanding in some other critical areas.

Knight's *Search for Identity* has been the state-of-the-art resource for students of the history of Adventist theology for nearly fifteen years.[1] No other book that he has authored includes such a wide-ranging survey of the Adventist theological landscape. Though purposefully brief, the amount of detail squeezed into this outline of the major developments in Adventist theology makes the book a mini-"reference work," but one that, in his inimitable style, reads almost like a story-book.[2] In his introductory note to the book, Knight tantalizingly mentioned the possibility of "four larger volumes" that would provide an expanded discussion of the development of Adventist beliefs.[3] This would be a treat to Adventist historians, theologians, and pastors, as well as many of the more studious among the laity. But the present volume stands apart in its power to give the reader a more than adequate grasp of the major theological developments of the first 150 years of the denomination.

Turning to Knight's treatment of the last half of the nineteenth century, one may wonder what he could have included in the discussion apart from a consideration of the determinative 1888 era and its issues. Since his purpose was to paint a sweeping picture of the general shifts in Adventist beliefs, he necessarily spent less time accounting for the development of beliefs less pivotal. But as Dr. Knight used to like to say in his classes, things don't happen in a vacuum. The Adventist Church wasn't born in a vacuum, and neither did the critical issues of the 1888 era just drop out of the sky.

As he brought out toward the end of chapter four of *A Search for Identity,* after the formulation of the doctrinal package known to sabbatarian Adventists as the "present truth," the church exercised great devotion and energy in proclaiming the newly found truths. The theological task that confronted the budding denomination was to "expand and expound upon their core pillar doctrines."[4] Among the theological "refinements" of the first decade after the Sabbath Conferences, Knight discussed the two-phase fall of Babylon, the pre-Advent judgment, the newly shut and open doors, and the manifestation of the prophetic gift in the remnant church.[5] Two of these, the pre-Advent judgment and the gift of prophecy as a mark of the remnant, have proven to be rather controversial at different times in Adventist history.

Knight's discussion of the acceptance of the pre-Advent judgment by sabbatarian Adventists is an example of *Search for Identity*'s underlying thesis, that Adventist beliefs have appropriately undergone change and development through time. This seems at first to be rather mundane and self-evident. After all, it is inevitable that some doctrinal change must take place if such understanding is to progress. But Knight spelled out the reality of this inevitable doctrinal change in a less comfortable way than Adventists were used to. As former General Conference president Neal C. Wilson noted, Knight raised "perplexing but legitimate questions."[6] Adventist historian Richard Schwarz, author of the denominational history textbook *Light Bearers to the Remnant*, had already pointed out that James White at first "flatly rejected" the concept of an investigative judgment.[7] But Knight, rather than just mentioning the fact, let us hear for ourselves the finality in White's voice: " 'This view is certainly without foundation in the word of God.' "[8] Such a display of disagreement by top church leaders on what they a few years later were proclaiming as part of "present truth" goes far toward establishing Knight's thesis, that the discovery of truth is an ongoing process.

The nature, purpose, scope, and timing of the pre-Advent judgment and the cleansing of the heavenly sanctuary have continued to be subjects of study, and have figured largely in discussions of the needed preparation for Christ's coming. Knight has addressed these concerns in many of his books, including his critique of M. L. Andreasen's last-generation theology, which sees God's vindication in the end-time judgment as dependent on the development of a generation of saints that completely overcomes sin. It was this identification by Knight of Andreasen as the source of last-generation theology that inspired my own doctoral research.[9]

The other newly established belief of the 1850s that has continued to provoke discussion is the understanding of the gift of prophecy as an end-time marker of the last-day people of God. In *Search for Identity*, Knight identified James White as a strong proponent of this theology in 1856. Accordingly, another of Knight's students, Theodore Levterov, was motivated to do doctoral research in this area.[10] In documenting how Adventists defended the existence of a prophet in their midst, Levterov significantly observes that the Adventists "never claimed that the true prophetic gift was limited only to Ellen White." Rather, they published accounts of those whom they believed had "genuine visionary manifestations."[11] This early, broader view of the "gift of prophecy" would later narrow to what Adventists in developed countries are more comfortable with today—that the gifts are a historic phenomenon, rather than a present reality.

In concluding his discussion of the formative period of Adventism, and as background to the issues that came to the fore in and around 1888, Knight identified four disturbing trends that had the potential to weaken the new denomination's theological position: (1) a drift toward legalism, (2) aggressive, debate-driven evangelism, (3) prioritizing doctrinal preservation, and (4) turning to Ellen White's writings for answers to biblical questions.[12] As background to the 1888 crisis, George showed how each of these trends set the stage for the full-blown struggle that erupted then. Going beyond what had been written before, he demonstrated that the precursors of the righteousness by faith debate were not only legalism, pride of opinion, and personality clashes, but also questions about the proper sources of doctrinal authority.[13] This is where his contribution to Adventist theology has been most valuable—in pointing out inconsistencies in the quality of the witnesses brought forth in defense of church teachings. Rather than going to the Bible, as Ellen White herself counseled, Adventist leaders were more concerned about who was in favor of a certain idea, and what had been taught in the past. The defense of past truths became more important than the discovery of present truth. And eventually, the words of Ellen White herself would become a new arbiter of Bible truth, against her own counsel. All of these epistemological and hermeneutical issues are brought to bear in Knight's analysis of Adventist theological development.

Knight has truly shaped the fields of Adventist history and Adventist theology, not to speak of Adventist education. As a result of his gifts in educating young people in scholarly research and writing, he has nurtured a generation of trained Adventist historians and historical theologians who are not afraid of what they will find, who learn to think critically for themselves, and who at the same time seek to differentiate the human from the divine in the sources they handle.

For many reasons, Adventists are indebted to George Knight. I am one of those who has personally benefited from his teaching ministry. When I resumed my MDiv studies at the Seventh-day Adventist Theological Seminary in 1996 (after a fifteen-year break) I had read some of his writings and looked forward to taking a class from him. Actually, though, it was while sitting in Jon Paulien's Salvation class that I first heard of "last-generation theology." Dr. Paulien informed us that, according to Dr. Knight, the writings of M. L. Andreasen had popularized this view. This was new to me, as I had always understood the last-generation view to be the standard Adventist take on eschatology. I enrolled in Knight's Development of Seventh-day Adventist Theology class to get a clearer understanding of his views, and was not disappointed. I found his lectures fascinating and stimulating.

His classes were always full, even though he was the only teacher I know who felt at liberty to lock the classroom doors to late-coming students (even at 7:30 A.M.!).

When at the end of my MDiv studies I felt a call to pursue a doctoral degree, it was natural for me to choose Adventist studies, with last-generation theology as a potential dissertation topic. Dr. Knight welcomed me to his group of select doctoral students. Shortly thereafter, though, I decided to switch to New Testament studies for employability reasons. The day after my decision, I met George riding his bike as I was walking home from school (the only time I ever met him like this). I told him about my change of mind. When he asked what had caused the change, I confessed that my wife had convinced me that I would be more employable as a New Testament teacher. He accepted this, but jokingly remarked that my wife (who is Korean) was not the traditional Asian woman who followed her husband ten paces behind. It was not the first time one of his lighthearted comments shook someone up a little. It freed me to rethink my decision (with my wife's encouragement), and in a short time I was back where my heart was—in Adventist studies. As I look back on it now, it was one of the best decisions of my life.

So I am personally indebted to George Knight, not only for keeping me in the field of Adventist studies, but also for opening my eyes to my own limitations. I came to Andrews University with a bit of suspicion. Having become somewhat familiar with Dr. Knight through some of his works, I was disinclined to accept his views in a number of areas. I had grown up in an era of theological controversy, in which it was natural for combatants to choose which side they would join. And even though I came to seminary with a new heart and mind and a desire to bring people together, rather than to separate them, I felt I was not in Dr. Knight's camp. But through the years, I began to realize that George didn't belong to either of the camps I had been familiar with. The more I read his works, and sat in his classes, and talked with him, the more I realized he didn't fit any preexisting mold. And I admired him greatly for that.

As I noted at the beginning of this piece, Dr. Knight has a way of making enemies on both sides of the Adventist "aisle." And I admire him for that too. It gives me hope that one day we can be brought together. Not by one side trouncing the other into submission, but simply by asking good questions, and exchanging honest answers.

A number of years ago, Knight confessed that he was no longer perfect.[14]

During my time at the seminary, I rather frequently saw in him what seemed to be the erstwhile perfectionist popping up. I don't remember any other professor who would hand out his tests facedown, and make students wait until everyone had a copy before signaling the class to begin. (This is the way a test *should* be administered if every student is to have the same amount of time to work on it, but most professors are far from the educational ideal.) In doctoral-level seminars, he had us check one another's citations for accuracy, and most of us were surprised at how far we were from perfect. Knight modeled an "ex-legalism" that, at the minimum, did not entail a lack of concern for detail! On the other hand, it was reassuring to see how *un*surprised he was by his *own* imperfections. In one seminar I had the opportunity to point out a small inaccuracy in *Search for Identity,* and I was reassured by Dr. Knight's simple admission of the error and his unwillingness for me to minimize its significance. Those not familiar with him may think they see a bit of a Texas swagger, but when you get to know him, you realize he is a genuinely humble person.

But although Knight exemplifies a Christian who is deeply aware of his own humanity, as a teacher he would never let his students get too comfortable. If they concluded from his casual attire and friendly classroom banter that they could relax and take it easy in his classes, they were in for a rude awakening. His life has demonstrated that redemption from perfectionism does not at all translate into mediocrity. As a teacher, he was an example of the truth of Paul's words, "Do we, then, nullify the law by this faith? Not at all! Rather, we uphold the law" (Romans 3:31, NIV). No, George Knight may not be perfect anymore. But in my book, he is still pretty close.

Endnotes

1. George R. Knight, A Search for Identity: The Development of Seventh-day Adventist Beliefs (Hagerstown, Md.: Review and Herald®, 2000).

2. Paul M. Evans, review of A Search for Identity: The Development of Seventh-day Adventist Beliefs, by George R. Knight, Andrews University Seminary Studies 40, no. 1 (Spring 2002): 154.

3. Knight, A Search for Identity, 11.

4. Ibid., 87.

5. Ibid., 77–86.

6. Neal C. Wilson, foreword to A Search for Identity: The Development of Seventh-day Adventist Beliefs, by George R. Knight (Hagerstown, Md.: Review and Herald®, 2000), 7.

7. Richard Schwarz, Light Bearers to the Remnant: Denominational History Textbook for Seventh-day Adventist College Classes (Mountain View, Calif.: Pacific Press®, 1979), 170.

8. James White, "The Day of Judgment," *Advent Review*, September 1850, 49, quoted in George R. Knight, *A Search for Identity*, 81.

9. Knight, *A Search for Identity*, 144–152; Paul M. Evans, "A Historical-Contextual Analysis of the Final-Generation Theology of M. L. Andreasen" (PhD diss., Andrews University, 2010). See below on how I came to a decision to study this topic further, under Knight's guidance.

10. Knight, *A Search for Identity*, 84–86; Theodore N. Levterov, "The Development of the Seventh-day Adventist Understanding of Ellen G. White's Prophetic Gift, 1844-1889" (PhD diss., Andrews University, 2011).

11. Levterov, "Development of the Seventh-day Adventist Understanding," 231.

12. Knight, *A Search for Identity*, 87, 88.

13. Ibid., 93–100. Cf. Schwarz, *Light Bearers to the Remnant*, 183–197; Department of Education, General Conference of Seventh-day Adventists, *The Story of Our Church* (Mountain View, Calif.: Pacific Press®, 1979), 243–248; Arthur W. Spalding, *Origin and History of Seventh-day Adventists* (Washington, D.C.: Review and Herald®, 1962), vol. 2, 281–303.

14. George R. Knight, *I Used to Be Perfect: An Ex-Legalist Looks at Law, Sin, and Grace* (Boise, Idaho: Pacific Press®, 1994).

## Chapter 9

# A New Look at Developments in Twentieth-Century Adventist Theology

Paul E. McGraw

George R. Knight's *A Search for Identity: The Development of Seventh-day Adventist Beliefs*, for two reasons, was a very important book when published in 2000. First, it took on the challenge of examining not just how Adventist beliefs had been formed to begin with but how and why they had continued to develop in the succeeding decades. Noting that such development was a reality and indeed a necessity, Knight looked for the connecting tissues of ideas between those developments and the contexts that nurtured them. His purpose was to provide an understanding of why the theological issues roiling the waters of Adventism at the end of the twentieth century were what they were and why they were significant. Secondly, the book attempted to discuss, in a popular form, what many have often perceived as esoteric theology, and in doing so, it made the history of contemporary Adventist theology readily accessible to a broad audience. That is one of the great achievements of this book.

An indication of the significance of the book is that Knight persuaded former

General Conference president Neal C. Wilson to preface the volume with "A Word to the Reader"—something that Elder Wilson did not do very often. The frank approach that Knight took in the book in discussing problematic episodes in Adventist history, and the provocative approach to explaining Ellen White's authority and to challenging long established Adventist orthodoxies risked the possibility that George's regular denominational publisher with its more traditional leadership might be disinclined to accept the manuscript. An endorsement from the former president would give the cloak of respectability it needed. Wilson commented that he had thoughtfully read the volume through three times, and although it raised "many perplexing but legitimate questions," he thought it suggested satisfying answers. The endorsement ensured publication.[1]

Knight sees the growth of Adventist theology during its first hundred years being shaped by its need to answer for itself three important questions: What is Adventist in Adventism? What is Christian in Adventism? What is fundamentalist in Adventism? In sensing the necessity to address these questions, he sees the movement seeking an identity for itself as a basis for understanding its mission. Thus the title of the work, *A Search for Identity*. By exploring these core questions, Knight seeks to do in a more serious historical theological study of Adventist history what Morris Venden sought to do in a homiletic mode a decade and a half earlier in his trilogy *Common Ground, Uncommon Ground,* and *Higher Ground*. Venden's work also challenged Adventism to understand its relationship to other Christian groups.

The importance of Knight's work, especially in the last half of *A Search for Identity*, is that he gives a clear explanation of how the dialectic tensions over theology in contemporary Adventism since the 1950s have arisen with the resurrection of the same three questions from its first century. The major strands of contemporary debate all relate to previous periods of crisis and the questions each crisis period sought to resolve. In this endeavor, George has succeeded in throwing much new light on areas of Adventism's previously neglected history. The importance of his work lies in its seeing important connections between the theological issues studied in earlier works on Adventist history (which focused mainly on nineteenth-century Adventism) to those that occurred in the twentieth century.

As a historian, a personal experience may explain the relevance of this connection and why *A Search for Identity* is such a significant work in Adventist history. While doing research at the Ellen White Estate in the late 1990s, I came across a letter written by Willie White to a friend recording his last visit with Arthur G.

Daniells. The letter described White, sitting at Daniells's bedside and the two recounting together their many life experiences. The letter was filled with both joyful recollection and regret for a relationship that had faltered in the years following Ellen White's death. Willie White recounted the better times in their relationship and emphasized one particularly enjoyable trip on the deck of a steamer where they "discussed eternal principles." I turned to one of the people who worked in the White Estate, who had been so helpful with earlier queries about documents, and asked if they had any idea to what experience Willie White might have referred. The reply I received is emblematic of why what Knight did in *A Search for Identity* was so vital. Asked for the date of the letter, I said 1934. The staffer replied, "Well if it happened after 1915, I really can't be of any help." For many other Adventists as well, nothing really important happened after Ellen White's death.

There are several reasons why Adventist scholars have done so little work on post-1915 Adventist history. First, is the basic problem of simply being able to acquire a historical perspective on issues in such close proximity to our own time. It is often difficult for contemporaries of an event to put personal experiences into an objective context. Often, those close to the incident either embellish or diminish the event based on emotions rather than objectivity. During the 1940s, both F. D. Nichol and LeRoy Froom attempted to analyze some twentieth-century issues, but their lack of historical perspective is often evident in their work. Another challenge for Adventist historians was that of moving past the most pivotal figure in Adventist history, Ellen G. White. It is this void that Knight's work helps to fill in the historiography of Adventist theology.

The early chapters of *A Search for Identity* attempt to explain how the question of what is Adventist in Adventism shaped the early Sabbatarian Adventist movement in the immediate post-1844 period. Knight then looks at the links between later nineteenth-century Adventism and that of the early twentieth century in the chapter "What Is Christian in Adventism." This chapter begins with an overview of the 1888 General Conference's focus on the importance of righteousness by faith and then explores the subsequent impact of that issue on Adventist theology. As Knight turns to the early twentieth century, he explains why not all the theological issues that emerged in the church are included in the book and he identifies five that he surveys briefly.[2] They include the Holy Flesh movement (1899–1901), the Kellogg or pantheism crisis (1901–1907), A. F. Ballenger's "rejection of Adventism's traditional understanding of the sanctuary and its ministries" (1905), and the challenge set forth by Jones and Waggoner when they suggested a move to a "pentecostal/holiness ecclesiology" (1899–1903). Knight briefly argues that such an ecclesiology as Jones and Waggoner argued for "denied the need for church organization since the Holy Spirit spoke directly to each church member."[3] George then concludes his explanation of the five exclusions with the "daily" controversy (1906–1910). While this controversy appears to deal merely with the meaning of one word in one verse of Daniel 8, it became important to Adventism because of its focus on the larger problem of the role of Ellen White's authority. Knight argues that these conflicts became dead ends and did not contribute to mainline theological development in the church. "No specific theological advances or changes came out of those five internal conflicts."[4]

One could argue, however, that at least two of these "internal conflicts" hold a significance greater than other simple short-run examples. At the least, two of the conflicts highlighted Adventism's tenuous relationship with the broader Christian community in America at the turn of the twentieth century. Calvin Edwards and Gary Land showed in their book *Seeker After Light: A. F. Ballenger, Adventism and American Christianity*[5] how Adventism's reaction to its brush with the burgeoning Pentecostal movement affected its theology as much by what it rejected as by what it retained. Ballenger attempted to push Adventism headlong into the center of discussion on the Holiness movement and, according to Edwards and Land, he almost succeeded.

Adventism at first appeared to embrace elements of the Holiness movement but it abruptly ended when the issue moved "beyond the traditional Adventist interest in character perfection to that of the physical perfection of the human body before the Second Advent."[6] While Knight chose not to do an in-depth study of what becomes known as the Holy Flesh movement, it could be asked what long-term effects this reversal had on twentieth-century Adventism.

A second issue that he mentions briefly, but does not focus on at length, is the so-called pantheism debate of the early twentieth century. The fact that two very important leaders at the time, John Harvey Kellogg and E. J. Waggoner, embraced a form of pantheism shook Adventism as it entered the twentieth century. Both Kellogg and Waggoner had great influence in the early twentieth century, and their thinking in this area could be seen as part of a search for a better theological rationale for the medical program. A larger underlying issue was whether the main focus of the movement should be on welfare work for the poor and marginalized or whether the focus should be on evangelistic preaching and the seeking of conversions. As Adventism emerged into the twentieth century, it was prepared to face issues such as its semi-Arian past and the fact that it would no longer countenance pantheism by its thought leaders. One could argue for the inclusion of each of these issues because of their effect on the trajectory of twentieth century Adventist theology. Yet the panoramic sweep of the book in general, (Knight acknowledges that of necessity he has to paint the picture with broad brush strokes) and limitations of space may have demanded their exclusion along with possibly many other events.

*A Search for Identity*'s contribution to understanding Adventist history from 1919–1950 is arguably one of the most important parts of this book. Knight takes a critical look at how much influence the Fundamentalist movement of the early twentieth century had on Adventist theology. Far too often previous histories of Adventism have minimized the impact of external forces. George's willingness to explore the effect of the Fundamentalist movement and how its arguments seeped into Adventism is very important.

Understanding how, against the background of an aggressive fundamentalism, Adventism tried to address the question, "What is fundamentalist in Adventism?" is enlightening. The easy, quick answer might be, virtually everything. Knight points out that some Adventist authors, noting that Adventists in keeping all of the commandments, including the Sabbath, considered themselves in a sense the only true fundamentalists. While the term *fundamentalist* comes from a twelve-volume series entitled "The Fundamentals," they were quickly distilled into a list of five that included the substitutionary atonement of Jesus, the virgin birth, the literal resurrection and second coming of Jesus, a literal reading of the Bible, including accounts of miracles, and the inerrancy of Scripture.

## Inerrancy

The first four of the Fundamentals could easily be accepted as core elements of Adventism. The final Fundamental, that of inerrancy of Scripture, would be the place where Adventism and Fundamentalism appear to diverge. Knight points out that while many within Adventism may have held to an inerrant view of Scripture, informed Adventist leaders who had worked closely with Ellen White rejected the idea. What he argues in *A Search for Identity* is that while fundamentalists pushed for the inerrancy of scripture, the battle within Adventism turned on whether or not the denomination should hold the writings of Ellen White to the same level as those of the Bible. Knight makes clear that Ellen White herself did not hold inerrantist positions in regard to the inspiration of the Bible, much less her own writings.

As mentioned above, the "internal conflict" over the "daily" had as much to do with the position of those who held to the "old view" of the daily on the nature of Ellen White's writings as it did to their position on the "daily" itself. They argued that Ellen White once wrote that the founders of Adventism were right on the topic. Yet when the issue reemerged at the turn of the twentieth century, rather than simply pointing combatants to her earlier comments on the subject, Ellen White emphasized that the topic was of minor importance and should not be allowed to become a divisive issue. Knight points out that those who pushed back against the "new view" of the daily, did so as much to protect Ellen White's writings as to argue a theological point. The challenge that Adventism faced in the 1920s stemmed from a misunderstanding by many within Adventism about the subject of inspiration as a whole.

George argues that a resolution passed by the 1883 General Conference Session had already answered the question regarding inspiration. It came about in a discussion about the republication of certain volumes of Ellen White's *Testimonies*. The official resolution prepared readers who might struggle with the idea that anyone could dare to edit a prophet. It specifically said that many of the letters published in the *Testimonies* were "written under the most unfavorable circumstances" and that the pressure to get them published at times allowed "imperfections to pass" uncorrected. This seemingly simple statement about possible grammatical errors led the 1883 General Conference to pass an official resolution as to the nature of inspiration. "We believe the light given by God to his servants is by the enlightenment of the mind, thus imparting the thoughts, and not (except in rare cases) the very words in which the ideas should be expressed." The resolution concluded by saying, "Such verbal changes be made as to remove the above named imperfections, as far as possible, without in any measure changing the thought."[7]

This perspective seemed to lose ground as the years passed. By the time the 1911 revision of *The Great Controversy* was published, many with a verbalist stance on White's writings were uncomfortable with the idea of revision, particularly when it was realized, as Prescott pointed out, that changing a word did change the thought. In a letter to S. N. Haskell in 1912, W. C. White went so far as to warn Haskell about trying to make his mother an authority on things such as history saying, "I believe, Brother Haskell, that there is danger of our injuring Mother's work by claiming for it more than she claims for it."[8]

Knight uses the dialogue from the 1919 Bible Conference to show that the acceptance of verbal inspiration was widespread in the years leading up to the 1919 Bible Conference. To take a verbalist view, however, he argues that one must then essentially ignore the previous stance of the church on the subject. Knight makes an important point when he observes that, "it is no accident that most of those Adventist leaders who were closest to Ellen White denied inerrancy and verbalism for both the Bible and her writings."[9] George points out that the Fundamentalist movement significantly influenced the younger leaders in Adventism in this area of theology.[10]

His work on this subject is important as it puts into context how the church moved from a historically moderate position on inerrancy to a widely held but unofficial stance that viewed the writings of Ellen White to be as inerrant as the Bible itself. This trend accelerated in the decade following Ellen White's death in 1915. By the early 1930s, the transition appeared to be complete. The June 1931 issue of *Ministry* magazine, in a section titled "Inspiration," quoted extensively from the *Princeton Theological Review* on the subject of verbal inspiration. The editors chose to quote without editorial comment that "if we do not accept verbal inspiration, then it is senseless, nonsensical, to speak of an inspiration of the Bible. The inspiration of the Bible as such is verbal inspiration and plenary inspiration."[11]

The ultimate result of this push toward a fundamentalist position on inerrancy was that by the 1970s and 1980s most Adventists had accepted inerrancy, believing it to be the traditional stance of the church. Knight's work on this subject of internal debate is important because it brought to light the fact that the popular position on the topic of inspiration has been different at various points in Advent history.

## Christology and last-generation perfectionism

Knight also traces the internal debate over the issue of the human nature of Christ, character perfection, and righteousness by faith. As Adventism edged closer to Fundamentalism on the issue of inerrancy, it moved in its own direction when it came to the question of salvation. One of the major figures of this era was

M. L. Andreasen, and Knight explains Andreasen's "last-generation" theology and how it pushed Adventism toward a much stronger position on character perfection. One of the central elements of Andreasen's theology was founded on the idea that Jesus came to earth with a fallen human nature. Andreasen did not originate the idea within Adventism. Knight points out that the book *Bible Readings for the Home Circle* in every edition from 1915 to 1949 said that Jesus was not only "incarnated in 'sinful flesh' but it stated that He had 'sinful, fallen nature' and was born with 'tendencies to sin.' "[12] According to Knight, such statements did not appear in *Bible Readings* from 1888 to 1915. It was only during the early twentieth century that you can find this element of an emerging theology in which character perfection was promoted by a widely circulated book. It was not until the 1949 edition that those remarks were removed. Knight points out that this period of time between the death of Ellen White and the 1950s is what is often contemporarily referred to as "Historic Adventism."

Even while Adventist thought was dominated by Andreasen and his "last-generation" theology, the 1930s and 1940s saw some within the church attempt to present a more moderate position which they hoped would make Adventism more acceptable to a wider cross section of American Christians. Together, F. D. Nichol, in his position as editor of the *Review and Herald,* and LeRoy Froom, as editor of *Ministry* magazine, worked to repair the image of Adventism in the minds of American Protestants. Nichol's 1944 work *The Midnight Cry* sought to give an accurate history of the Millerite movement while debunking some of the arguments Protestant groups made to marginalize Adventism through the use of the term *cult.* Along with Nichol's attempts to legitimize Adventism, LeRoy Froom's four-volume series, *Prophetic Faith of Our Fathers,* first published in 1946, also sought to show that Adventist theology, in particular its interpretation of prophecy, was not aberrant but founded in historic Christian faith.

The work of Nichol and Froom produced a push back against some of the more radical fundamentalist positions within Adventism. In 1953, the publication of the first of seven volumes of the *Seventh-day Adventist Bible Commentary* appeared. Along the same lines as the works of Nichol and Froom, the commentary sought to give Adventism a voice of its own in articulating its beliefs.

The area where *A Search for Identity* does some of its most helpful work is when it casts light on the background of certain more recent theological conflicts in the church. If much of Adventism's history, following the death of Ellen

White in 1915, has been ignored, the period of the 1950s and following has received even less attention until recently. Some of the important developments that Knight highlights during this time include the establishment of the Seventh-day Adventist Theological Seminary, which Knight points out was intended more for the training of religion teachers than that of prospective pastors. The Biblical Research Fellowship organized during the late 1940s and became a place where Adventist religious scholars could join together, present scholarly papers on various topics, and receive feedback from their colleagues. By 1951, the Biblical Research Fellowship was integrated into the General Conference as the Office of Biblical Research.

One person who had a substantial impact on an emerging generation of Adventist leaders and pastors beginning in the 1940s was Edward Heppenstall. Where Andreasen's theology dominated Adventism in the 1930s and 1940s, Heppenstall's renewed focus on righteousness by faith and the "new covenant experience"[13] had extensive influence upon the next generation. Knight points out that "Heppenstall's theology was definitely a more cross-centered, Christ-centered, evangelical form of theology than that of Andreasen and his followers." He goes on to point out that Heppenstall's theology was a direct counter to Andreasen's "last-generation" perfectionist theology.[14]

## Inter-faith dialogue

The 1950s became a dividing point in Adventist theological history. LeRoy Froom's efforts to legitimize Adventism in the eyes of evangelical and fundamentalists since the early 1930s grew in recognition with the publication of *Prophetic Faith of Our Fathers*. Through a unique series of events in the early 1950s, he, along with his fellow Ministerial Department colleague Roy Allan Anderson, came into conversation with prominent fundamentalists over the legitimacy of Adventism as a Christian faith.

Their meetings with Walter Martin would come to be called the Evangelical Conferences. *A Search for Identity* shines an important light on these meetings and how they portended the future of Adventism's debates both internally and with the broader Christian world. These conferences first took place with Walter Martin, who planned to write a book on how Adventism was a "cult," and then with Donald Grey Barnhouse. Barnhouse was a Presbyterian pastor based in

Philadelphia, whose weekly sermons were heard on radio across the United States. Froom, Anderson, and W. E. Reed, convinced Martin and Barnhouse that Adventism was indeed orthodox in its theology. When, in 1956, Barnhouse declared his conclusions in an article he published in his fundamentalist periodical *Eternity Magazine* entitled "Are Seventh-day Adventists Christian?" it led to a division among fundamentalists and Adventists alike. The dividing point came when Barnhouse referred to Adventists who differed from what Froom and Anderson explained as Adventist positions at the "lunatic fringe."[15] Many of the positions Barnhouse believed were held only by the "lunatic fringe," including the belief that atonement was not complete until 1844. Actually, it was a position held by numerous Adventists (if not most) since 1845. Barnhouse encouraged fellow fundamentalists and evangelicals to disregard extremist's voices and only countenance what the "sane leadership" of the church said Adventists believed. This segmenting of Adventism by Barnhouse became apparent with the 1957 publication of *Seventh-day Adventists Answer Questions on Doctrine.* M. L. Andreasen, despite having retired, reemerged to argue for traditional Adventist beliefs.

Knight takes a strong stance on the issue when he infers that Froom, who was one of the principal authors of *Questions on Doctrine,* was less than honest with Martin and Barnhouse about the differences between his beliefs and those of rank-and-file Adventists. On issues such as the nature of Christ, Froom implied that Adventism had always held to a pre-Fall position on the nature of Jesus, not a post-Fall one. "Froom, Anderson, and their colleagues were not completely candid when they gave Martin and Barnhouse the impression that 'the overwhelming majority never held to those divergent views,' " Knight asserted.[16] Especially during the 1930s and 1940s, numerous Adventists believed just as Andreasen preached in his "last-generation" theology that only a Savior who suffered the same weakened physical condition and the same propensities toward sin that every human experiences, could be our Savior. Barnhouse had grown up near a large Adventist community in Mountain View, California, and knew that most Adventists he met held to the fallen nature of Christ. When he encountered Froom, Anderson, and Reed, he finally found Adventists who agreed with him on the pre-Fall nature of Christ, and they just happened to be the leadership of the church—thus his "shock." Andreasen, however, and others who shared his theology, pushed back strongly against Froom and *Questions on Doctrine.*

Knight, in the "Annotated Edition" of *Questions on Doctrine,* presents important and extensive documentation exposing the two conflicting views held by Adventists through the years, both perspectives also reflected in Ellen White.[17] George's assessment of the controversy over the nature of Christ leads to a very important point. Andreasen viewed the nature of Christ as a "foundational pillar" to Adventism, but Knight points out that "while it is true that it was a core aspect of his [Andreasen's] theology, the founders of the Adventist message certainly didn't view it as a pillar."[18] A Search for Identity addresses several other "theological tensions" from the last half of the twentieth century, ranging from the Desmond Ford and Walter Rea controversies in the early 1980s to the revival of a form of Andreasen's theology in the 1888 Message Study Committee. Although he devotes more attention to such issues than the five at the turn of the twentieth century, it is still difficult by the time A Search for Identity was published in 2000 to perhaps have the full benefit of distance in shaping a historical perspective in viewing them.

While Knight makes important points about various issues that Adventism encountered in the twentieth century, what is of even greater importance is the methodology his work exemplifies. The real gift of A Search for Identity comes from that very methodology. By looking back at Adventist theology through a historical lens, Knight brings into focus theological issues and historical discussions that have fallen into the recesses of the collective Adventist memory. This work brings these issues to the forefront and shows that whether understood by the majority of the rank-and-file Adventists or not, each issue actually played a substantial role in the theology held to by many early twenty-first-century Adventists. One of the most important benefits of this book is that by recounting its history, Knight shows that Adventism has never been static theologically. Whether realized or not, at any given time Adventism makes its way from tension to crisis and back to tension again. By doing this, it continues to follow the path of its founders who believed in the reality of present truth and the concept of progressive revelation.

One of the values of history is to allow us to look back over broad swaths of time and see how the concepts of present and progressive revelation work themselves out in practice. Knight's Search for Identity offers a helpful brief survey that does exactly that and alerts us to the fact that change in Adventism in inevitable as it seeks to understand more clearly its role and mission in each new generation.

Though limited by format and audience, the book shows how Adventism sought to work out its theology when faced with new perspectives, both within its own ranks and in reaction to beliefs among other conservative Christian groups.

Adventism can be grateful that it has had the diligent work of George R. Knight to help remind it of this perspective as it moves forward.

The impact of George Knight on my development as a historian is very easy to identify. I remember the event vividly. During the summer of 1987, I had just completed a class in modern church history from Daniel Augsburger and began to realize my love of Christian history. While I had taken church history as an undergraduate, something about the way Augsburger presented the story struck a chord with me that summer. In the second summer session, I signed up to take a course, "The History of Religion in America," from George Knight. I knew who he was, and had read some of his work, but never imagined that class would have the lasting impact that it did. I'll never forget the first class period when George somewhat offhandedly quipped, "Remind me to tell you sometime why I don't like Adventists." He repeated that line from time-to-time throughout that session, and it seemed that everyday someone reminded him of his promise. I believe it was the last class period that the highly anticipated story came out. I can only remember parts of it but more importantly how eager almost everyone in the class was to find out why George Knight didn't like Adventists. For me, however, the most important thing I learned by the end of that class was that I had found my intellectual passion—American religious history and particularly the Adventist part of it. That class in the summer of 1987 piqued my interest in American religious history, and I began to use my electives for Adventist history courses. I took "The Development of Adventist Lifestyle" and then an independent study on the issue of religious liberty during the next school year, and I was hooked.

I stayed in contact with George during the next eight years as I pastored. I was very grateful for his advice and encouragement about pursuing more graduate work in history. By the time I finished my dissertation, almost fifteen years after that summer class in 1987, there was no question in my mind that when I wrote the thank-you section I would have to acknowledge his influence. Knight's written works play a role in my Adventist Heritage class to this day. They have provided many of the foundational elements that guide my understanding of Adventist history and for that I will be forever grateful.

## Endnotes

1. George R. Knight, *A Search for Identity: The Development of Seventh-day Adventist Beliefs*, Adventist Heritage Series (Hagerstown, Md.: Review and Herald®, 2000), 7, 8.

2. Ibid., 126.

3. Ibid., 126.

4. Ibid., 127.

5. Calvin W. Edwards and Gary Land, *Seeker After Light: A. F. Ballenger, Adventism, and American Christianity* (Berrien Springs, Mich.: Andrews University Press, 2000).

6. Knight, *A Search for Identity*, 127.

7. "General Conference Proceedings No. 32," *Review and Herald*, 1883, 741.

8. W. C. White to S. N. Haskell, October 31, 1912.

9. Knight, *A Search for Identity*, 137.

10. Ibid.

11. "Inspiration," *Ministry* 4, no. 6 (June 1931): 21.

12. *Bible Readings for the Home Circle*, 1915 ed. (Washington, D.C.: Review and Herald®, 1915), 174.

13. Knight, *A Search for Identity*, 172.

14. Ibid.

15. Ibid., 164.

16. Ibid., 165. See also George R. Knight, ed., *Seventh-day Adventists Answer Questions on Doctrine*, critical ed., Adventist Classic Library (Berrien Springs, Mich.: Andrews University Press, 2003).

17. Ibid., 522–526.

18. Knight, *A Search for Identity*, 170.

## Chapter 10

# The Definitive Interpreter of Minneapolis 1888

Woodrow W. Whidden

W hile Knight's first book-length publishing success was *Myths in Adventism* (Review and Herald®, 1985),[1] the book that really put him on the wider Adventist stage was his well-timed biography of A. T. Jones, *From 1888 to Apostasy: The Case of A. T. Jones* (Review and Herald®, 1987).[2] The *Myths in Adventism* volume was a surprising success, but it was mostly a harbinger of what would develop into one of if not the most prodigious and astonishingly productive scholarly/ad populam writing careers in Adventism since that of Ellen G. White.

## Impact of 1888 themes on Knight and his major works

Prodigality, however, is not the key thesis of this reflection. Rather, the real significance of the Jones biography is that it became the source from which would flow not only Knight's writings on the 1888 phenomenon, but also his other foundational works in Adventist studies. His research on this project led to further studies covering Adventist history and theology (including the life and work of Ellen White) and to his contribution as a major Adventist author and editor of lay-oriented Bible commentaries and devotional books.

More specific to this essay, however, are his subsequent works on 1888, Minneapolis, and its complicated legacy. His very next book, after the Jones biography, would be *Angry Saints* (Review and Herald®, 1989), to be followed almost a decade later by *A User-Friendly Guide to the 1888 Message* (Review and Herald®, 1998). As suggested above, these works would also provide a fertile spawning bed for Knight's important theological treatises, including *My Gripe With God* (Review and Herald®, 1990), subsequently revised and released as *The Cross of Christ* (Review and Herald®, 2008), the first volume in the Library of Adventist Theology series; and *The Pharisee's Guide to Perfect Holiness* (Review and Herald®, 1992), subsequently re-released as *Sin and Salvation* (Review and Herald®, 2008) in the Library of Adventist Theology.

It is also noteworthy that two other volumes in the theological genre emerged from his work on 1888 issues: his further reflections on personal salvation *I Used to Be Perfect* (Pacific Press®, 1994, later republished by Andrews University Press, 2001) and his historical interpretation of Adventist theology entitled *A Search for Identity* (Review and Herald®, 2000), especially pages 90–127.

## The salvation theme—a major driver in Knight's agenda

For Knight, the issues of personal salvation proved to be major "drivers" of his productive writing agenda. In fact, one suspects that a strong undercurrent in his writing career has been to exorcise the theological "demons" that have haunted him since his initiation into mid-twentieth-century Adventism. This should not be understood as a manifestation of disrespect for the initiators of his conversion to Christianity in general or Adventism in particular. But it was, in fact, a most perfection-oriented ("historic") brand of Adventism that he had initially adopted. And the results of this encounter eventually led him, as he later reflected on it with tongue in cheek, to try to become history's first perfect Christian. When, however, this ambitious goal failed to materialize, a period of profound loss of faith in both Christianity and Adventism ensued.

Thankfully, Knight was ultimately able to regain his theological bearings and personal Christian faith mainly, he reports, through the influence and prayers of his college religion teacher at Pacific Union College, Dr. Robert Olson. It was this subsequent renewal that led to his steady emergence as a Christian thinker and apologist, Adventist historian, theologian, and educational philosopher—all eventually embodied in his remarkable teaching, public speaking, but most importantly for posterity, in his publishing and editorial career. At the very core of these important transitions in both his spiritual journey and in his career has been an almost unrelenting effort to come to terms with the crisis of Minneapolis and its subsequent negative and, ultimately, positive developments. The popularity of his books clearly indicates that many readers resonate with his insights.

## Knight more intentionally wrestles with the theology of 1888

While the Jones biography (1987) inaugurated his "1888 pilgrimage," it was not his most definitive treatment of the issues related to Minneapolis and its tortured aftermath. By his own admission, "the greatest weakness" of his treatment of the Minneapolis meetings in the Jones biography "was the discussion of the meaning of Minneapolis itself." In retrospect, he concluded that he "overemphasized the experience to the detriment of the content of the 1888 message." While still "holding to the primacy of the experience"[3] it was only with the publication of *Angry Saints* in 1989 that Knight would begin to decidedly clarify the theological implications of the Minneapolis event and its lengthy aftermath.

To be more specific, Knight's most definitive treatment would come with the publication of *A User-Friendly Guide to the 1888 Message* (1998). It should also be mentioned that Knight produced the latter volume during the years of his participation in the Primacy of the Gospel Committee, which was the last General Conference–sponsored dialogue with the late Robert J. Wieland and Donald K. Short and other leading spokespersons for the 1888 Message Study Committee. These deliberations concluded in the spring of 2000 (after five years of semi-annual meetings, each lasting three to four days), under the shared chairmanship of two vice presidents of the Seventh-day Adventist General Conference. Furthermore, it was George who wrote the official response of the General Conference membership of the Primacy of the Gospel Committee to the historical and theological interpretations of Wieland, Short, the 1888 Message Study Committee, and, to a lesser degree, Pastor Jack Sequeira.[4] Not surprisingly, Knight's response to such teachings, in the context of the Primacy of the Gospel Committee, reads like a concise resume of the contents of his *User-Friendly Guide to the 1888 Message* (1998). Thus, with this brief historical overview in hand, we now address the question of what have been Knight's key contributions to the historical and theological meaning of the 1888 Minneapolis General Conference Session, its complex background, and controversial aftermath.

## Key contributions to the meaning of 1888

Most certainly Knight was not entering virgin territory in denominational publishing history when he began writing on the significance of the 1888 conference. It seems safe to assert, however, that when he did explore the contours of this territory his work embodied the most decisive historical and theological review of any of his predecessors in sorting out the complex issues in the protracted, testy debates over the meaning of 1888. What then are the key components of Knight's work? What distinguished this scholarly effort that arose out of a most decisive move in his personal pilgrimage as an Adventist historian, theologian, and enterprising editorial impresario?

## Myth busting

The first key issue is his effective demythologizing of A. T. Jones and E. J. Waggoner. This was most likely not a conscious move for Knight. But as I began my own pilgrimage of understanding in the early 1970s, I clearly recall the almost mythic status accorded those two key personalities. While there had been a fairly widespread perception that the crucial "Messengers" of 1888 had left the Seventh-day Adventist Church, there was also a notorious lack of knowledge as to just how far they had strayed away from the "truth" of Adventist theology (and moral sensibilities). And Knight's Jones biography was effectively the first major revelation that would seriously qualify their legendary status in Adventist history. For me, the reading of the Jones biography and my own writing of a Waggoner biography (*E. J. Waggoner* [Review and Herald®, 2008]) have provided some of the most painful moments of disillusionment in my experience as an Adventist historian. In fact, during my work on the Waggoner biography, I sometimes found myself simply overwhelmed with spontaneous grief.

## Research based on primary documents

A second factor was that Knight consistently based his research on the primary documents related to the debates about the meaning and message of Minneapolis. He studiously refrained from giving credence to any popular hearsay in Adventism's legendary lore. This has been a notable feature of Knight's scholarship, whether it involves his own publications and lectures on the 1888 issues, or his roles as director of dissertations and theses involving key 1888 figures and issues. Such efforts have significantly expanded the knowledge base for 1888 studies and have provided a sounder context for reaching more informed conclusions on the controversial historical, theological, and ecclesiological issues.

Other notable contributions that have achieved wider notice by Knight's work as an editorial impresario on 1888 issues include Gilbert Valentine's volume on W. W. Prescott entitled *W. W. Prescott* (Review and Herald®, 2005) and Clinton Wahlen's master of divinity thesis, "Selected Aspects of Ellet J. Waggoner's Eschatology and Their Relation to His Understanding of Righteousness by Faith, 1882-1895" (Andrews University, 1988). Wahlen also published a subsequent article entitled "What Did E. J. Waggoner Say at Minneapolis?" *Adventist Heritage* 13, no. 1 (Winter 1988).

## Historical, social, and theological backgrounds

The third distinctive characteristic of Knight's contribution emerges from his rich portrayal of the key historical, social, and controversial theological backgrounds. This portrayal has provided a more nuanced setting for understanding the 1888 General Conference and its heritage in Adventist history. While considerable portions of this material have probably not originated from Knight's path-breaking research, he has provided and collated an unprecedented, variegated presentation that helps to explain why the Minneapolis conference was so controversial and why the subsequent opposition to the major "Messengers" (especially Ellen White, Jones, Waggoner, and Prescott) was so intense. Most certainly, earlier interpreters such as L. H. Christian, L. E. Froom, Norval Pease, and A. V. Olson had laid a good and mostly solid historical context, but it was not until Knight's work that we get a truly comprehensive portrait that illuminates the unfolding of the key issues. George has skillfully and forcefully pulled together the following crucial aspects: (1) helpful profiles of the key players (such as Uriah Smith, G. I. Butler, and others); (2) the rise of powerful national movements seeking to make the United States officially a "Christian nation," including a national Sunday law and required Bible readings and prayers in the public schools; (3) the debates over the meaning of the "law in Galatians" (whether it was the "moral" or the "ceremonial" law) and the interpretation of the "horns" of Daniel 7; (4) the so-called California Conspiracy; and (5) the sad and portentous apostasy of D. M. Canright.

## Theological authority

The fourth contribution made by Knight concerns the contentious question of who exercises authority when it comes to determining the "truth" of the concepts associated with the theological discussions of 1888. Clearly, the most immediate issue relates to who has the *penultimate* authority to settle even the matter of what aspects should properly be included in the list of 1888 issues (Jones and Waggoner, or Ellen G. White). But the *ultimate* locus of authority involves the question of the primacy of Scriptural authority in the varied attempts to settle the 1888-related doctrinal issues.

In pursuit of these issues, we will first turn to the question of who has the effective *penultimate* authority? Again, let's be reminded that the point in question here includes what themes should be included in the "1888 Message," whether they were the subject of what was preached at Minneapolis, whether they were published in reports or documents coming directly out of the actual Minneapolis meetings themselves, whether they were concepts also included in the later writings of Jones and Waggoner or whether they might be part of the interpretive perspectives of Ellen G. White. Next, we will seek to demonstrate how the 1888 event eventually spotlights Adventism's *Sola Scriptura* foundations. And, finally, we will seek to point out Knight's positive conclusions concerning what the 1888 Message truly was and is for Seventh-day Adventism.

## *Penultimate* authority

So who has the *penultimate* authority to define what the "message" of 1888 and its aftermath really was? Knight's analysis has forthrightly moved forward on the assumption that the more immediate and *penultimate* authority must be ceded to Ellen G. White. Clearly, acknowledging her staunch support for Waggoner and Jones at Minneapolis and during the years subsequent to the meetings, her widespread participation in the revivals that occurred in the more immediate years after 1888 and the many writings that she produced in support of what she saw as the message of "Christ and His Righteousness," Knight clearly grants her "pride of position" as the premier *penultimate* authority as to what was the true meaning of 1888.

Furthermore, when one looks at the volume and intensity of Ellen White's efforts and the levels of opposition to her and to A. T. Jones and E. J. Waggoner, especially from Uriah Smith, G. I. Butler, and their supporters, it is very clear that if it had not been for Ellen White's prophetically authoritative and persistent support and clarification, Jones and Waggoner would have been summarily shunted aside. In other words, the very survival of Jones and Waggoner as spokespersons for the new emphasis was in reality due to the authoritative influence of Ellen G. White! Thus, it seems almost self-evidently axiomatic that her prophetic authority carried far more weight in seeking to define what the actual message of 1888 was all about theologically, rather than some supposedly inherent, self-authenticating authority residing in the theology of Jones and Waggoner.[5]

Knight has made two important points on this issue. First of all, Ellen White never gave Jones and Waggoner her unqualified support in the sense that she provided them with some "kind of blank check in theological matters."[6] In response to those who see Jones and Waggoner as determinative of the matter, he responds with the following rationale: "Some with a burden for the 1888 message in the late twentieth century" have felt led to "do their Bible reading basically through the eyes of Jones and Waggoner and to get their basic theology from them on the ground of Ellen White's endorsements. Then after having obtained their theological structure from the 1888 messengers, they begin to plug in Bible texts and Ellen White quotations to prove their points. Unfortunately, this procedure leads them to adopt both the 1888 messengers' helpful ideas and those that may be erroneous. . . . In the meantime, their theology has shifted from a biblical perspective to a Jones and Waggoner perspective."[7] With this rationale in mind, Knight proceeds to document and outline a litany of very questionable concepts that have greatly complicated the theological "blank check" reliability of Jones and Waggoner.

The list of problematic concepts include the following: (1) Waggoner taught

"that there was a time when Christ proceeded forth and came from God" and
thus affirmed that Christ was not eternally preexistent with the Father, a position
clearly contrary to Ellen White (see DA 530). (2) Waggoner taught that "Christ
could not sin," clearly contradicting Ellen G. White's position that Christ was
quite "capable of yielding to temptation (EGW MS 57, 1890)." (3) Both Jones
and Waggoner advocated that Sabbath keepers were just as responsible to work on
Sunday as they were to rest on the Sabbath when a Sunday law was in effect, and
that if they did not do so they would receive the "mark of the beast." Ellen White
clearly contradicted them by saying that "refraining from work on Sunday is not
receiving the Mark of the Beast." (4) Both Jones and Waggoner advocated ideas
on church organization clearly at odds to her understanding. (5) In the year 1893,
Jones claimed that "there were no conditions in salvation." Ellen White rebuked
Jones, stating that "the Bible is full of conditions" (Ellen G. White to A. T. Jones,
April 9, 1893). (6) Jones and W. W. Prescott rashly pushed to the fore the prophetic claims of Anna Rice as a new Adventist prophetess while Ellen White flatly
denied any such claims for Rice and rebuked Jones for his rashness in supporting
them. (7) Furthermore, Knight has pointed out how Ellen White never explicitly
supported their views on the humanity of Christ and Waggoner's later teaching
on universal legal justification.[8] Thus, with these facts in mind, it becomes very
problematic to make Jones and Waggoner the authoritative spokespersons for the
1888 message. While they played an important role in shaping it, it was not their
privilege to finally define it. Quite clearly, then, the more sensible and balanced
perspectives of Ellen White should have the primacy when it comes to the *penultimate* authority used to define the theological significance of the 1888 message.

## *Ultimate* authority

Regarding the *ultimate* authority to be used in testing the "theological truth"
of the issues of 1888, Knight clearly supports Ellen White's clarion call to base the
whole message of 1888 on the Bible and the Bible alone. "*We must never forget
that the Bible is the basis of all theological thinking* and that we must test the ideas
of all other writers by God's Word."[9] And George has consistently put his "biblical
money" where his writing and speaking "mouth" has spoken. His actions have
matched his convictions in the numerous biblically based theological expositions
and commentaries that he has edited and written.

## The theological and practical meaning of the 1888 message for today?

So what is the essence of Knight's understanding of the 1888 message for Seventh-day Adventists? He suggests that a comprehensive answer is needed to address this question and lists nine "propositions."[10] We can sum up the substance of these propositions as follows:

As I have interacted with Knight through the years, from the very beginning I have sensed that the heart of his theological understanding of 1888 and his overall theology has to do with Ellen White's central burden for Jones and Waggoner and 1888: the Advent movement clearly needed to be more intentionally focused on the person and work of Christ, especially as these themes provided the setting for the manner in which saving grace is communicated. Furthermore, Knight has not been slow to emphasize how such grace should suffuse all of the teachings of the church, especially its great emphasis on the themes of distinctive Adventism— "Present Truth." He has repeatedly sounded this theme in echoing Ellen White's great burden to exalt Christ and His saving grace.

But Knight, though a bit slow in coming to terms with 1888's persistent theological issues, does finally come full circle as he concludes his expositions with a strong appeal to "truth-burdened" 1888 gurus to really personify the loving grace of Jesus in their witness to Christ, not only to their fellow Adventists, but also to a lost world. We could sum up his overall theme in this way: If the professed "remnant" would be more kind and tender-hearted and loving and lovable in their dealings with one another (both Adventist partners in dialogue and non-Adventists), there would be a great revival of primitive godliness and the work would soon climax with the coming of Jesus. Thus, in his theological reflections, he has instinctively returned to his original emphasis on the importance of actually living out the expositions of grace that so captivated Jones and Waggoner and their *penultimate guide,* Ellen G. White.

It seems appropriate to bring this theological reflection to a close with one final theological/historical suggestion: when one reflects on the theological currents in twentieth and early twenty-first century Seventh-day Adventism, it seems that Knight's basic perspective has given voice to what I have chosen to call the Reformation/ Wesleyan Evangelical impulse in Adventist theological development. Building on the work of such figures as L. E. Froom, Edward Heppenstall, Kenneth Strand, Raoul Dederen, and Hans K. LaRondelle (to name only the most prominent), Knight has steadily and eloquently given voice to their central concerns in a readable and prolific manner. And the heart of this impulse has been to uplift the Christ of the Triune God-head as the atoning sacrifice for the sins of the world. This Christ has been portrayed as the Author of prevening (calling and convincing), converting/regenerating, justifying, sanctifying, and glorifying grace as our Advocate with the Father in the setting of the great pre-Advent judgment. Knight has sought to do this in a way that upholds all of the great Protestant *"solas"* (Scripture alone, grace alone, faith alone, and Christ alone), while drawing on the best of the American Puritans, John Wesley, the Restorationists, and their Millerite progeny. He has done all of the above in terms of a solid historical, biographical, and biblical perspective, while persistently allowing these genres to enrich his theological exposition and practical, devotional insight.

## Concluding reflections

Yes, for all of the above substantive theological emphases, we are in Knight's debt. But our indebtedness must also include his astonishing prodigality and persistence as a researcher, expositor, personal and public mentor, teacher, writer, editorial impresario, and practical advocate for the deeper life with God. Finally, one suspects that even for those who have chosen to challenge him, he has probably been one of their greatest goads to seek a deeper clarity for the best of their own convictions. And for that, even they, along with his loyal admirers, should be grateful to God.

### Endnotes

1. Reprinted in 2009 as "An Adventist Classic 25th Anniversary Edition."

2. Revised and published as A. T. Jones: Point Man on Adventism's Charismatic Frontier (Hagerstown, Md.: Review and Herald®, 2011).

3. Angry Saints, 12.

4. While not fully agreeing with Wieland and Short and their associates, Sequeira has adopted the essential core of their teaching on the humanity of Christ and "Universal Legal Justification," the latter being a teaching that claims that at the cross the whole human race was "unconditionally justified" and that such an act of justification could only be forfeited by not exercising personal faith in Christ.

5. I have based what has been said in this paragraph and the following paragraphs on Knight's User-Friendly Guide, 68–72.

6. Ibid., 73, 74.

7. Ibid., 79.

8. Ibid., 74–76.

9. Ibid.

10. Ibid., 81–116, 165–167.

# Chapter 11

# George Knight's Contribution to Adventist Theology

Denis Fortin

Perhaps no other Adventist author or theologian in recent time has had as much of an impact upon my understanding of Adventism as George Knight. Although I never had him as a professor, since he joined the Seventh-day Adventist Theological Seminary the year I completed my master's degree, as a young pastor I became fascinated with his books on Adventist history and theology. His thoughts and reflections seemed to resonate with my own spiritual journey. A convert to Adventism as he is, I also had difficulties with understanding a church community that created its own dysfunctional situations and personalities. I also asked myself the question of how one could be a Seventh-day Adventist, expecting the soon coming of Christ and preparing oneself for eternity, yet finding myself in some of the most unchristian and troublesome situations, with people who seemed to have no sense of what it means to walk with Jesus. Knight helped me in finding an answer—an answer that I still appreciate today.

The "celebrations" marking the centennial of the 1888 Minneapolis General

Conference and the number of books published in connection with that event marked the beginning of my own personal acquaintance with George as a speaker and author. Beginning in 1988 and for a few years afterward, I read a number of books on Adventist history and theology. I was intrigued with this centennial and what it meant for us as a faith community. For my thirtieth birthday, my wife gave me Knight's latest book, *Angry Saints*,[1] which along with his earlier book on A. T. Jones,[2] began to shape my understanding of Adventism. Through those years I read almost everything Knight published, and slowly I also began to understand better the perfectionist approach to life that had strongly influenced my earlier years as a new Adventist. Since then, I have joined the seminary faculty and became one of Knight's colleagues and came to appreciate even more his contributions. His mentorship has meant a lot to me in the transformation of my doctoral dissertation into a published monograph[3] and in the framing of the *Ellen G. White Encyclopedia*.[4]

Beyond his major contributions to our understanding of Adventist historical developments and eschatology, Knight's theological contributions are best seen in three of his books:

- *I Used to Be Perfect* (1994, 2001)
- *My Gripe With God: A Study of Divine Justice and the Problem of the Cross* (1990), republished as *The Cross of Christ: God's Work for Us* (2008)
- *The Pharisee's Guide to Perfect Holiness: A Study in Sin and Salvation* (1992), republished as *Sin and Salvation: God's Work for and in Us* (2008)

It is obvious throughout George Knight's theological works that the writings of Ellen White have influenced him to a large extent. Although another essay in this volume draws attention to his contributions to Ellen White studies, I would like to start my evaluation of his insights into Adventist theology by referring to a seminal essay he wrote in the first volume of his series on Ellen White. In the last chapter of his book *Meeting Ellen White*, he presents "An Examination of Ellen White's Major Themes," in which he briefly describes the seven major themes of her writings: (1) the love of God, (2) the great controversy, (3) Jesus, the cross, and salvation, (4) the centrality of the Bible, (5) the second coming of Christ, (6) the third angel's message and Adventist mission, and (7) practical Christianity and the development of Christian character.[5] To a large extent, these major themes in the writings of Ellen White are also Knight's theological themes, and he explores each of them at various levels in his books.

As I reflect on Knight's theological contributions to Adventist theology, I will focus mainly on key elements of his doctrine of salvation. Three loci or themes are especially worth exploring: (1) the nature of human sin, (2) the atoning work of Christ, and (3) the meaning of salvation and the sanctified life of the Christian. Overall, his theology of salvation is Arminian and Wesleyan Methodist, and steers away from controversial aspects of Adventist theology found in proponents of universal legal justification[6] and final generation perfectionism.[7] Another element that becomes clear in his theological construct is that Knight's theology does not adhere to a Reformed view of atonement, one that centers *only* on the event of the cross within the philosophical framework of the timelessness of God, but rather affirms a linear view of atonement and the plan of salvation in which "all aspects of Christ's life, ministry, and death are important. . . . The atonement as seen in Christ's work is not a point [in time, as in Reformed theology]—it is more like a line."[8] All that Christ has done for the salvation of humanity and the vindication of God's character—His willingness to die for humanity even before the foundation of the world, His life, His death, His resurrection and His heavenly ministry—is part of the *process* of atonement.[9]

## The nature of human sin

Foundational to Knight's theology is understanding his concepts of love and sin, and the relationship between the two. While for him, "Love to God and neighbor is the centerpiece of Christianity,"[10] love can be perverted and becomes the cause of sin, or SIN, as he writes. Therefore, for him "SIN is love. SIN is *agapē* love—that special kind of God-like love that is central to the New Testament."[11] "SIN is love focused on the wrong object. SIN is to love the object more than the Creator of the object. It makes no difference whether that object is an external thing, another person, or one's own self. To love anything or anyone more than God is SIN. SIN is love aimed at the wrong target accompanied by a way of life lived in the direction of that aim. Thus we have SIN, which leads to sins."[12]

Hence, with this approach to human sin, Knight falls within the Christian theological tradition that views sin as an alienated state of being before it becomes a series of bad actions, or sins. Sin is part of the human fabric we inherit at birth—it is an ontological reality of human life. "The crucial point to recognize is that SIN is much more than a series of unrelated actions," he argues. "It reflects a state of heart and mind."[13] And, consequently, the point he is driving at is "that an inadequate doctrine of SIN will of necessity lead to an inadequate doctrine of salvation."[14]

Here, one notes that Knight's theology of sin is in response to an Adventist view that sees it primarily as the outward transgressions of known commands. For this view, sin is only a willful decision or action, an outgrowth of one's decision to rebel against God's will. But for George sin goes much deeper than that. "Distrust of God stands at the very foundation of the sin crisis."[15] "Sin is the arrogant desire to be the god of our own lives,"[16] and that desire is inherited at birth. We are born with a sinful and egotistical mind-set that is in rebellion against God. The solution, therefore, is not and cannot be within humanity's grasp. Nothing that we do or decide to do can solve this situation. The plan of salvation must be totally God's initiative.

But also at the core of Knight's understanding of sin is the predicament in which humanity finds itself because of the sin of Adam and Eve. Our first parents "fell when they redirected their love from God to themselves. SIN is a rebellious, broken relationship with God that puts my self and my will on the throne of my life. Out of that broken relationship flows a series of sinful actions (sins)."[17] Thus, "at the core of Satan's temptation to Eve was the inference that God could not be trusted because He was arbitrary in prohibiting her from the tree 'in the midst of the garden'—that His commandment was unfair."[18] For Knight, the sin of Adam and Eve was first a distrust of God—it was a deceptive thought process that led to their decision to eat the forbidden fruit. It is this mind-set that humanity inherits at birth. We are thus born with a relationship to God that is already broken—we are born lost and in need of a Savior.

It is in this context as well that Knight's theme of the great controversy enters his theology. Adam and Eve's sin was much more than the eating of a forbidden fruit—it was a decision on their part to love their own selves rather than God. They did not trust God but rather believed Satan's lie that God was unfair and arbitrary in giving them rules for their lives. At the center of this controversy, therefore, is God's character of love and justice, and at the heart of the plan of salvation is God's decision to vindicate His character before the universe. For

George, the future of humanity is bound with God's, and our justification is tied to His.[19] Christ's work of atonement is consequently at the center of the divine solution to the sin problem.[20]

## The atoning work of Christ

From Knight's perspective, Adam and Eve's decision to rebel against God, at Satan's instigation and falsehood regarding the true character of God, meant that God would sacrifice Himself to procure the only adequate moral solution to the sin problem and the redemption of humanity. "God apparently knew that some things can't be explained satisfactorily. *He therefore chose not to answer Satan's accusations through rational argument or a full-blown 'theology.' Rather, He chose to demonstrate His love in action. That demonstration would highlight and bring to a climax the principles of both sides in the cosmic struggle between good and evil.*"[21] Therefore, it is at the cross that "*the principles of both God's and Satan's kingdoms are exhibited in their full maturity.* The cross clearly testifies that God 'loved the world.' "[22]

The centrality of the death of Christ on the cross is another important element of Knight's theology. A number of key concepts carefully interlock, and in the end his theology of the cross is unequivocally Protestant and Evangelical.

After wrestling with the biblical concept of the wrath of God, so dominant in some passages of the New Testament, George concludes that "God's anger is as real as sin is real."[23] "*God's wrath is not opposed to His love. Rather, it is an outgrowth of that very love.* The more love, the more indignation at sin and its results, and thus the more wrath. The opposite of love is not wrath, but indifference."[24] "The good news is not that God is not wrathful," he argues, "but that Christ bore the penalty of (God's judgment on) sin for all who believe in Him."[25]

Knight believes it is the purpose of the atoning work of Christ to protect the sanctity of God's law and moral government, and whatever God does to solve the sin problem "must be in harmony with His holiness, justice, and love. Beyond that, God's plan must heal people's alienations, free the redeemed from slavery to sin, remove their death penalty, cleanse them from defilement, and save them from divine wrath."[26] Hence, the death of Christ on the cross is God's ultimate and only acceptable solution.

Many theories of atonement have been proposed in the past two millennia of

Christian theology about the reasons for the death of Christ on the cross, but for Knight those theories are not all equal. The New Testament uses picture-words to describe Christ's work for lost sinners (propitiation, redemption, justification, reconciliation, cleansing), and they help us understand the process of salvation. However, such picture-words are metaphors rather than exact descriptions. But Knight does not believe biblical references to sacrifice and substitution are such picture-words—those two concepts are not metaphors but a reality. The sacrificial, substitutionary atonement of Christ on the cross is not a metaphor, or a theory, or an image.[27] Grounding his understanding on the descriptions of the Old Testament sacrificial system and its references in the New Testament, George argues that "the sacrificial system was a powerful object lesson on both the results of sin and the cost of its remedy for those who remained sensitive to its meaning."[28] "At the very heart of substitution is the thought that Christ in His death did something that we could not do for ourselves."[29]

For Knight, the substitutionary sacrificial death of Christ is the basis of all theories of atonement—it must be the dominant perspective to make all others relevant. "The theory that Christ died to win us over to God's love and to inspire us to live our lives after the pattern of His life ... has a great deal of truth in it, but taken as the primary reason for Christ's death, it dismisses the great bulk of Bible evidence claiming that Jesus bore our sins and died our death so that we might be 'redeemed ... from the curse of the law' (Gal. 3:13) with its death penalty (Rom. 6:23)."[30] "While Christ's death reveals God's love to us, it does much more than that—it removes the sentence of God's just condemnation from us."[31]

God had to deal with sin responsibly, and the cross is the solution. God takes upon Himself the just penalty of sin and the wrath it incurs, and thus His forgiveness is morally possible.[32] The biblical images and metaphors of the death of Christ are all dependent on the substitutionary sacrifice of Christ. They each meet a different aspect of human need, emphasize God's saving initiative of grace, growing out of His love, and teach that God achieved His saving work through the blood of Christ in His substitutionary sacrifice.[33] Along with John Stott, Knight concludes from the many references to "Christ's blood in these great salvific themes that sacrificial 'substitution is not a "theory of the atonement." Nor is it even an additional image to take its place as an option alongside the others. It is rather the essence of each image and the heart of the atonement itself.' None of the other images 'could stand without it.' "[34]

Thus, at the crucial moment of the great controversy between Christ and Satan, "The life of Christ demonstrated that God was right and Satan wrong. God's law of love could be perfectly kept"[35] and "Christ's death on the cross sealed Satan's defeat."[36] For Knight, "*The cross demonstrated two things—God's love and justice, and Satan's hate and deceptiveness concerning God's character. . . .* The love of God in giving His Son and utter hatred of Satan were both plain to see for the onlooking universe. Beyond that, *all could recognize that God had maintained His holiness and justice in the way He had handled the sin problem. He neglected neither the requirements of the law nor its just penalty. All was accounted for at Calvary. The cross put divine forgiveness on a moral basis.*"[37]

## The meaning of salvation and the sanctified life of the Christian

For Knight, this understanding of the death of Christ on the cross is God's solution to the sin problem. Another aspect of the plan of salvation is God's invitation to humankind to accept the death of Christ as their substitute and have their hearts transformed, to be refocused from their own selfish mind-set back to God and others. "Such a new-birth experience implies—no, it demands—a ground shift in all that we do and all that we think."[38]

The death of Christ allows for the justification of humanity, for those who accept by faith what Christ has accomplished. There is no universal legal justification because salvation requires human beings to accept by faith the sacrifice of Christ on their behalf. Justification "is God's legal declaration that those who have accepted the sacrifice of Christ as their substitute are no longer under the condemnation of the broken law. Justification is a legal declaration, and it is totally by grace."[39] Thus "faith is grabbing hold of grace, God's unmerited forgiveness in Christ. Faith is grabbing hold of what we don't deserve."[40] Such a faith and trust in God's provisions in Christ then starts a life of commitment and growth.

One last aspect of Knight's doctrine of salvation is his understanding of the Christian life, and the relationship between justification, sanctification, and perfection. While for purposes of abstract theoretical discussion, "we can isolate justification and sanctification from each other, ... in daily living they are intricately linked together"[41] and "sanctification is nothing less than the process by which Christians become progressively more loving."[42] For him, the Christian life is "founded upon the crucifixion of the self-centered life principle of SIN and the resurrection to a new life based upon the other-centered LAW of love."[43] But it is important to recognize that "Christianity is not merely a way of dying, but also a way of living."[44] And furthermore, the Christian life is to be patterned after Christ's life of self-giving and service.[45]

Thus, the substitutionary sacrifice of Christ is the foundation of humankind's salvation. "While it is true that Christ's work of atonement is something He did and is doing for us by His death, resurrection, and heavenly ministry, it is also the case that His work cannot be completed without what He must do within us." In Knight's theology, the work of Christ for us demands "a human reaction in believers."[46]

Knight's struggle with perfectionism plays an important part in his construction of a doctrine of salvation. Perhaps it can be said that his entire life has been a struggle with this concept, and his understanding of perfection is congruent with his understanding of love and sin. It centers on his understanding of the love of God and the relationship between God and humankind. "Perfect love is not perfect performance, perfect skill, or perfect human nature," he argues. "Rather, it is rendering obedience in relationship to both the God of love and the great principle undergirding His LAW."[47] In summarizing his view of perfection, he states that "biblical perfection is not the abstract standard of flawlessness found in Greek philosophy but an individual's perfect relationship with God and his or her fellow humans. Biblical perfection involves ethical conduct, but it involves much more than mere behavior. It centers on maturing the relationships that were ruptured in the rebellion of the Genesis fall but are restored to individuals at conversion."[48] "Thus being perfect is a dynamic state in which dedicated Christians continue to advance in Christian living."[49] Quoting Ellen White in *Christ's Object Lessons,* he affirms, "The object of the Christian life is fruit bearing—the reproduction of Christ's character in the believer, that it may be reproduced in others."[50] *"Perfectly reproducing the character of Christ is reflecting His love"* in our relationships with others.[51]

## Conclusion

An aspect of George Knight's theological contributions that has always warmed my own heart is his focus on the grace of God. I think his writings on the doctrines of sin, atonement, and salvation make it abundantly clear that his faith in God and understanding of the plan of salvation rests on His grace. At the end of his book *The Cross of Christ* he reflects on the human component of the plan of salvation, or more accurately the lack of human involvement. Adventism has wrestled for decades with the need of human participation in the plan of salvation to put an end to the great controversy between good and evil. But as Knight emphasizes, such participation can never amount to much. "The simple fact is that the plan of salvation is God's work, not humanity's. It was Christ who lived the perfect life as a human being and proved that God's law could be kept; it was Christ who died for every person by absorbing the death penalty that resulted from the broken law; and it is Christ who currently ministers in heaven on behalf of those who believe in Him and accept the merits of His death and resurrection. Atonement is all of God. . . . Christ's work will stand whether or not any human beings accept it. . . . The Bible never gives humanity too prominent a place in the plan of salvation. The great controversy is between God and Satan, not Satan and humanity. Whether or not any human being ever demonstrates God's power in living a 'spotless' life, the atonement will have been completed through the demonstration of Christ's sinless life, death, resurrection, and heavenly ministry. His sinless life is the great fact of the ages; His death demonstrated that principles of both God's and Satan's kingdoms; His heavenly ministry extends the fruits of His accomplished victory to those who have faith in Him; and His comings at the beginning and end of the millennium will complete the work of atonement. The biblical message is that salvation is from God alone."[52]

This grace-focused and Christ-centered perspective on the doctrine of atonement and human merit is fundamental to understanding George Knight's theology of salvation, and I believe it is his major contribution to Adventist theology, one that has steered us away as a faith community from salvation by works and human accomplishments (something that we have been very prone to believe), and one that has given the glory to God for what He does in our lives through Christ our Savior.

## Endnotes

1. George R. Knight, *Angry Saints: Tensions and Possibilities in the Adventist Struggle Over Righteousness by Faith* (Hagerstown, Md.: Review and Herald®, 1989).

2. George R. Knight, *From 1888 to Apostasy* (Hagerstown, Md.: Review and Herald®, 1987).

3. Denis Fortin, *Adventism in Quebec: The Dynamics of Rural Church Growth, 1830–1910*

(Berrien Springs, Mich.: Andrews University Press, 2004).

4. Denis Fortin and Jerry Moon, eds., *Ellen G. White Encyclopedia* (Hagerstown, Md.: Review and Herald®, 2013).

5. George R. Knight, *Meeting Ellen White: A Fresh Look at Her Life, Writings, and Major Themes* (Hagerstown, Md.: Review and Herald®, 1996).

6. See George R. Knight, *Sin and Salvation: God's Work for and in Us* (Hagerstown, Md.: Review and Herald®, 2008), 85–87.

7. See Knight, *Sin and Salvation*, 170–192.

8. George R. Knight, *The Cross of Christ: God's Work for Us* (Hagerstown, Md.: Review and Herald, 2008), 81.

9. I have also addressed this linear concept of atonement in Ellen White's thought in the article "The Cross of Christ: Theological Differences Between Joseph H. Waggoner and Ellen G. White," *Journal of the Adventist Theological Society* 14, no. 2 (Autumn 2003): 131–140.

10. George R. Knight, *I Used to Be Perfect: A Study of Sin and Salvation*, 2nd ed. (Berrien Springs, Mich.: Andrews University Press, 2001), 39.

11. Knight, *I Used to Be Perfect*, 18.

12. Ibid.

13. Ibid., 19.

14. Ibid., 20.

15. Knight, *The Cross of Christ*, 19.

16. Ibid., 28.

17. Knight, *I Used to Be Perfect*, 63.

18. Knight, *The Cross of Christ*, 20.

19. Ibid., 23.

20. For a good analysis of George Knight's theology of the doctrine of sin, I recommend Jamie Kiley, "The Doctrine of Sin in the Thought of George R. Knight: Its Context and Implications" (MA thesis, Andrews University, 2009).

21. Knight, *The Cross of Christ*, 25; emphasis in the original.

22. Ibid., 25; emphasis in the original.

23. Ibid., 41.

24. Ibid., 39.

25. Ibid., 40.

26. Ibid., 42.

27. Ibid., 61, 62.

28. Ibid., 48.

29. Ibid., 54.

30. Ibid., 51.

31. Ibid., 65.

32. Ibid., 66, 67.

33. Ibid., 78.

34. Ibid., 79.

35. Ibid., 91.

36. Ibid., 95.

37. Ibid., 95; emphasis in the original.

38. Knight, *I Used to Be Perfect*, 22.

39. Ibid., 42.

40. Ibid., 43.

41. Knight, *Sin and Salvation*, 91.

42. Knight, *I Used to Be Perfect*, 49.

43. Ibid., 45.

44. Ibid., 127.

45. Ibid., 133.

46. Ibid., 132.

47. Knight, *I Used to Be Perfect*, 74.

48. Ibid., 76.

49. Ibid., 79.

50. Ibid., 93.

51. Ibid., 94. See also 96, 97.

52. Knight, *The Cross of Christ*, 141, 142. This last paragraph includes a clear rejection of final generation perfectionism and its advocacy of God's need of human moral perfection to vindicate His character before the universe in order to win the great controversy with Satan.

# Chapter 12

# The Knight Approach for Ellen White Studies

Michael W. Campbell

During the past thirty years, George R. Knight has played a leading role in transforming Ellen White studies into a significant field of rigorous academic study within the Seventh-day Adventist Church. Previous approaches were largely polarized between popular hagiography of Ellen White and harshly critical assessments of her life and teachings.[1] Knight sought a middle path. With his educational qualifications and his personal theological journey of struggle with the meaning and authority of her writings, he was uniquely prepared to study them, and to assess her continued influence and authority within the Seventh-day Adventist Church.

This essay will examine Knight's contributions to Ellen White studies by surveying three specific areas of study: pursuing historical contextualization, simplifying hermeneutical methods, and lastly, affirming her continued prophetic role within the Seventh-day Adventist Church. His most significant contribution to the field of Ellen White studies came through the research conducted by doctoral students whom he advised as he expanded his writing and research beyond just the field of education to church history. Those students have gone on to exercise significant influence through their own writing in the field of Adventist studies, while a significant number have actually been hired by the White Estate.[2]

This contribution can perhaps be best seen in the plethora of topics that some of his doctoral students have covered in Adventist studies. Gil Valentine researched the life and thought of William W. Prescott as Knight's first doctoral student in 1982.[3] Later students wrote about early Adventist educators such as Goodloe Harper Bell (by Allan G. Lindsay), Frederick Griggs (Arnold Colin Reye), and Edward Alexander Sutherland (Warren Sidney Ashworth).[4] Jerry Moon explored the contours of the relationship between Ellen White and her son, Willie C. White.[5] Alberto R. Timm and Merlin D. Burt, both of whom subsequently worked for the White Estate, wrote on the historical development of early Sabbatarian Adventist theology.[6] Julius Nam analyzed the book *Questions on Doctrine* that became the focal point of controversy about how Ellen White's writings were later used and interpreted, and Theodore N. Levterov covered the development of early Ellen White apologetics.[7]

## Contribution to Ellen White studies

George R. Knight rose to prominence within the Seventh-day Adventist Church after writing the book *Myths in Adventism* in 1985.[8] This volume did a great deal to demythologize Ellen G. White, particularly in connection with many traditional understandings of Adventist education. Knight, who earned an EdD from the University of Houston, was at that time teaching in the School of Education at Andrews University. Soon, however, after exploring the history of Adventist education, he would venture increasingly into the field of Ellen White studies. Part of this was a personal journey. He had spent time as a Seventh-day Adventist pastor, but had left the ministry in frustration over the issue of perfectionism. As he has remarked on numerous occasions, he intended "to become the first perfect Christian since Christ."[9] He found he was not able to.

Knight wrestled with the issues of perfectionism and the inspiration and authority of Ellen White's writings during the 1980s and 1990s through his guidance of seminary students and his own theological studies. His writings were still largely unnoticed in terms of Ellen White studies, however, until he wrote a series of four books about Ellen White during the late 1990s. At one point, he considered limiting himself to a one-volume work, but later felt that the series would be more approachable and more likely to be read as a series of smaller works. It appears that the approach worked, since these volumes helped to cement his status as the best-selling contemporary Seventh-day Adventist author.[10]

The first volume of Knight's series, *Meeting Ellen White: A Fresh Look at Her Life, Writings, and Major Themes* (Review and Herald®, 1996) sought to interpret her life and ministry by investigating three eras: her early life (1827–1850), her prophetic guidance to the Sabbatarian Adventists and early Seventh-day Adventist Church (1850–1888), and her prophetic guidance for an international church (1888–1915). In the second volume, *Reading Ellen White: How to Understand and Apply Her Writings* (Review and Herald®, 1997), he introduced Adventist readers to a hermeneutic for approaching inspired writings. His approach was to inductively discover the basic principles of interpretation from Ellen White's life and writings and then utilize illustrations or case studies to demonstrate that interpretation.

He went on to paint a broad historical and cultural landscape in *Ellen White's World: A Fascinating Look at the Times in Which She Lived* (Review and Herald®, 1998). Unlike most Ellen White apologists, Knight recognized the American Civil War (1861–1865) as the defining event of her generation and therefore her life, and then examined various religious, socioeconomic, and political influences that surrounded her.

And finally, in *Walking With Ellen White: Her Everyday Life as a Wife, Mother, and Friend* (Review and Herald®, 1999), he presented his subject as a human being who was not as glum and negative as some have depicted her. He noted that she enjoyed beauty and adventure, and had a winsome personality. On the other hand, she did, however, experience tension and conflict in her marriage that once led to a brief separation, and she made mistakes as a parent. Yet despite her flaws, God was able to use her in a remarkable way.

Together, these four volumes, though written in a popular format, constituted Knight's most cogent contribution to the field of Ellen White studies.

## Historical contextualization

As both a scholar and an apologist, George Knight has intentionally sought to provide historical context for understanding Ellen White. Whereas previous as well as contemporary writers, in the broader development and flow of twentieth-century Seventh-day Adventist theology, have argued that one must accept Ellen

White's authority in order to be a committed Seventh-day Adventist, he has consistently argued that this is an erroneous and dangerous misconception. Seventh-day Adventists from the very beginning have emphasized *sola scriptura*—the primary authority of inspired writings is the Bible. It fails to take into account a correct understanding of the basic question of the relationship of Ellen White's writings to those of the Bible. "The unfortunate record of history," George writes, "is that some modern Seventh-day Adventists are more apt to set forth Ellen White as a doctrinal authority than were the founders of their movement."[11]

He argues that all of the unique teachings of the Seventh-day Adventist Church were in place before Ellen White received their confirmation. In her early work in the area of doctrinal development, he asserts, her life and ministry involved "confirming" the results of the biblical study of others.[12] To explore the background of this issue in greater depth, he encouraged some of his PhD students to focus their dissertations on this issue and related topics. Such studies confirmed for him that only with the passing of time had some Adventists begun to insist that acceptance of Ellen White's prophetic ministry needed to be forced as a doctrinal tenet upon new members. She shied away from referring to herself as a "prophet" but rather self-identified as "the Lord's messenger."[13] Yet it was the emphasis upon *sola scriptura* by the early pioneers that led them to embrace the possibility of prophetic manifestations. The Bible was always their primary spiritual authority.[14]

In providing this important historical contextualization, Knight helped to demythologize Ellen White. Whereas previous scholars tended to focus on her amazing accomplishments—for example, the fact that she was the most translated female author and the supernatural aspects of her visions such as the length of time she held a Bible up in vision—Knight, while noting her accomplishments, also highlighted some of her flaws, thereby avoiding the standard hagiographical portrait of her life and ministry. While Ellen White was clearly a significant leader and co-founder of the Seventh-day Adventist Church, a careful analysis of the historical context indicates that she recognized her unique role as that of God's messenger to lead people back to Jesus Christ and the primacy of Scripture.[15]

## Hermeneutical methods

In numerous places, Knight argues that unbiblical views of inspiration are largely responsible for the misuse, or even abuse, of Ellen White's writings. If that is true, then a more reliable and biblical hermeneutical methodology is necessary. He has simplified these in such a way that he leaves little wiggle room for even the most strident Ellen White "basher" to reject their relevance.

Knight argues that the only safe way to interpret Ellen White correctly is to read her writings within a biblical framework and in the light of her own claims.[16] A serious pitfall is to regard Ellen White as an infallible commentator upon the Bible. Instead, he notes, she usually spoke homiletically. There is a significant difference, Knight observes, between exegesis and exposition. Ellen White viewed herself as using the Bible primarily in the latter endeavor. The difference was a matter of authority. Although her writings came from the same inspired source, they served to point readers back to the authority of the Bible.

Throughout his writing and in his public speaking, George Knight has urged people to read Ellen White's writings for themselves. He suggests that people start by reading her foundational works, such as *Steps to Christ* or one of the volumes of the Conflict of the Ages series, such as *The Desire of Ages*. Even Ellen White noted that those most opposed to her writings are the ones who do not read them.[17] Thus, a humble posture of faith that allows the Holy Spirit to lead is ultimately the best way to discern spiritual truth.

## Eschatological identity

Unlike other Ellen White apologists, George Knight does not spend a great deal of time defending her prophetic identity using the "testimony of Jesus" as equated to the "spirit of prophecy" in the King James Version of Revelation 12:17 and 19:10. It wasn't Ellen White who made Adventism, he argues. Instead, it was Sabbatarian Adventists' unique sense of prophetic identity arising out of their understanding of the three angels' messages in light of the unique end-time message of the Seventh-day Adventist Church. What made Ellen White's role significant was her profound influence in effectively communicating these insights along with their missiological implications.[18]

Ellen White's role in the development of Adventist theology and lifestyle would hold true with many other teachings that were not unique to her. For example, ever since her "health reform" vision of June 5, 1863, Ellen White's health teachings have been a perpetual source of controversy. Knight, on the other hand, bypassed this whole discussion by declaring that it wasn't the uniqueness of Ellen White's health teachings that was significant. While she certainly was on the "cutting edge" in comparison to other health reformers of her day, what made her distinctive was her ability to integrate health reform with Adventist theology.[19] Thus, Knight argues, healthful living was significant because of the role God's people had to play at the end of time, but at the same time he also avoided extreme Adventist positions advanced by M. L. Andreason known as "last-generation theology" that defined perfectionism as a state of sinlessness (or by extension following a strictly regimented diet).

## Conclusion

We can largely describe Knight's contribution to Ellen White studies as using the best of Adventist scholarship to shift this field from largely reactive to proactive in addressing issues relating to the life of Ellen White and the authority of her writings. Knight did this by being by far the best-selling contemporary Adventist author and through a cadre of doctoral students who have made their own contributions—including those within the Ellen G. White Estate. All of this has resulted in what we can describe as the "Knight Approach" to the field of Ellen White studies. His influence within the broader field has been far greater than had he taken a post at the helm of the White Estate.

In many ways, Knight's journey within the field of Ellen White studies reflected his personal experience—a journey away from perfectionism and a misuse of her writings to one that admired her theological balance and a move toward a moderate hermeneutic of inspired writings. As the Seventh-day Adventist Church wrestled increasingly with issues related to the authority of her writings, Knight was uniquely prepared through his own spiritual journey and academic credentials to help others understand her writings in a much more "healthy" and balanced way.

The "Knight Approach" to the field of Ellen White studies has helped convince both members and theologians that a "correct understanding of inspiration" is "of crucial importance" for the Seventh-day Adventist Church. Knight perceptively recognized that the majority of issues in Ellen White studies grew out of an incorrect and biblically unsound understanding of inspired writings. He has sought to reverse this tide through his writings and by training a new generation of thought leaders.

## Endnotes

1. An example of a serious scholarly attempt at assessing Ellen White's contribution that laid a foundation for Knight's work is, Roy Graham, *Ellen G. White: Co-founder of the Seventh-day Adventist Church* (New York: Peter Lang, 1986). Early apologetic responses by Adventist thought leaders include Francis D. Nichol, *Ellen G. White and Her Critics* (Washington, D.C.: Review and Herald®, 1951); T. Housel Jemison, *A Prophet Among You* (Mountain View, Calif.: Pacific Press®, 1955); Denton E. Rebok, *Believe His Prophets* (Washington, D.C.: Review and Herald®, 1956). There appears to be a gap in Adventist apologetic literature during the 1960s that was filled largely by the ministry of Robert W. Olson (1920–2013) and who was the director of the Ellen G. White Estate from 1978 to 1990. It appears that Olson and Knight significantly influenced one another. (Interview with Robert W. Olson in 2004).

2. Students of Knight who went on to serve in White Estate positions include Ted Levterov (Loma Linda University [LLU]), Merlin Burt (LLU and Andrews), Alberto Timm (Silver Spring, Md.), Alan Lindsay (Avondale, Australia), and Michael Campbell (LLU).

3. Gilbert Murray Valentine, "William Warren Prescott: Seventh-day Adventist Educator" (PhD diss., Andrews University, 1982).

4. Allan G. Lindsay, "Goodloe Harper Bell: Pioneer Seventh-day Adventist Christian Educator" (EdD diss., Andrews University, 1982); Arnold Colin Reye, "Frederick Griggs: Seventh-day Adventist Educator and Administrator" (PhD diss., Andrews University, 1984); Warren Sidney Ashworth, "Edward Alexander Sutherland and Seventh-day Adventist Educational Reform: The Denominational Years, 1890–1904" (PhD diss., Andrews University, 1986).

5. Jerry Allan Moon, "William Clarence (W. C.) White: His Relationship to Ellen G. White and Her Work" (PhD diss., Andrews University, 1993).

6. Alberto R. Timm, "The Sanctuary and the Three Angels' Messages, 1844–1863: Integrating Factors in the Development of Seventh-day Adventist Doctrines" (PhD diss., Andrews University, 1995); Merlin D. Burt, "The Historical Background, Interconnected Development, and Integration of the Doctrines of the Sanctuary, the Sabbath, and Ellen G. White's Role in Sabbatarian Adventism From 1844 to 1849" (PhD diss., Andrews University, 2002).

7. Juhyeuk [Julius] Nam, "Reactions to the Seventh-day Adventist Evangelical Conferences and *Questions on Doctrine*, 1955–1971" (PhD diss., Andrews University, 2005); Theodore N. Levterov, "The Development of the Seventh-day Adventist Understanding of Ellen G. White's Prophetic Gift, 1844–1889" (PhD diss., Andrews University, 2011).

8. George R. Knight, *Myths in Adventism: A Thoughtful Look at Misconceptions About Ellen White and Adventist Life That Have Long Caused Controversy in the Church* (Hagerstown, Md.: Review and Herald®, 1985).

9. George R. Knight, *The Pharisee's Guide to Perfect Holiness* (Nampa, Idaho: Pacific Press®, 1992), 131.

10. Based upon personal conversations I have had with Adventist publishing personalities.

11. George R. Knight, *Meeting Ellen White* (Hagerstown, Md.: Review and Herald®, 2001), 24.

12. Ibid., 25.

13. Ellen G. White, *Review and Herald*, July 26, 1906, reprinted in *Selected Messages* (Washington, D.C.: Review and Herald®, 1958), bk. 1, 31–35.

14. Ibid., 29.

15. George R. Knight, *Walking With Ellen White* (Hagerstown, Md.: Review and Herald®, 2000),

117. Knight would later nuance this statement by stating that Joseph Bates and James White were the "leading" ministers of their time until after they both passed away.

16. George R. Knight, *Reading Ellen White: How to Understand and Apply Her Writings* (Hagerstown, Md.: Review and Herald®, 1997), 25, 29.

17. Ellen G. White, *Selected Messages*, bk. 1, 45, cited in *Reading Ellen White*, 45.

18. George R. Knight, *Ellen White's World* (Hagerstown, Md.: Review and Herald®, 2001), 86.

19. Ibid., 36.

# Chapter 13

# Champion of an Academic Press

Ronald A. Knott

George Knight is a man known for not wasting time. Thus, it is no surprise that he quickly made a mark for himself when he arrived at Andrews University to begin teaching in the fall of 1976. A decade earlier, he had finished an MA and MDiv from the seminary, and after some years as a pastor, teacher, and high school principal, he had completed an EdD in education from the University of Houston. Now, at only thirty-five years old, he was back at Andrews as a new assistant professor of Educational Foundations in the School of Education.

Documents in obscure files at Andrews University Press show that almost immediately upon his arrival, he began planning the start of what would become the most vigorous and significant literary career in the Adventist world in the second half of the twentieth century.

It began with a type-written, neatly organized three-page document, submitted to Andrews University Press with a cover page carrying the date of January 17, 1977—just four months after the start of his teaching career at Andrews.[1]

Perhaps only George Knight, who would become well-known both for his vision and self-confidence, could have guessed the significance of his little document. In retrospect, the rest of us can now see that it launched that formative and sustaining influence he would wield for the next forty years on Adventism's academic publishing output, and particularly on the continuing existence of the church's only regularly established academic publishing house.

Andrews University Press had been established in 1969–1970 to provide an engine and outlet for Adventist academic publications and to burnish Andrews' reputation as a university seriously committed to scholarship and research. Siegfried Horn, then dean of the seminary, led out as best he could on day-to-day matters, as editor of a "monograph series." Then Larry Geraty, and later James Cox, assumed that responsibility.[2] But there wasn't any formal staff. Tiny as it was, the press nevertheless received keen administrative and academic attention, apparently disproportionate to its size and scope, because the university and others clearly understood its importance to the Adventist educational enterprise. Throughout the first half of the seventies, Richard Hammill, the university president, chaired the press board. The secretary of the board was the academic vice president, Grady Smoot, and the membership included what, in retrospect, is a hall of fame of Andrews academic luminaries of the time: Horn, Geraty, Hans LaRondelle, John Waller, Sakae Kubo, Kenneth Strand, Wilfred Futcher, and others.[3] Because the press had no formal staff, the board members took an active role in helping with the manuscript processing and correspondence that employees would later handle.

By the time Knight submitted his document, the press had already published, among other things, five volumes in the *Heshbon* archaeological series, Alger John's *Short Grammar of Biblical Aramaic,* and Sakae Kubo's *A Reader's Greek-English Lexicon of the New Testament,* the latter two still in print today. Other titles were already in the works, including Joseph Battistone's *The Great Controversy Theme,* and Niels-Erik Andreasen's *Rest and Redemption.*

Knight's document was a proposal for a book called *Philosophy of Education: An Introduction in Christian Perspective.* He originally described the book as a text for education students in Adventist colleges and universities, but the concept soon broadened. The press board received the proposal warmly, voting at two different meetings that year to encourage him to develop the book. They also were impressed with the specific form of his proposal, voting "to consider this proposal *a model to be circulated to future authors* desiring to publish through the AU Press."[4] The new professor had begun to make his mark.

Thus began George Knight's academic publishing career, and a lifetime association with Andrews University Press through (1) his published works, (2) his leadership in the press as a longtime board member and director, and (3) his personal influence on its future through his mentoring of later personnel. This short historical and personal essay, written by the current director of that press, will briefly address these three areas to make the modest claim that George Knight should be considered the single most formative influence in the existence of an Adventist academic publishing house. In the discussion following, the reader must always keep in mind that in considering Knight's involvement with the press, we are looking at a very small section of a much larger canvas of his activities, one that portrays many other important, and even monumental things, Knight was doing at the very same time he was helping to grow a serious academic publishing institution for the church.

## Published works through Andrews University Press

With the encouragement of the press board votes in regard to his 1977 proposal, Knight began work on his text. By the spring of 1979, Robert E. Firth, the newly appointed half-time director, reported to the board that he expected Knight's manuscript in September.[5] This information could only have been based on some assurance from George. Those familiar with Knight's practice of keeping his promises and hewing to his schedule would thus not be surprised to learn that in September, right on schedule, Firth was writing to Peter De Boer, chairman of the education department at Calvin College: "We have just received a new manuscript *Philosophy and Education: An Introduction in Christian Perspective*[6] by Dr. George Knight of Andrews University that we will be considering for publication. There is apparently nothing quite like it on the market. . . . Would you be willing to read this manuscript and give us your reactions in writing, by about the end of October?"[7] The peer review process, involving two other reviewers, concluded in January.[8] Knight made revisions according to the critiques, and the board voted on May 8, 1980, to publish the work in a print run of one thousand copies.[9]

By December of that year, the book was back from the printer and on the market. Reviews in a variety of journals were almost uniformly complimentary, even while one or two sniffed at the unimaginative title.[10] A reviewer for *Religious Education,* the journal of the Religious Education Association, said the book is "characterized by its clear and simple writing, its orderly logical presentation, and, above all, by the honesty, modesty and tentativeness of its claims." Further, "on methodological grounds alone, the book would be of interest to religious educators of all faiths, and also, interestingly enough, to those educators who are secular humanists. I would especially recommend the book to my fellow Catholics interested in the present controversy regarding the nature and the calling of Catholic higher education."[11] The reviewer for *Christianity Today* called it "an excellent survey of the relation of education and philosophy [that] deserves serious consideration as a textbook in educational philosophy."[12]

Long before these reviews, many Christian college education departments had already gotten the word of an interesting new resource, due to Firth's vigorous marketing efforts, which consisted of sending out flyers and review copies. Just two months after the book's release, he received a request from the academic dean at Liberty Baptist College in Lynchburg, Virginia (now Liberty University) for a copy of the book. Firth tersely replied that he had already sent *nine* complimentary copies to faculty at Liberty, and the press was looking for textbook adoptions, and not simply to "build professors' personal libraries." "Is there a need for more copies at your institution for the purpose of making a decision?" he asked with some irony. The dean wrote back, apologizing for the requests, and assured Firth that the sending of the nine copies complimentary copies would be rewarded with textbook adoptions.[13] The same week (just eight weeks after publication), Firth was replying to requests from professors at Wayne State University, Southern Illinois University and Eastern Kentucky University, saying that the press had "been deluged with requests" for complimentary copies of book but could not "afford to fill all the requests from state institutions where adoptions seem highly unlikely. Please send us more information."[14]

George Knight's writing career was launched, and Andrews University Press had a bestseller on its hands. Following as it did the highly popular and financially profitable *Temperament Inventory* by Robert Cruise and Peter Blitchington, the press leadership could see things beginning to move. Knight's book went through eleven printings totalling twelve thousand copies in ten years. Based on the $8.95 retail price of the first edition, it is reasonable to estimate sales revenue of more eighty thousand dollars. That was a very big deal for the press. A second edition came out in 1989 and went through about eighteen thousand copies in ten years. A third edition in 1998 had a *first printing alone* of ten thousand copies. A fourth edition was published in 2006, and has already sold more than twelve thousand copies. Its four editions up to the present have sold more than fifty-seven thousand copies, making it the highest grossing title in the history of the press (outside the *Andrews Study Bible*), with sales revenue of approximately $720,000.[15]

To have a potentially long-lived, widely adopted textbook in its publication line-up, or a more popular item like the *Temperament Inventory,* is the dream of every small university press. It can provide a desperately needed steady revenue stream to fill in the gaps left by the fits and starts of small-run monograph publishing. Even from the vantage point of 1981, *Philosophy and Education* clearly had the potential to become such a textbook. Could Knight produce another one? Firth's letters to those disappointed professors at the state universities pointed to another obvious market for another textbook, a repurposed version of *Philosophy of Education,* and he and Knight were quick to exploit it. On March 8, 1982, just fifteen months after the release of *Philosophy and Education,* Knight presented to the board a "proposition" to publish the book with a new title and cover, and in a "form which would be saleable to state universities and colleges," by "omitting the specific references to Christian education."[16] The board voted the proposal.

Knight and the press staff worked extremely quickly. Or, more likely, Knight and Firth had been working on the project long before they formally brought it to the board. In May, just nine weeks after the approval of the proposal Firth reported to the board that the book was *already at the printer.*[17] Eight weeks later, in July 1982, *Issues and Alternatives in Educational Philosophy* was on the market, and gave immediate promise. Comments solicited by the press from professors at public universities were almost uniformly strong in praising the book for its "brevity and comprehensiveness," and, among many other good things, its "substance without over-weighted ponderosity." As a telling indication that Knight and the University Press in 1982 were not, perhaps understandably, on the very cutting edge of societal evolution, one professor from Youngstown State University wrote that "the book is very male-oriented and very multi-culturally insensitive. I could not use it in good conscience."[18] Nevertheless, the book was an immediate hit for Knight and for the press. Thirty-one years later, it has gone through many printings, and like its counterpart, is now in its fourth edition, with some thirty-six thousand copies sold and gross sales of approximately $360,000.

Those who later heard the midcareer Knight describe his general professional plan of releasing a new book about every year[19] would see the pattern developing well in the early 1980s. Even while *Philosophy and Education* (effectively released in January 1981) and *Issues and Alternatives* (July 1982) were in process, Knight was planning his next project, a collection of historical/biographical essays about the early founders and leaders of Adventist education. The authors of the essays were well-known church leaders, scholars, history professors in Adventist education, and recent doctoral students in the School of Education working under George's supervision in various areas of Adventist educational history. Knight organized the project and served as general editor. The first mention of the project in press board minutes occurs in February 1983, though it seems obvious that Knight and Firth had been collaborating for some time. Publication was voted in May, calling for a printing of one thousand copies in a clothbound edition. By the fifth of August, Firth was sending out complimentary and review copies of *Early Adventist Educators*.[20]

Knight now had his third book in three years and was on his way. But the route was changing. *Early Adventist Educators* marked the beginning of a major career change for Knight. Book reviews understandably treated the book as history, with varying degrees of approval. A reviewer from Southeast Missouri State University, writing for *Vitae Scholasticae,* somewhat sarcastically noted that because the book was written about Adventist educators, "from Adventist sources, published by an Adventist press chiefly for Adventist educators," it would "provide an apparently accepted Adventist view of the development of Adventist education."[21] At least two other reviewers likewise faulted the work for not integrating an understanding of the Adventist educational development with its wider cultural context.[22] Nevertheless, the appreciation for the work among Adventists obviously foreshadowed Knight's shift from the comparatively esoteric world of academic educational philosophy toward more popularly accessible denominational history and historical theology. Just two years after the publication of his first focused work in Adventist history, Knight, in 1985, made that shift more symbolically complete when he moved from teaching in the School of Education to the Church History Department at the seminary.

He had a much bigger field to plow—or perhaps harvest—in writing for a more general Adventist audience. That meant that the relatively small and academically focused reach of Andrews University Press was not the regular place for publishing his future works. Although by way of exception in 2001 the press did release a second edition of his popular *I Used to Be Perfect* that went on to sell more than twenty-five thousand copies. His next major project released through the press was in 2003 when he edited the press's annotated edition of *Questions on Doctrine*. However, his need to publish elsewhere definitely did not mean that his influence at the press would diminish. Rather, it simply turned another direction, equally important.

## Leadership for the press

The young professor had favored Andrews University Press with his first book publishing idea in 1977. He had quickly followed up its publication with two other more promising ideas. So it was obvious that administrators saw him as someone who would be a good resource for developing more good ideas for the still fledgling press. He became a regular member of the press board and attended his first meeting on October 20, 1981. It was the start of what became, at eighteen and a half years, the second longest tenure on the press board, just short of the record still held by the late Kenneth Strand. Strand's engagement on the board was focused primarily through the lens of his responsibility as editor of *Seminary Studies,* which for many of those years the press board supervised. Knight's tenure, which ran until May of 2000, was more that of a generalist, a member at large, and an idea man, to help steady the direction of the press now that it had, with his publications and the *Temperament Inventory,* the reality of some solid successes.

He made the press a priority in his professional life. Of the nineteen press board meetings held during the three year period from April of 1982 to May of 1985, Knight missed only one. It was the meeting at which the press board appointed him as associate editor of *Seminary Studies.* That action doubtless came in recognition that his strong credentials as a published scholar and editor should now be put to good use in the seminary, immediately following his recent relocation there from the School of Education.

Throughout the 1980s, the press continued to grow and develop under the leadership of Robert Firth. Knight was providing the focused guidance and expertise of one whose publishing reputation with an educated but popular readership in the church was skyrocketing with the publication of his *Myths in Adventism* (1985), *From 1888 to Apostasy* (1987), and *Angry Saints* (1989). In 1987, the press board, chaired by Arthur Coetzee, discussed some complexities in how the university conducted research and publishing activities beyond the reach of Firth's role at the press. The board appointed an *ad hoc* committee to consider the matter, and naturally looked to Knight, along with Firth and the university treasurer Robert Lemon, to bring a report.[23] In 1989, when Firth and the board wanted a standing subcommittee, called the Book and Occasional Papers Committee (or more commonly just Book Committee), to handle much of the detail work in finding, developing, and vetting new manuscripts, it made Knight the chair.[24]

The press had for years considered Robert Firth's role as director a half-time position, supported with a full-time secretary/typesetter, and student workers to take care of the warehouse and shipping. After masterfully directing the press for eighteen years, Firth stepped down 1990. Delmer Davis, from the School of Arts and Sciences, became director for two years, and occasionally doubled as chair of the press board. Knight was away from the press for most of Davis's second year. In the fall of 1992, the board named Knight director of the press. His first board meeting as director was on October 20, 1992, exactly eleven years to the day since his first meeting as a member of the board on October 20, 1981.

Knight took on the job, now counted as a quarter-time position in his work load, even while he was moving into the height of his influence at the seminary and on the wider church stage. He served as director for three years, producing a respectable record of titles, while trying to address marketing issues and develop a mission statement that is still operative today.[25] He also had the unusual distinction for much of his tenure of simultaneously being chair of the press board, director of the press, and the highest royalty-earning press author.[26]

New ideas have always been his emphasis. His restless and inquisitive nature frequently proposed new initiatives, with a particular emphasis on marketing.[27] Among the publication ideas he proposed were a line of children's materials for the General Conference Sabbath School Department, a new line of more popularly oriented books that wouldn't compete with the other Adventist publishing houses, and books to serve the Hispanic market.[28] Often people heard him say, in his half-apologetic but deliberately provocative way: "We've got to find something to support our habit." In this case, the "habit" was regular serious, high-quality but usually unprofitable academic publications, which were to Knight, committed as he was to the press, as alluring as illicit drugs are to an addict. The "something" was "bread and butter" money-making products, such as his educational philosophy books or more popularly oriented volumes, to pay for all those "drugs."

Many of Knight's "something" ideas never went anywhere. In this sense, what supposedly has been said of Churchill as a war leader could, with only mild exaggeration, also apply to Knight. "He had 50 new ideas every day, only five of which were any good. But that was four better than anyone else."

His steadily increasing responsibility at the seminary and the wider church stage called him to hand the director's role back to Davis in 1995, and Knight returned to perhaps his more natural role as a board member, in which he provided ideas, counsel, and opinions regarding the viability of manuscripts. In the midnineties other staffing arrangements at the press changed. The board upgraded the full-time office staff position that had previously functioned as typesetter and a kind of managing editor, and changed the title to director, the first time a nonacademic carried the title, but still under close supervision by the board chair. By the early 2000s, staffing had evolved again into a professional level staff director, along with an editor—both positions at three-quarter time for several years.

During the summer of 1999, I became director of Andrews University Press. George Knight had been a close friend, teacher, and professional mentor for nearly twenty years. I think he had long viewed me as a bit of an agitating reformer, something like himself. I suspect he had been influential in recommending me to the press board and university administration for the press job.

So it was natural that I immediately turned to him for counsel on a wide range of project ideas. He was the first person with whom I discussed the idea for an *Andrews Study Bible* in the early fall of 1999. Eventually published in 2010, it had Knight serving in a key role on the editorial team as the contributor of the theme notes. During the same conversation in his office in the seminary, I raised the idea of publishing a new edition of *Questions on Doctrine* (*QOD*). I had long admired the book as an excellent example of good Adventist apologetics, and was vaguely aware that it had essentially disappeared because of controversy. Knight, I was excited to learn, was supervising research on all the controverted issues surrounding the book, and was enthusiastic about releasing a new edition in what he conceived as a new series, called the Adventist Classic Library. The Annotated Edition of *QOD* came out in 2003, with Knight providing all the new content, including extensive annotations and historical and theological essays. The volume has sold more than five thousand copies, generating more than $93,000 in sales.

Collaborating with Knight on *QOD* provided some unintended but valuable experience on working through professional disagreements between friends. The new edition was to include an updated, annotated bibliography in which George would provide a brief comment on Adventist books published since 1957 that were particularly relevant to specific topics in *QOD*. One Friday afternoon, I was in the local Adventist Book Center and found a recently published book from one of the church's other publishing houses dealing specifically with one of the controverted *QOD* topics. In fact, it discussed *QOD* on the topic at some length. I checked Knight's annotated bibliography and saw that it didn't include the title. The following week, I called Knight and mentioned what I thought had been an innocent oversight. But I learned that it wasn't an oversight. He didn't want the book included. I insisted that it should be, or the book and the press would rightly be criticized for appearing to manipulate the historical record of important publications on the topic. We talked past each other for some time, with tension mounting. George even said he would withdraw from the project if I insisted on including the citation. Fortunately, the matter turned out to be a misunderstanding. When he understood that I wasn't requiring him to say *anything nice* about the book in his annotations, he readily agreed to list what he found to be a misguided book.

In the spring of 2000, a reorganization of the press board meant that after eighteen years of association Knight would no longer be involved, as both author receiving royalties and as board member. This had been a challenging adjustment for my friend and mentor. It was clear to me in the off-hand jokes Knight attempted to make in the months following that being off the press board was a definite disappointment for him. However small a slight it might have been in the scheme of other big things he was doing, it still hurt him. And it only made more obvious the point that the church's only regularly established academic publishing house held a very special place in the heart of George Knight.

## Personal influence

Other articles in this volume are describing the big picture of George Knight's monumental contributions to Adventist thought and self-understanding. It's important to mention some of the other less tangible contributions too, as they relate to the press. By his teaching and personal example in my own interactions with him for nearly thirty years, George, more than anyone I have met, has asserted the preeminence of accuracy in scholarship, not only in the treatment of content, but particularly in the use of scholarly apparatus. He has made it clear to me that the published scholar must take careful, personal responsibility for the smallest details, right down to the correct placement of commas in a bibliographic citation. While accepting the contributions of content and copy editors, he never relies on them to "sweat the small stuff" or clean up messes he has left behind, as some authors seem willing to do. He does all that himself. Perhaps some of us have had professors who gave lip service to a high standard, but relied on the teachers of the requisite research course to get this across to students. Not George Knight.

In the fall of 2000, I took his doctoral seminar in the development of Seventh-day Adventist doctrines. At the beginning of the course he made it clear that in addition to the advertised academic content, he would also use the seminar as a training exercise in the mechanics of how to write a serious academic paper. Throughout the semester he gave us clear instructions of his expectations. I had known Knight for nearly twenty years by this time. I, like many others, considered him an honored mentor. I knew he was a polite but forceful personality who meant what he said. But I didn't take his instructions seriously enough until I received back from him the first draft of my sixty-page paper. While he liked my research, my writing, and my argument, he clobbered me on the sloppiness of my citations. Apparently, he had read many of the footnotes with care, red-marked numerous careless flaws in the bibliographic form of my citations, and had gone to the James White Library (or his own at home) to check the accuracy of my quotations, which, alas, fell far short of his modest standard of an unrelenting 100 percent. It was an effective way of teaching me that responsible scholarship really means responsible scholarship. And doubtless this has been formative for many of his other admirers and protégés.

During my time with the press, Knight is the only author I know who takes his same kind of care with his own manuscripts before he hands them over to us. And he does the same with typeset proof copies we send to him for approval just before we go to print. He reads them word by word, citation by citation, quotation by quotation, comma by comma, rechecking every detail of his own work—and ours.

Thus, his example for me in the classroom and at the office has had an important influence on how we operate the University Press on this point. After the humiliation of publishing a work by another author that got savaged by a reviewer for the sloppiness of quotations and citations, we instituted a new practice. When we are about to accept a new manuscript for publication, we send a student worker to the library to check the accuracy of a representative sample of quotations, along with their bibliographic citations. If we find more than a very few of the most minor mistakes, we return the manuscript to the author. We gently make it clear that we will be happy to reconsider the work for publication when the author can certify that he has rechecked every quotation and citation for 100 percent accuracy. Admittedly, it's a stern, cold policy. But I had not the least hesitancy to invoke it, because I developed it out of the confidence I had in the high personal example and pedagogical practice of George Knight. It was justified both by what he taught me, and by what he showed me.

## Conclusion

These days, George Knight usually drops by Sutherland House[29] whenever he is in Berrien Springs. He comes just to say hello, to briefly discuss a new manuscript he hopes we will publish, to bring me up to date on what he is doing, and to catch up on how things are going for the press and how his books are selling. Always affirming and encouraging, he insists that he is proud that the press has filled out to the point where it needs four full-time employees. "Back when I was involved, we used to run this out of my back pocket," he is fond of saying. What that means is that George Knight was doing so many other things in his professional life, detailed elsewhere in this book, that his back pocket was the only empty space he could find for the press. And it was a deep pocket.

It is a singular pleasure to be able to talk serious shop with someone who has more than just an abstract or administrative interest in the past and future of the press; with someone who has invested real talent and loving attention, as an author, board member, director and informal counselor for thirty-six years—ever since he wrote that first, "model" book proposal in 1977. In this small section of that much larger canvas of his professional life, George Knight has laid out a remarkable record. All told, his works carrying the Andrews University Press imprint, which represent just a fraction of his publishing record, have generated sales of approximately $1.2 million and been read by scores of thousands. But that, of course, is only part of it. His investment of intellectual energy and influence has been worth even more. Considering the challenges facing all academic publishing operations, it is a truism to say that his is a record without which Adventist higher education would not today have a regularly established academic publishing house. But we do. And so George Knight, more than any other, is responsible.

## Endnotes

1. George R. Knight, *"Philosophy of Education: An Introduction in Christian Perspective—A* Research Proposal for the Andrews University Monograph Series in Education" (unpublished manuscript, January 17, 1977).

2. Robert E. Firth, "Andrews University Press: History and Functions" (unpublished manuscript, undated). Firth was the first official director of the press and served from 1978 until 1992.

3. Minutes of Andrews University Press Committee, Andrews University Press. During forty-three years, the governing board for the University Press has operated under five names: Andrews University Press Committee (March 1970–May 1972), Andrews University Press Board (October 1972–July 1978), Andrews University Press Board of Directors (July 1978–November 1979), Scholarly Research and Publications Board of Andrews University (November 1979–June 1987), and Scholarly Publications and Andrews University Press Board (October 1987 to present). Firth and his successors kept meticulous records of the minutes of the press board. Press staff have recently developed a database record of all attendees of the 158 press board meetings, under various names, from March 1970 to April 2013. All future references to these minutes will simply cite "Minutes," with the appropriate date.

4. Minutes, March 15, 1977, and November 30, 1977.

5. Robert E. Firth, "Directors Report to the Board" (unpublished manuscript, May 10, 1979, implied).

6. The title in Knight's original 1977 proposal was "Philosophy of Education," and the original Adventist college textbook audience was broadened to target Christian higher education.

7. Robert E. Firth to Peter De Boer, September 27, 1979.

8. The reviewers were De Boer; George Akers, professor of religious education at Andrews; and Maurice Hodgen, dean of the graduate school at Loma Linda University. See Maurice Hodgen to Robert E. Firth, January 9, 1980; Peter De Boer, "Some Critical Commentary Re George Knight's Manuscript: *Philosophy and Education: An Introduction in Christian Perspective"* (unpublished manuscript, November 1979); George H. Akers to Robert E. Firth, October 17, 1979.

9. Minutes, May 8, 1980.

10. Findley B. Edge, review of *Philosophy and Education*, by George R. Knight, *Review and Expositor* (Winter 1982): 185. Edge began his review with the following: "The rather prosaic title of this book does not do justice to the importance of the issues it discusses."

11. Joseph A. Varacalli, review of *Philosophy and Education: An Introduction in Christian Perspective*, by George R. Knight, *Religious Education* (Spring 1983): 301.

12. Norman Harper, "Life as Faith and Learning," *Christianity Today*, July 16, 1982, 58.

13. Robert E. Firth to Russell G. Fitzgerald, February 11, 1981.

14. Robert E. Firth to Arthur Brown, February 16, 1981; Robert E. Firth to Emil R. Spees, February

18, 1981; Robert E. Firth to William A. McKenney, February 18, 1981. Firth's letters to all three were virtually identical.

15. This number is compiled and estimated from various records available in the files and current databases of the University Press.

16. Minutes, March 8, 1982.

17. Minutes, May 18, 1982.

18. "Comments Received on *Issues and Alternatives*" (undated). The typewritten document has no author or date but has handwritten notations indicating that it was being worked on in October 1982.

19. Personal knowledge of the author.

20. Robert E. Firth to Everett N. Dick, August 5, 1983; Robert E. Firth to Myron F. Wehtje, August 5, 1983. Dick was a preeminent Adventist historian living in retirement in Lincoln, Nebraska, and Wehtje was professor of history at Atlantic Union College in South Lancaster, Massachusetts. Both men had been peer reviewers of the book before it was published.

21. Frank Nickell, review of *Early Adventist Educators*, edited by George R. Knight, *Vitae Scholasticae* 3 (1984): 255.

22. F. Michael Perko, review of *Early Adventist Educators*, edited by George R. Knight, *Church History* (Fall 1984): 562; James Findlay, "Nineteenth-Century Protestantism and American Education," review of *Early Adventist Educators*, edited by George R. Knight, *History of Education Quarterly* (Spring 1986): 125.

23. Minutes, October 7, 1987, and November 18, 1987.

24. Minutes, January 31, 1989.

25. Minutes, April 6, 1993, and February 1, 1994.

26. Only very rarely had his predecessors in the director's role been also listed in the Minutes as chair of the press board. Usually, they were listed as secretary. Eleven of Knight's sixteen board meetings as director had him listed as chair.

27. April 6, 1993.

28. Minutes, October 20, 1992, and March 1, 1994.

29. Sutherland House is the oldest building on the Andrews University campus. It was built originally as the home of Edward A. Sutherland, the educational reformer who brought Battle Creek College to Berrien Springs in 1901. Sutherland House has been the home of Andrews University Press since 2005.

# Chapter 14

# An Adventist William Barclay

Gerald Wheeler

O n hearing the name George R. Knight most Adventists would probably think of a church historian or maybe theologian. Those who knew
him in his early graduate teaching career might remember him for
his work in the philosophy of education.[1] His two volumes on that
subject have become a standard, have been used as textbooks at many colleges and
universities and have gone through several editions. Most, however, on hearing
his name would probably not immediately think of a Bible commentator. Yet
such books have become a major strand of Knight's published works and have had
a significant influence in the church.[2]

One of Knight's significant—but sometimes overlooked—projects has been
his Exploring series, devotional commentaries on various books of the Bible
launched in 2003. But this was not his first entrance into the genre. Back in the
1990s, he had worked with Pacific Press® Publishing Association to develop the
Abundant Life Bible Amplifier series, served as its general editor, and wrote the
Matthew volume for it. The set reached at least fourteen volumes, but when it

failed to meet sales expectations, the publisher phased it out, to George's great disappointment.[3] But he did not give up on the concept.

Knight then produced three adult daily devotionals that were basically commentaries on major blocks of biblical material: *Walking With Jesus on the Mount of Blessing* (Hagerstown, Md.: Review and Herald® Publishing Association, 1996); *Walking With Paul Through the Book of Romans* (Hagerstown, Md.: Review and Herald® Publishing Association, 2002); and *Turn Your Eyes Upon Jesus* (Hagerstown, Md.: Review and Herald® Publishing Association, 2013). The first title covers the Sermon on the Mount section of the book of Matthew while the latter title follows the life, ministry, and return of Christ in the Gospels and the rest of the New Testament. In addition, Knight was also one of the contributors to the *Andrews Study Bible*.[4]

But George desired to do more than just daily devotionals or notes for study Bibles. He wanted full commentaries that avoided some of the problems encountered in the Bible Amplifier series. An admirer of the highly popular *Daily Study Bible* set of New Testament commentaries by the renowned Scottish interpreter William Barclay, he sought to emulate it—and improve upon it by providing additional resources in it. As a result he conceived his Exploring series and released them through the Review and Herald® Publishing Association.[5] He visualized it as "a series of user-friendly commentaries aimed at helping people understand the Bible better. While the books have the needs and abilities of laypeople in mind, they will also prove beneficial to pastors and other church leaders. Beyond individual readers, the 'Exploring' format will be helpful for church study groups and in enriching participation in midweek meetings."[6]

As with the Barclay series, George wanted his devotional commentaries to be helpful "in the daily life of believers in the twenty-first century." He did not intend the series to be a technical one. "Rather than focusing on the details of each verse, the 'Exploring' volumes seek to give readers an understanding of the themes and patterns of each biblical book as a whole and how each passage fits into its context. As a result, they do not attempt to solve all of the problems or answer all the questions related to a given portion of Scripture."[7]

Knight breaks the complete text of each biblical book into "bite-sized" segments with the commentary following each portion. For the New Testament books he has done his own translation, and for Old Testament books he used the updated *New American Standard Bible*. "The commentary sections aim at being long enough to significantly treat a topic, but short enough for individual, family, or group readings."

The format of each volume includes an introduction covering such areas as author, date, and original recipients of the specific biblical book; occasion, date, and purpose of the book; major themes of the book; relationship, if any, with other writings of the Bible, the relevance of the book for the twenty-first century; and a list of works cited. The biblical text and commentary then follow the structural outline of the scriptural book itself. He has also provided online study guides for each commentary volume. To enhance the visual interest of the pages he employs many drop-ins and call-outs. Knight also weaves in some archaeological and social background material to help bring out the meaning of a text. His work shows a wide reading in other commentators and theologians.

In choosing which books to write on and in what order, George followed the sequence of biblical books being studied in the Seventh-day Adventist *Adult Sabbath School Bible Study Guides.* The list of completed titles includes the following:

*Exploring Hebrews* (2003)
*Exploring Mark* (2004)
*Exploring Galatians and Ephesians* (2005)
*Exploring Ecclesiastes and Song of Solomon* 2006)
*Exploring the Letters of John and Jude* (2009)
*Exploring Romans* (2010)
*Exploring Thessalonians* (2012)[8]

Although he deals with all the major themes and implications of each biblical book and writes in a way that would be understandable and appreciated by even non-Adventists, as a Seventh-day Adventist scholar Knight does focus on issues of special interest to Adventists in the context of the texts themselves, such as the Sabbath in Mark,[9] the heavenly sanctuary in the book of Hebrews, the law in the book of Galatians, the state of the dead in Ecclesiastes, death, resurrection, and the Second Coming in 1 Thessalonians, the human nature of Christ in the epistles of John, etc. A major emphasis, of course, is righteousness by faith. It is a theme that runs through much of his writing, especially his historical and theological works on the 1888 Minneapolis General Conference Session. But in his commentaries he approaches the topic within the context of the scriptural text itself.

George is by nature a perfectionist, a trait he has to fight against in theological matters. But his strong sense of detail has served him well in many other ways.[10] As he has candidly discussed in many of his books, he knows all the arguments and texts that perfectionists employ—because he has used them and tried to live by them himself in the past. Thus as he reads and comments on Scripture, he is always alert for the biblical emphasis on salvation only through the life, death, and ministry of Jesus Christ. His overriding motif is always one of grace. That is, salvation is not what human beings do, but what God has done.

Naturally, in his commentary on the book of Romans, Knight would put this front and center. He sums up by declaring, "One of the most important things we can say about Paul in the letter to the Romans and in his entire ministry is that he put God at the center. What the Lord had done for him personally in Christ was never far from his mind. He knew where the center was. While doctrine and how one lived were important to Paul, they were never the most important. Everything, he believed, stood in relationship to the grace of God, the sacrifice of Christ, and the ongoing work of the Holy Spirit.

"Christianity for Paul was the extreme opposite of self-centeredness or those religious practices that lead people to focus on themselves and their achievements for God. For the apostle, God was all in all, and even human achievement reflected what He does in people." Knight asserted further, "With God at the center, it is little wonder that Paul started his book by referring to himself as a slave to Christ (1:1) and concluded it with praise to God (16:27)."[11]

In his commentary on Galatians, he states, "The heart of Paul's gospel is that Jesus 'gave Himself for our sins' that we might be delivered. Salvation is not the result of our actions but of His. It is not the consequence of some great thing that we as human beings do as an offering to or an appeasement of God, but something done for us by Jesus who bore our sins and took our place on the tree of Calvary (Gal. 3:13). Here we have the core of Paul's understanding of the good news. 'The gospel,' he writes to the Corinthians, is that 'Christ died for our sins in accordance with the scriptures, that he was buried, that he was raised on the third day' (1 Cor. 15:1-4, RSV).

"The very foundation of the gospel is that salvation rests on what God has done for us in Christ rather than on something we must do for Him. It is that teaching that the false teachers who have invaded the Galatian congregations now challenge."[12]

While Knight emphasizes that salvation is by grace and faith in that divine act, he also reminds us that salvation has obligations. Salvation calls for obedience—obedience defined by divine law. "Paul's theology has as its foundation free grace accepted by faith, but it is not a lawless theology. For him every Christian has two obligations. The first is their duty to love God, and the second is to love other people. Beyond that, the apostle directly ties those responsibilities to the Ten Commandments in Romans 13:8-10, in which he explicitly links love to one's neighbor with the commandments on the second table of the Decalogue. . . . The way of faith means that a Christian is free from keeping the law as an avenue to salvation, but the way of faith also means that a Christian for the first time has the liberty and the power to live God's law of love from the right motive."[13]

Elsewhere in his commentary on the books of 1 and 2 Thessalonians, he emphasizes "a theme that runs all the way through Paul's writings and even throughout the entire New Testament—becoming a Christian leads to a new way of life. In other words, 'getting saved' is not something that merely happens in people's inner being but is an experience that finds expression in how they live their lives. Repeatedly we find that pattern reflected in Paul's letters. Thus Romans, Galatians, Ephesians, and other epistles consistently move from theological concerns related to salvation to ethical issues in daily living. Herman Ridderbos identifies that move as the shift from the 'indicative' to the 'imperative,' from declarations about the process of salvation to commands as to how salvation will affect a Christian's life (Ridderbos, 253-258). As a result, Paul constantly teaches that the gift of grace includes the call to obedience."[14]

But, he reminds us, obedience is not just for its own sake. It must be done out of love. A frequent refrain in Knight's sermons and writing is about meeting a "saint" who is meaner than the devil. Obedience must always be manifested in love. In his comments on 1 John 5:1–5, George points out that "intertwined with it we find a replay of the three tests of genuine Christianity that have been so prominent throughout the letter. The tests of belief or truth, love, and obedience have shown up repeatedly in the first four chapters.

"First John 5:1-5 resurrects John's three tests in an intertwined triumphant finale, with faith and belief appearing in verses 1, 4, and 5; love in verses 1, 2, and three; and the necessity to obey in verses 2 and 3. What we need to understand is that those three threads form a unit in John's thinking, with all of them combined being the full test of a genuine Christianity that overcomes the world. Two out of the three won't do. All three are required—for everyone always. And the tragedy is that the secessionists that he is warning his readers about lack all three.

"The apostle's logic as it unfolds in the tightly packed verses of 1 John 5:1-5 is that

1. those who believe Jesus is the Christ must of necessity love the Father and His children (verses 1, 2a).
2. one cannot love the Father without obeying His commandments and overcoming (verses 2b-4a).
3. one cannot overcome the world without belief in Jesus as the Son of God (4b-5).

"The sequence begins and ends with faith and belief in the incarnate Christ. That understanding is crucial. Without that central affirmation and reality all else is lost. And without the incarnate Christ there can be no plan of salvation. Thus John's repeated attack on those who deny the foundational truth that frames his discussion in 1 John 5:1-5. It is within that framework of belief that he treats the necessity of love and obedience. Outside of it, they have no meaning."[15]

Knight concludes his discussion of the book of Hebrews by describing it as "a letter so full of what God has done for us in Christ, [that] it is encouraging that the final word of blessing is one of continuing grace as we head into an unknown future. The good news of Hebrews is that the God who has done so much for us in the past, who is doing so much for us now through the heavenly ministry of Christ, will continue to care for those who walk by faith until we finally arrive at the heavenly Jerusalem (12:22), the city 'whose designer and builder is God' (11:10)."[16]

Throughout his commentaries, George tries to make the teachings of Scripture practical, to relate them to actual daily life. For example, in his discussion of prayer in the book of Ephesians, he observes, "That means that prayer must be constant. Victorious Christians live in an atmosphere of prayer. Rather than praying merely when a crisis arrives, or at meals, or in the evening and the morning, prayer must become a part of our life throughout the day." He continued, "that doesn't mean that we are on our knees all day long, but rather that we can utter a prayer to God as we drive down the road or as we meet a person and aren't quite sure what to say in a particular situation. It is from a life of constant and consistent prayer that we gain strength and wisdom to live the Christian life."[17]

But it is not just any kind of prayer that we need. Commenting on Jude 19 and what church members needed to do to combat the false teachers of Jude's day, Knight warns us that "in the war against spiritual darkness, human prayer is not adequate. It must be prayer 'in the Holy Spirit,' a teaching that implies that Jude's readers are empowered by the Spirit, since they pray in Him, while the false teachers are without the Spirit (verse 19)."[18]

His approach to the Song of Solomon illustrates both how he takes the content of Scripture seriously, then seeks to apply it to real life. Rejecting the old tradition of the book as religious allegory (God's love for the church), he interprets it as patterned after the genre of ancient love poems.[19] Then he explains how a biblical concept of sexuality should shape the believer's thinking and life.[20] While the biblical poem is not a wooden allegory, it can still teach us about our relationship with God, because "it is also a faithful picture of our relationship with the God who made us male and female. As a result, our relationship with God parallels that which we have with other humans. Never fully satisfied, we are ever stretching beyond for fuller relationships. The Song's final invitation leaves us with a feeling of desire for our earthly beloved, and, by extension, a longing for our heavenly Beloved who made us in such a way that we can enjoy love here on earth as both a taste of Eden and a foreshadowing of things to come."[21]

George Knight has written his devotional commentaries from a pastoral heart. Even more than what a text might teach, he has sought to get across to his readers what a passage means in the reality of their daily lives. In the process, he has made not only a great contribution to Adventist scholarship, but also to Adventist spiritual life. He illustrates how a scholar must not only be a teacher but a spiritual guide.

## Endnotes

1. His work also touches strongly on the sociology of religion, especially as it relates to the functioning and outlook of an eschatologically focused church.

2. As a denominational publishing house editor, I have long encouraged Adventist religion scholars to write for the general church public, believing that to do so would help ease and bridge the suspicion that sometimes exists among both leadership and the ordinary member toward the academic community. Knight has been one of the few to do exactly that, greatly enhancing, I believe, his credibility throughout the church.

3. Knight has commented that several aspects of the format and marketing approach developed by the publishing house may have doomed the entire project almost from the beginning.

4. Berrien Springs, Mich.: Andrews University Press, 2010.

5. He did most of the copy editorial and proofreading work on them himself.

6. From "Exploring the 'Exploring' Idea" introduction.

7. Ibid.

8. As of the time of this writing he is completing the volume on the book of Daniel. Feeling a need to cut back on his prolific output, he plans to be more restrictive in what he writes in the future.

9. *Exploring Mark,* 78–82.

10. His years of directing Andrews University Press taught him many aspects of publishing. That awareness makes him much easier to edit. Taking great care with his writing, he still handwrites all his manuscripts and has me do the editing on paper instead of computer screen so that he can immediately see all changes and save time. Knight tolerates my hostility toward passive tense and repetition in any form, while I have come to accept his more conversational and even occasionally sermonic style. The quarter-century editorial relationship between us has worked well as we have come to know each other's idiosyncrasies.

11. *Exploring Romans,* 303. The sizable content and range of the series means that any material cited has been chosen only as representative (and somewhat random) samples of his style and themes.

12. *Exploring Galatians and Ephesians,* 33.

13. Ibid., 131.

14. *Exploring Thessalonians,* 119.

15. *Exploring the Letters of John and Jude,* 154.

16. *Exploring Hebrews,* 254.

17. *Exploring Galatians and Ephesians,* 300.

18. *Exploring the Letters of John and Jude,* 276.

19. *Exploring Ecclesiastes and Song of Solomon,* 153.

20. See especially ibid., 149–157, 160, 205–208.

21. Ibid., 234.

## Chapter 15

# Challenges to Adventist Mission

Jon L. Dybdahl

## Introduction: The centrality of mission

George Knight leaves no doubt as to how important mission is in his thinking.[1] Two of his key books on mission begin their introductory "A Word to the Reader" section with the same words: "Mission is what the S.D.A. church is all about. It is the only reason for the denomination's existence."[2] When Knight writes on the subject of Adventist history, he puts mission front and center in the purpose statement he makes: "The book seeks to develop the central lines of Adventist history with a special interest in the growth of its concept of mission."[3] He declares in another place that his brief history of Adventism deals with the centrality of mission and is the only history of Adventism written from a missiological perspective.[4]

Missiology today covers a broad range of topics. While the study of the history and theology of mission are crucial for mission studies, its scholars also spend much time dealing with the issues related to the communication of the gospel as it interacts with other religions and cultures. Knight makes little attempt to deal with the broad sweep of missiology but centers his efforts in key areas which he believes are at the core of the challenges we face in Adventist mission today. Dr. Knight concentrates on the areas he knows best, the places where his expertise lies—Adventist history and the current situation in the church.

## The missiological vision

We can summarize Knight's missiology as follows. The Adventist Church has a unique biblically based apocalyptic vision that it must share with all nations in a Christ-centered way. This mission vision made us more successful than the other groups born out of the Millerite movement. The passage of time, however, has led to developments that threaten the Adventist mission vision. They include (1) a neglect of our apocalyptic vision, (2) overemphasis on the details of the apocalyptic vision, (3) "beastly preaching" that leaves Jesus out of apocalyptic, and (4) a top heavy organization that perpetuates itself and deemphasizes mission. The list could go on. Unless we admit we have challenges and deal decisively with them, our church will have serious problems and lose its mission vision.

This missiological vision has had wide dissemination in the church both through Knight's prolific pen but also by his international speaking and teaching ministry. Probably no Adventist writer other than Ellen White has written so much and spoken so widely. Careful reading of Adventist history and a passionate concern for the health of the church he loves characterizes George's work in missiology. Knight does not shrink from drawing conclusions he deems appropriate even if they provoke opposition in some quarters. His writings in missiology demonstrate clearly his knack for the catchy title. You don't have to be interested in Adventist history to want to know who the fat lady is, what the devil is up to, and how the church is being neutered. Part of the genius of his work lies in his ability to speak to both the scholar and the typical member in the pew.

If one reads Knight's missiological works carefully, it becomes clear that his publications are not works on mission composed from the beginning as books. They began as articles written for a magazine or journal publication or as sermons intended for an audience of church members or ministerial staff. The articles or sermons he then compiled or expanded into a book. This allows for pivotal articles to appear in more than one place. Knight himself acknowledges that "several"[5] chapters in "Devil" originally appeared in the "Fat Lady." In actuality, ten of the twenty chapters in "Devil" appeared earlier in the "Fat Lady." One might be tempted to say that George, at his core, was more of a missiological preacher than a missiological writer.

As far as I know, no official survey has been taken to evaluate the worldwide impact of Knight's work. The best I can do is to cite anecdotal evidence and give testimony to the impact in my life and thinking, believing there may be others with similar experiences. We move to that evaluation now.

## The five pillars

I see five key issues that we can call pillars of Knight's missiology. Each of them needs to be stated and then evaluated as to their impact on Adventist thought and psyche.

First is the apocalyptic vision. This is his conviction of the key role of Adventist apocalyptic which combines belief in the imminence of a premillennial literal return of Jesus, a pre-Advent judgment, a historical view of Daniel and Revelation, and the importance of the Sabbath. It also includes a passion to share this with the world. Together they form the heart of what George's theology is about. At the end of his book "Vision," Knight talks about the response his message evoked the first two times he presented it publically to a large audience. Those hearing him were hundreds of ministers in the Pacific Union and Australian Union.[6] In the Pacific Union, the audience ranked the slate of the various speakers who spoke at the meetings as to how valuable they were. Knight's presentations were rated both the most valuable and the least valuable. It needs to be noted that the "most valuable" votes were five times the "least valuable" votes. This demonstrates both how divisive the topic is and how positive was the general response.[7] Comments from hearers said that they could now preach the Adventist apocalyptic message with assurance of truth, felt more confidence in the pre-Advent judgment, and could now see the major parts of the apocalyptic vision in context. I had the privilege of being at the Australian meetings and can vouch for the truth of the response George claims for the meetings.

I would go on to say that in my estimation much of his success in preaching the apocalyptic vision and the positive response of people is based on the second pillar of his missiology—the centrality of Jesus in apocalyptic. While the apocalyptic vision is important it can never be separated from Jesus. Christ is to be central to eschatology. He is not only the judging Lion (apocalyptic) but also the Lamb slain for the redeeming of humanity. George's message is never an apocalyptic without grace, love, and salvation. His balanced presentation was a major factor in the general positive response to the apocalyptic vision message.

A third major plank in Knight's missiology is the view that Adventists have been successful in mission. A major argument for that success is how much better we have done number-wise than the other denominations born out of the Millerite movement. While it is encouraging to see this and certainly helpful, it is clearly not the only way to view the issue, and it does seem to ignore a comparison that may be somewhat sobering. I will say more about this later.

Part of the success argument is the global spread of the Adventist Church, a fact related to Bible passages such as Matthew 28:18–20, and 24:14, and Revelation. 14:6. For a long time, Adventists defined and measured their global spread by the number of countries where the Adventist Church had an officially organized program and members. The official Adventist yearbook chronicled the growth. Since 1990 and the global mission initiative, we have begun to view the world in million person population segments. This gives us a more precise gauge of where the church is (and is not) and offers a clearer picture of the work remaining. Knight does not enter into the discussion of the specifics of measuring the task. He is satisfied with general statements about the worldwide advance of the church that he suggests is biblically foretold, and I believe most of the church would see things the same way.

The fourth core pillar of Knight's missiology is that the church is in serious trouble as it looks to the fulfilling of its mission. Based on his analysis of history and the current situation in the denomination, George believes that the church is in serious difficulty in at least two areas—loss of apocalyptic vision and institutionalization that forces it to lose its mission priority and emphasize self-preservation over reaching the world for Jesus. I suggest that most thinking Adventists who have taken the time to reflect would agree with his analysis—at least in the church of the global North (North America, Europe, Australia).

As a fifth core teaching, Knight believes that these problems are so serious that minor tinkering or tweaking will not suffice. We need a major overhaul of the church organization and theology if we want to fulfill our mission and accomplish what God has called us to do. Again, it is difficult to say how widely George's ideas are accepted. Certainly many thoughtful Adventists have either heard him speak on this topic or have read some of his books. I would suspect again that the biggest impact on Adventist thinking has come in the global North and perhaps secondarily in South America. My work and travels in Africa and Asia suggest that Knight's influence has been minimal in these areas but that the passage of time will see that situation change.

The greatest influence on me personally is Knight's articulation of a comprehensive apocalyptic vision. I suppose that, like many others, I have experienced a dimming of such an apocalyptic vision. The passage of time with no Second Coming, the shrill voices of those who seem to see only an apocalyptic vision with no Jesus, those whose reading of current events leads them to continue time setting, and the "beastly preaching" George describes[8] (failing to put Jesus and the love of God at the center of our preaching) have all contributed to a lack of fervor about the apocalyptic vision. Knight's balanced approach, which sees Jesus clearly in Revelation as the center of apocalyptic, appeals to me. His broad outlines avoid quarreling over details but at the same time give clear exposition of the overall picture of the passages that have been so key to Adventist eschatology. While I may not see eye to eye with all that George says, he passionately and articulately defends a vision that describes our mission clearly and can deliver us from the neutering he fears is taking place.

## A broader vision

Knight has performed such a valuable service to the church and means so much to me as a personal friend that I find it hard to make some suggestions, but that is part of my assignment. If we could clone George or give him another life to speak and write I would suggest that he broaden his audience and context. Basically writing and speaking in and to an Adventist milieu, he talks about Adventist history to deliver a message to Adventists. I would like to suggest that he reach out more broadly in two main ways.

First, I would love to have him begin to deal with the issue of world religions. Christianity, even counting nominal members, composes about 33 percent of the world's population. Adventist missionaries to other cultures have in the majority of cases reached out first to other Christians. Even in countries where Christians were a small minority, Adventists have traditionally gone first to those tiny Christian communities. Our missionaries designed Bible studies, pamphlets, and evangelistic sermons mainly for those from a Christian background. There are hopeful signs that this is changing. We do have a reform message for other Christians, but that does not complete our mission. The global mission initiative voted in 1990 took some important steps. While George did mention this initiative, he fails to point out one important part of that initiative.[9] In connection with the Global Mission initiative the church has established five religious study centers to work with the major religious blocs in the world (Buddhists, Hindus, Muslims, Jews, and urban/secular/postmodern people). These centers were commissioned to study methods and create resources for reaching out to these various religious blocs. They have taken initial steps to find ways to use creative projects to communicate with these people. In addition to this shift in evangelistic method, the new mission emphasis has raised many theological and organizational questions. That has made necessary the formation of a special mission committee, created by church leadership, to discuss and make recommendations concerning these issues. The committee has produced documents that have made an impact. It was response to a mission issue that led to the formulation of a new fundamental belief, number twenty-eight (now number eleven), concerning demonic powers and the importance of the devotional life. The church's general session voted the belief in 1995.

Would George be interested in broadening his vision? Would the preaching of the apocalyptic vision be the same in a Muslim setting? How would one preach the books of Daniel and Revelation in a Hindu context? If we are serious about taking a message to the whole world (every tribe, nation, tongue, and people), we must admit that it should include the world of the followers of Muhammad, the Buddha, Karl Marx, and others.

Second, it would be extremely helpful, in my view, to widen the horizons of his comparisons with other Christian groups. As part of his argument for the success of Adventist mission, George compares Seventh-day Adventists with the other Christian bodies that arose out of the Millerite movement.[10] Although we were originally the smallest of the six groups that Millerism spawned, now more than one hundred years later only four remain and Adventists are the largest many times over. Although these facts are not in dispute, taking a broader view might make the comparison look a bit different.

This would be especially the case if one were to compare the Seventh-day

Adventist Church to the charismatic movement. It is clearly the fastest growing major bloc in Christendom today. David Barrett, probably the foremost Christian statistician of mission, in 2010 numbered Pentecostal/charismatics at 613 million adherents and believes that by 2025 the figure will be 800 million.[11] It will make this movement about 50 percent of all Christians globally.

Why should we compare Adventists to the Charismatic movement? Charismatics have a close historical theological kinship to Adventism. Pentecostals emerged mainly from Wesleyan Holiness churches in the nineteenth-century Methodist tradition. Ellen and James White and many other early Adventists had the same heritage.

Even more important is the centrality of the belief in the imminent, literal, premillennial second coming of Jesus. Pentecostal scholar and historian Allan Anderson of the University of Birmingham (UK) says the charismatic movement has five main features.[12] The number one key belief that Anderson deals with is the literal premillennial imminent second coming of Jesus. The presence and power of the Holy Spirit is a key belief but charismatics see it as the fuel for the mission of spreading a global revival that would lead to a return of Jesus. They take Matthew 24:14 seriously (as among Adventists) as a justification and motivation for evangelism worldwide.

Another key similarity between Adventism and the charismatic movement is the belief in the continuity of spiritual gifts. Adventists early on saw Ellen White's ministry as a fulfillment of the biblical teaching of spiritual gifts. Pentecostals believe also in the present day validity of spiritual gifts. Much of the early opposition to the charismatic movement among evangelical Protestants resulted from a dispensational/cessationist view of spiritual gifts. These conservative Protestants believed such spiritual gifts were for the apostolic age and ceased when it ended. Adventists and charismatics have always rejected the cessationist theology. Realizing this, it should not seem strange that some Adventists played a key role in the earliest years of the Azusa Street revival, which most see as the birth place of the Pentecostal movement.[13]

In conclusion, we can say, although its date of beginning is later for the charismatic movement, many core theological beliefs are similar to Adventists. It seems fair to call the two movements close cousins. One could then ask George, is it not possible to compare the mission success of the Adventists with that of the charismatic movement? This huge movement, which began in 1900, may have some things to teach us that the failed Millerite groups cannot. I would love to see him reflect on this comparison. Perhaps that may change the way we evaluate our "success."

## Other contributions

Knight leaves other legacies besides his speaking and writing. For me, he means much as a longtime personal friend and esteemed colleague. We go back to undergraduate theology major days at Pacific Union College. He, an eager new convert, married and a bit older than most of us sat together with me, a third generation Adventist who had just switched to theology from pre-med. We drank in Carl Coffman, Robert Olson, Fred Veltman, Leo Van Dolson, W. T. Hyde, and Eric Syme. Later, George stayed with Kathy and me during an evangelistic campaign in Idaho. We remain good friends until today. That is the kind of person he is—a loyal friend.

I would suggest he should also be seriously appreciated as an editor. His editing work has resulted in the mentoring and promotion of others whom he has recruited to help with the various books and series of books he has edited. Not only did George help many start their writing career, they also had the assurance that if their writing was part of a Knight project it would surely get published.

George was also willing to participate in the projects of others, even if he was already busy with other things. He seemingly could always find time for one more project or piece of work and invariably meet his deadlines. For me, this was personally visible in his contribution of a piece on the remnant for a book on Adventist mission as well as his writing and editing of introductory articles for the *Andrews Study Bible.* Many of his colleagues are better (and probably more prolific) writers because of the support we received.

## Conclusion

In summary, I would call George a missiological prophet. Like Jeremiah of old, he loves God's people so much that he is willing to risk opposition to declare the truth about what is wrong and then call for repentance. He leaves minor issues to the side and goes straight for the heart of the matter. The church owes him a great debt of gratitude that it hopefully will demonstrate by heeding his message.

## Endnotes

1. This chapter gives special attention to the following writings of George R. Knight: *The Fat Lady and the Kingdom* (Nampa, Idaho: Pacific Press®, 1995) (abbreviated as "Fat Lady"); *If I Were the Devil* (Hagerstown, Md.: Review and Herald®, 2007) (abbreviated as "Devil"); *The Apocalyptic Vision and the Neutering of Adventism* (Hagerstown, Md.: Review and Herald®, 2008) (abbreviated as "Vision"); *Anticipating the Advent: A Brief History of Seventh-day Adventists* (Nampa, Idaho: Pacific Press®, 1992) (Abbreviated as "History"); "Remnant Theology and World Mission," in *Adventist Mission in the 21st Century*, ed. Jon L. Dybdahl (Hagerstown, Md.: Review and Herald®, 1999), 58–95, (abbreviated as "Mission").

2. "Fat Lady," 7; "Devil," 9.

3. "History," 6.

4. "Devil," 11.

5. Ibid.

6. "Vision," 106,107.

7. Ibid., 107.

8. "Vision," 21.

9. "Fat Lady," 75, 76 .

10. "Devil," 233–236; "Fat Lady," 129–132.

11. *International Bulletin of Missionary Research* 34, no. 1 (January 2010): 36.

12. Alan Anderson, "Spreading Fires: The Globalization of Pentecostalism in the Twentieth Century," *International Bulletin of Missionary Research* 31, no. 1 (January 2007): 9.

13. Steve Daily, *The Prophetic Rift II* (Portland: Better Living Publishers, 2000), 1–14.

# Chapter 16

# Reflections on the Church and Unity

Barry D. Oliver

lthough it is more than twenty-five years ago, I remember well the time when I was doing research at Andrews University with George Knight as one of my supervisors. The research focused on the development of Adventist organizational structure. George drew from the work we did together and, of course, from his own research to later publish his *Organizing to Beat the Devil: The Development of Adventist Church Structure* in 2001.[1]

In the course of the research, I read most of what the Adventist press had published on the topic of organization from 1860 to 1988. I could not help but notice how often the authors talked about unity. What's more, it seemed that the more responsible the position held by the author, the more he (I do not remember any "she"!) talked about it. Of course, this was just a subjective impression on my part at the time. I certainly did not do any kind of objective analysis. But I do remember being somewhat disconcerted by what I perceived to be this overemphasis on unity. I thought to myself, *Can't these guys talk about anything else? Surely they do not have to keep on and on about unity.* Of course, they did discuss other things. But particularly those in positions of administrative leadership did speak a lot about unity!

But . . . now that I have been asked to serve at a senior level in the church as president of the South Pacific Division, it would be fair to say that I have changed my tune somewhat. I have actually found myself becoming more understanding of the emphasis on the need for unity. Some may say that I "have sold my soul." I may just have to live with that. You see, dealing on a daily basis with circumstances and forces that have the potential to destroy the unity we enjoy can stir within you a heightened awareness of its value!

## The Bible, unity, and the Seventh-day Adventist Church

The New Testament appeal for unity is unequivocal. The prayer of Jesus for His followers in John 17:14–23 and the words of Paul in Ephesians 4:1–6 are rich theological passages. Whatever else we would like to say or think about these passages, it is clear that unity is not an optional extra for the church. Unity is intrinsic to who we are. To promote disunity is to compromise the very nature of the community that Christ has established.

But the unity spoken of by Jesus and Paul is not unidimensional. It is multidimensional. Rather than uniformity, it is rich in its diversity. Paul himself used the imagery of the human body to describe this unity of belief, purpose, and function. It is a dynamic unity just as the human body is dynamic, and it must adapt to changing circumstances and environments while retaining its integrity as the body—the body of Christ.

How does this dynamic unity of belief, purpose (mission), and function play out in the global Seventh-day Adventist Church? How can the structures of belief, purpose, and function continue to build a strong global church community as we move further into the twenty-first century?

First, for unity to exist in the church as a whole there needs to be a strongly and widely held structure of belief that defines in and of itself a boundary which provides an important aspect of identity for the church. If there is no structure of belief that describes the components of the belief system, unity simply cannot exist. Unity cannot exist in a vacuum of belief.

That belief structure is both inclusive and exclusive. It enables those who accept it to be included in the community. The church has processes based on

Scripture and its ecclesiastical practices that outline the steps an individual needs to take in order to be included in the community. The church describes the essential components of the belief structure in its statement of twenty-eight fundamental beliefs. Inclusion within the community continues as the individual subscribes to this statement.

On the other hand, the belief structure is exclusive. It enables those who do not choose to accept its components to remain outside the community or indeed to step out of the community. By being both inclusive and exclusive it facilitates unity among those who are members of the church community. If there were no boundaries of belief there would be anarchy of belief. Not only cannot unity exist in a vacuum, neither can it exist in a state of anarchy.

The second structural boundary determinative of unity is the purpose or mission structure of the church. It is gratifying that the mission of the global church has in recent years been reframed to reflect the commission of Jesus to His disciples in Matthew 28. Now expressed in terms of the primary task of disciple-making, it recognises the unique nature of the Seventh-day Adventist movement as expressed in the three angels' messages of Revelation 14.[2]

However, it is noteworthy that there is not the same commonality across the church when it comes to the statement of purpose or mission as with the statement of belief. Even a superficial perusal of those church-related entities which have published their own mission statements quickly reveals a host of different statements. Now, of course we should recognize that various entities are set up under the larger umbrella of the church for different purposes. The objectives of a health institution are very different from those of an educational institution, which are very different from those of a risk management service which are very different from the General Conference Auditing Service, and so forth. However, given the specific differences, anecdotal evidence suggests that we do not display the same degree of oneness in the various statements and implementation of our macro-mission as we do when it comes to our fundamental beliefs. This is quite amazing in the face of the often pragmatic nature of the functionality of the Seventh-day Adventist Church.

Does this reflect a lack of commitment to the global mission of the church as stated in its global mission statement? And does it indicate a lack of unity of purpose? Perhaps some do not see a statement of mission as important. They may consider action as more important, the perception being that we need to get on with the job. But of course such an approach begs the question, "What job?" I would suggest again that function without unity of purpose leads to anarchy. To the extent that mission is not articulated and implemented, unity is lacking.

The third structural boundary that contributes to unity is the functional or operational structure. The functional structures of the church are many. We could consider the nature and function of the local congregation, the conference, the union, or even the General Conference and its divisions. But despite considerable temptation to do so I am not going to discuss the efficiency and effectiveness of the layers of church organization. Rather, I refer to three operational documents that provide the structural boundaries for the functions performed by the church. Those three documents are the *Church Manual;* the Constitution of each constituency; and policy. If one were to enquire as to why the Seventh-day Adventist Church operates with such consistency around the world, there would be no need to look any further than these three documents. They together define the operations of the church from the local congregation to the General Conference. Without them there would indeed be a functional vacuum. To disregard them would result in operational anarchy. To the extent that those responsible for the operations of the church lack knowledge or fail to comply with these documents, unity suffers.

These structures—belief, mission, and function—provide the boundaries that govern the identity of the Seventh-day Adventist Church. Unity is a function of the maintenance of these boundaries. And we are talking about unity here. We are not promoting uniformity. Some forces within the church do tend toward uniformity. A state of uniformity will inevitably lead to the destruction of unity. The forces necessary to maintain such uniformity in a community of any kind may be totalitarian in nature and will not result in unity despite the best intention of those who perpetuate the totalitarianlike regime. The church is no different from any other social or political group in this respect. The principle of free choice is vital in the church. Confidence in the church and its leadership and a healthy unity are cultivated in a context of informed choice. The representative governance system of the Seventh-day Adventist Church is well positioned to encourage such choice.

## A current case study of how unity can work in the church

From time to time issues arise in the church that could threaten the unity we enjoy as Seventh-day Adventists. Some of these issues are local. A few become more global in scope. The debate over ordination, and particularly ordination without respect to gender, is an example. Extended discussion with respect to it has occurred within the church since the 1980s. It is not my task here to defend or promote any particular viewpoint with respect to ordination. Like most of us, I do indeed have a viewpoint that I believe is right. As Seventh-day Adventists, we have always valued very highly being right.

But the primary issue for us in this discussion is what happens to unity in the church when there are strongly held positions that differ on what is right. That is certainly the case here. One only has to listen to the passion with which people debate the issue on the floor of the General Conference Executive Committee, or a General Conference session, or more recently at some union sessions to know that strongly held convictions exist on both sides of the argument. What do we do? What are the options? Can we respect and uphold unity and diversity so that the church is strengthened?

Whatever we do, we must ensure that we are true to our Seventh-day Adventist history and heritage. Since the latter half of the nineteenth century whenever we have had to make difficult decisions about matters of belief, purpose, and function, we have always asked the question, "What is it that best serves our mission?" George Knight has effectively shown us that since the 1980s as the church entered what he calls its "3rd cycle or organization" with a period of what has been "sustained agitation," the question has been whether the church will be flexible enough to adjust and change. He challenged us as to whether we will gain our identity from organizational structures or from our mission.[3]

Further, in being true to our history and heritage, we need to remember that flexibility has been an indispensable attribute in the significant deliberations of the church. Ellen White herself often demonstrated this principle in the counsel she gave to the leaders of the denomination. For example, on the day before the official opening of the 1901 General Conference Session, she declared, "God wants a change . . . right here . . . right now."[4] The following day when reiterating the concerns that she had communicated in no uncertain terms on the previous day, she added, "according to the light that has been given me—and just how it is to be accomplished I cannot say—greater strength must be brought into the managing force of the Conference."[5] While she called for change and flexibility she did not attempt to dictate at key times in our history the shape that structures were to take. She left that to due process.

As we grapple with the issue of ordination with respect to gender, we will have to make choices. None of these choices are particularly easy to work with, because we are a global church. Size and geography, let along language and culture, tend to complicate things. Some have commented that it would be so much easier if we were structured congregationally. But that is not an option for us. A global mission calls for a global structure.

The first option is that we do nothing. Well, technically, it is an option; but in actual fact it is not a realistic one if we wish to maintain unity in the church and fulfill our mission. If we do nothing, entities within the church will choose to do their own thing irrespective of any position held by the church, and those kinds of actions will act like a cancer eating away at the unity of the church.

That action on the part of various entities is in fact a second option. They can choose to make decisions irrespective of the will of the greater body. Again, the unity of the church could come under grave threat. What could happen is that entities holding viewpoints that differ from the dissenting entities may choose to react to the dissenting entities by an action of their own to maintain a viewpoint that separates rather than unifies. And that could lead to action on issues other than the one that presented itself initially. Many issues always exist in the church, and unilateral action by one entity with respect to a particular issue could indeed be the catalyst for another entity to take the opportunity to use the situation to respond to still a different issue altogether. The "ties that bind" can all too easily be snapped but for the grace of God. Again mission would be compromised.

A third option is that we appeal for patience and agree to study the issue further. It is indeed appropriate that we thoroughly study any issue with the potential to divide the church. Scripture, the writings of Ellen White, church history, society and culture, all need to be investigated in order to bring to bear as much light on the issue as possible. But what happens if as a result of extended study difference still remains? What if in the opinions of different entities the "right thing to do" differs? Study alone will not ultimately solve such a problem if the results are inconclusive or alternatively conclusive one way for some and another way for others.

If that is the case, two options remain. The first is that the church splits: those who support ordination without regard to gender go in one direction and those who advocate ordination specific only to one gender go in another direction. Imagine the ramifications if that were to happen. Such a situation would be devastating for the global church. It is likely that at least two denominations would form. There would be legal battles to decide on how to split the resources of the church between the new entities. The fallout would continue for years. Again, mission would be compromised.

The second and so much more amenable option would be for the church to reach a consensus, agreeing that different entities could take one of two alternative approaches to the issue of ordination. Agreement would be reached at a global level that those entities that chose to ordain without respect to gender could do so, and that entities that decide to ordain with respect to gender could also do so. The unity of the church would thus be maintained through the mutual agreement of the church irrespective of differing practice. And most importantly, such an approach would not compromise mission but strengthen it as congruence would still exist between the structures of belief, purpose and function in the church.

If the church chose to follow this last option it could then amend the primary operational documents of the church (*Church Manual,* constitution, and policy) to accommodate the situation. A practice would be followed similar in many respects to that which exists with respect to the ordination of deacons and elders right now in the global church. After all, there does not appear to be a distinct ordination described in the New Testament exclusive to those whom today we refer to as ministers.

Finding a solution among these and perhaps other options listed in this example is the task that the global church must remain committed to—if we are to remain a global church family. Such a solution can maintain the integrity of our belief structure by acknowledging that ordination with or without regard to gender is outside the boundary provided by our statement of twenty-eight fundamental beliefs. We can agree that the practice does not impinge on the fulfillment of our global mission. And we can surely consent to modify our essential operational documents in order to reflect our mutual decision. Whenever in our history we have faced a situation such as this, we have taken the decision that will best fulfill our mission. Our unity has always been a function of our commitment to our God and the mission He has given to us.

## A final word on unity in diversity

The primary challenges to unity are not structural but attitudinal. The Seventh-day Adventist Church does not derive its unity because of its structures but because of its people. And its people are diverse.

I remember when George and I were consulting together as I worked on my dissertation at Andrews University back in the mideighties, he expressed a number of times his concern for the ongoing unity of the church. He voiced with some alarm his fear that the church may not exist in its present form into the coming new millennium. Of course, he was right to the extent that the church needs to be continually reinventing itself and responding to changes in the environment. I think, however, that he was possibly fearing something somewhat more radical than that.

As I have described the example of ordination, it is readily evident that such a situation is a threat to the church. But I am quietly confident that we will be able to avoid that outcome? Why? Because of the people and their commitment to the mission of the Seventh-day Adventist Church. There are two things that I regard as antidotes to schism in this church. The first is allegiance to the church, and the second is involvement in its mission. They are twin sisters, foundational to unity. Both must be present. One without the other will not do it. After all, what is the point of allegiance without involvement? Without involvement no one knows anything of my allegiance. But involvement without allegiance can be even worse. It is pointless. Mission is nowhere in sight. Such involvement is aimless and it may be destructive. Unity is the casualty.

This church exists because there are people who have given to God and the church their allegiance, and they act on it. Coming from "every nation, kindred, tongue and people," they go to "every nation, and kindred, and tongue, and people" (Revelation 14:6). They are one but they are different. Structural diversity requires structural adaptation. Unity is ultimately dependent on the recognition that diversity exists. If we are ever to solve this conundrum, we cannot forget it.

## Conclusion

This essay has reflected on just a few aspects of unity (and diversity) in the church. It has considered unity in the light of the church's mission and certainly has not covered all aspects of the topic and the example explored. Some may see things very differently. That is all fine.

But this much is sure. While there may be diversity in the church with respect to how we express unity in this global church, there should be no uncertainty acknowledging that unity in diversity is an essential aspect of the character of our church and that we compromise it to our peril. Our church has no future if we do not practice unity and promote it through the diversity formed by the sociological, cultural, and geographical forces at work within it. It is appropriate that we remember Jesus' prayer and Paul's imperative for our church: "I in them and you in me—so that they may be brought to complete unity" (John 17:23, NIV). "Be completely humble and gentle; be patient, bearing with one another in love. Make every effort to keep the unity of the Spirit through the bond of peace" (Ephesians 4:2, 3, NIV).

## Endnotes

1. George Knight, *Organizing to Beat the Devil: The Development of Adventist Church Structure* (Hagerstown, Md.: Review and Herald®, 2001).

2. The mission statement of the General Conference reads as follows: "The mission of the Seventh-day Adventist Church is to make disciples of all people, communicating the everlasting gospel in the context of the three angels' messages of Revelation 14:6-12, leading them to accept Jesus as personal Savior and unite with His remnant Church, discipling them to serve Him as Lord, and preparing them for His soon return." I refer to this statement as our "macro-mission."

3. Knight, *Organizing to Beat the Devil*, 8.

4. "Talk of Mrs. E. G. White, Before Representative Brethren, in the College Library, April 1, 1901, 2:30 P.M.," MS 43a, 1901. This manuscript together with MS 43, an edited edition of Ellen White's speech, is available in the Ellen G. White Research Centre Branch Office at Avondale College.

5. *General Conference Bulletin*, 1901, 25.

# Chapter 17

# Neither Amish nor United Methodist: Adventist Lifestyle Today

### Alberto R. Timm

I n the early 1990s at the Andrews University Theological Seminary, a few colleagues and I were taking George R. Knight's insightful doctoral seminar on "Historical Methodology." One day I asked him how he could be so provocative and not get into trouble with the leadership of the church. He vindicated his style by arguing first that, for instance, his book *Angry Saints* (1989)[1] "has to be titled *Angry Saints* in order to sell; if it would be just *Holy Saints*, nobody would ever buy it." Then he added, "The liberals like my provocative style, but get frustrated with my conservative conclusions. The conservatives believe I'm too irreverent. So I end up losing both groups!"[2]

Knight's provocative style also emerges when he deals with Seventh-day Adventist lifestyle. For example, in his book *I Used to Be Perfect* (1994), the first chapter—"SIN Is Love"—begins with the following words:

"Eating cheese is not SIN!

"I figured most of you would agree with me on that point. So I'll see if I can't antagonize the rest of you.

- Eating rats, snakes, and snails, or even hogs is not SIN.
- Sabbath breaking is not SIN.
- Murder is not SIN.
- Theft is not SIN.

"SIN is prior to all these things. They may be sins—maybe—but they are not SIN.

"SIN is love."[3]

Undoubtedly, George likes to challenge his listeners/readers to think things through, allowing them to expand their horizons. As he told me once, "A good teacher is someone who leads his students to surpass him or her." But the above-quoted statement also demonstrates how easily one can distort the actual meaning of apologetic and/or provocative texts by simply isolating some sentences (such as "Murder is not SIN") from their literary and historical contexts and purposes.

Trying as honestly as possible to reflect Knight's own thoughts, the present article deals with his endeavors to provide foundational principles for understanding and improving the overall Seventh-day Adventist lifestyle.[4] The discussion takes place under the following four main categories: (1) taking time and place into consideration; (2) distinguishing between universal principles and elements of time and space; (3) applying the principles consistently; (4) choosing between the ideal and the real; and (5) avoiding the Amish and the United Methodist extremes.

## 1. Taking time and place into consideration

George R. Knight began his class on "Development of Seventh-day Adventist Lifestyle" (Winter 1991) saying that "Seventh-day Adventists did not fall directly from heaven into New England."[5] By this he implied that there exist significant interplays between biblical principles and the sociocultural contexts in which the denomination was born and developed. One of his favorite books for understanding at least part of that context is Otto L. Bettmann's *The Good Old Days—They Were Terrible!* (1974).[6] Helpful insights on the context in which Ellen White lived and wrote several of her counsels on lifestyle appear in *The World of Ellen G. White* (1987), edited by Gary Land,[7] and Knight's own *Ellen White's World* (1998).[8]

Among the examples Knight used to highlight the importance of contextual studies are two contrasting statements by Ellen White about eating eggs.[9] In the first (from the late 1860s) she warned, "Eggs should not be placed on your table. They are an injury to your children."[10] Yet in the second one (from 1901) she recommended, "Get eggs of healthy fowls. Use these eggs cooked or raw. . . . I say that milk and eggs should be included in your diet. . . . And eggs contain properties which are remedial agencies in counteracting poisons."[11] Knight began chapter 1 of his book *Reading Ellen White* by stressing the contrast between those two statements, and leaving the reader to struggle with the question: "Which statement is the inspired counsel on the topic?" Not until chapter 11 did he explain that, while Mrs. White made the first statement to "a family whose children were struggling with sensuality," the second one addressed someone whose "deprived diet eventually led to deficiencies that seriously threatened his health."[12] Thus, we can harmonize the tension by putting each of those statements in its proper context.

For Knight,[13] to some extent, elements of time and place also shaped White's statements urging schools to teach girls "to harness and drive a horse" so "they would be better fitted to meet the emergencies of life";[14] warning people to avoid the "bewitching influence" of the "bicycle craze";[15] counseling administrators not to buy an automobile because it would be both a needless expense and "a temptation to others to do the same thing";[16] and suggesting that women shorten their dresses to "about nine inches from the floor."[17] Using his characteristic sense of humor, Knight warned of the danger of just shortening their skirts by eight or nine inches, without taking into consideration that it was "from the floor." Since many styles have changed across time,[18] to shorten some modern dresses or skirts by that many inches would "put the bottom of the hemline somewhere above the top of the waistband."[19]

Therefore, one way to use White's writings "improperly is to ignore the implications of time and place and thus seek to apply the letter of each and every counsel universally."[20] But on the other hand, there is also the danger of overestimating the role of time and place in the inspired writings. One has to realize that universal principles that we cannot ignore permeate her writings.

## 2. Distinguishing between universal principles and elements of time and space

Another significant contribution by George Knight for the understanding of Seventh-day Adventist lifestyle is his attempt to establish dialogue between universal principles and elements of time and space in the inspired writings. In his *Ellen*

*White's World,* he addressed the topic of "Ellen White and Her World" by saying that "the most basic thing we can say about Ellen White is that she was immersed in her world; she was a nineteenth-century person who faced nineteenth-century issues with a nineteenth-century frame of reference."[21] Taking this statement out of its own context, one could easily argue that Knight downplays Ellen White's writings to such a low level that her lifestyle counsels end up being nothing more than a nineteenth-century cultural expression.

Yet, while dealing with "Ellen White and Our World," Knight adds, "But if we are going to get the most from her writings, we need to move beyond surface reading and begin to uncover the universal principles that undergird her counsels."[22] This, for him, is a threefold task, implying (1) "to seek out the principles of Christian living through a Spirit-guided study of the Bible and the writings of Ellen White"; (2) "to relate the principles we have found to our personal lives and social context"; and (3) to "have a good grasp of the current situation to which we are going to apply the universal principles."[23]

Knight sees three different approaches that people can use while dealing with principles and the particulars of time and place. One takes both of them together. Another does not even see the principles. And a third one (more balanced) goes back to study the particulars in their own context, in order to take out the principles and apply them to their own current culture.[24] Such approaches can also be employed in regard to Ellen White's counsel that girls should "learn to harness and drive a horse."[25] The first group would try to require all girls from our boarding schools to "learn to harness and drive a horse." The second one would simply discard this statement as outdated and meaningless. The third group would consider that, in order to "meet the emergencies of life," girls should learn today how to drive a car and replace a flat tire.

But even with these concepts in mind, one might find that it is far easier to enunciate and even illustrate them than to apply them in the practical interpretation of the inspired writings about lifestyle. In some cases readers might find themselves wondering: Where do I draw the line? Which specific universal principle should prevail? Are there cases (such as to rest one day in seven) in which the principle involved is already defined (such as the seventh-day)? Even though we may not be able to solve all the problems that might show up, we have to be as consistent as possible in dealing with lifestyle issues.

## 3. Applying the principles consistently

Overall consistency in lifestyle matters reflects itself in two basic dimensions. The first one is the task of drawing sound principles from the whole body of the inspired writings dealing with a given topic. George Knight argues that we should base our conclusions on and harmonize them with "the overall tenor of the body" of those writings. He adds that "when we read the balancing and mediating passages on a topic, rather than merely those polar ones that reinforce our own biases, we come closer to Ellen White's true perspective."[26]

For instance, she offers various counsels on the proper position in prayer.[27] Volume 2 of her *Selected Messages* has a chapter on "Proper Attitude in Prayer" that says at the beginning: "Where have our brethren obtained the idea that they should stand upon their feet when praying to God? . . . Both in public and private worship it is our duty to bow down upon our knees before God when we offer our petitions to Him." The chapter ends with the statement: "It is not always necessary to bow upon your knees in order to pray. Cultivate the habit of talking with the Saviour when you are alone, when you are walking, and when you are busy with your daily labor."[28]

From studying White's various counsels on prayer, Knight concluded that the position for the main Sabbath morning prayer was always, "where possible, to be kneeling. But nowhere in her writings do we find her advocating kneeling for benedictions, invocations, grace before meals, and so on. Her general teaching is that it is 'not always' necessary to kneel for every prayer. Such appears to be not only her teaching but also her practice."[29]

The second dimension in which the overall consistency in lifestyle matters reflects itself is by also applying those principles to parallel lifestyle issues not explicitly addressed in the inspired writings. However, as Knight pointed out, the basic criteria of some people is whether or not Ellen White mentioned something explicitly in her writings. If we followed that approach we then could assume that "God forbade the wearing of gold bands but did not frown on the possession of gold Cadillacs,"[30] and that she spoke only against playing "checkers but not monopoly."[31]

For Knight, "if we don't have principles we will very soon end up with a Mishnah."[32] So to avoid this danger, we have to define the sound principles and then carry them over to parallel matters. In doing so, we may face a serious tension between the ideal to be reached and the limitations of the real world in which we live.

## 4. Choosing between the ideal and the real

One of George Knight's most significant contributions for the understanding of Seventh-day Adventist lifestyle is his attempt to dialogue with the tensions between the ideal and the real in applying inspired counsels to the practical life. For example, in 1894 Ellen White declared that "never can the proper education be given to the youth in this country, or any other country, unless they are separated a wide distance from the cities."[33] But ten years later (1904), when the denomination established Washington Training College (now Washington Adventist University) on a property of only twenty acres close to the nation's capital, Ellen White could confirm that "the securing of this land was in the Lord's providence."[34] Justifying such procedure, she added, "But in the cities there are many children who could not attend schools away from the cities; and for the benefit of these, schools should be opened in the cities as well as in the country."[35]

Knight recognizes that, without giving up her ideals, White was also *flexible* enough to recognize that "circumstances often prohibited the accomplishing of the ideal."[36] For him, "The answer is that rural education for all children was the *ideal* that the church should aim at 'so far as possible.' But the truth is that the hard facts of life make such education impossible for some. Thus *reality* dictated a compromise if Christian education were to reach children from poorer families. Ellen White understood and accepted the tension between the ideal and the real."[37]

But we should never confuse such adjustment of *counsels* to the surrounding circumstances with a "situation ethics" that would give up even universal principles in the contextualization process. It is worthwhile mentioning that in one of his classes in the Seventh-day Adventist Theological Seminary, Knight spoke of two opposite questions. One is the anti-Christian question: "Can I do this on the Sabbath and still be saved?" The other one is the Christian question: "What is the best way to observe the Sabbath?"[38] In other words, a genuine Christian should always live by ideal and not by exception! This approach should be taken seriously in these days when Seventh-day Adventism is facing many sociocultural challenges.

## 5. Avoiding the Amish and the United Methodist extremes

George Knight has warned that Seventh-day Adventism is passing through "the life cycle of the church" suggested by David O. Moberg, comprising the following five stages: (1) incipient organization, (2) formal organization, (3) maximum efficiency, (4) institutional, and (5) disintegration.[39] Knight believes that in many ways the denomination is now in stage 4 and needs to make some radical changes in order to regain its maximum missionary efficiency.[40] In this process, *"Adventists cannot escape the dilemma between being meaningful or being neutered."*[41]

Trying to learn from the experiences of other denominations, Knight warns that Adventists should avoid not only the Amish traditionalist lifestyle but also the United Methodist culturalist trend. For him, both groups failed "to distinguish between universal Christian principles and the particulars of time and place," but they ended up in opposite directions. While the Amish "have sought to transfer the world of the sixteenth century into the twentieth" (now the twenty-first), the mainline Methodists have followed the route of "uncritical assimilation" (Jürgen Moltmann) to contemporary culture. Adventism today faces both temptations: " 'Ghettoization' on the one hand and 'uncritical assimilation' on the other. One sector of the church would pull it one direction, and another wing would pull it the other."[42]

On matters related to Seventh-day Adventist standards and values, Knight suggests that, *"The great temptation for Adventism will be to shut its eyes and hope the problems will go away. But such a course is suicidal. In the long run, ignoring the problems and challenges will lead to an ignoring of the standards themselves. The church (and its members) must face the problems seriously and strenuously if it expects the coming generations to take its time-honored standards seriously.* We cannot have one without the other."[43]

## Concluding remarks

George Knight once mentioned that a basic problem related to Seventh-day Adventist lifestyle is that the church still tends to use nineteenth-century answers in response to twentieth-century (now twenty-first-century) questions.[44] With his provocative and sometimes even polemic style, Knight has been able to draw people's attention to several crucial lifestyle issues. Of the many topics he addressed in his writings and lectures, I highlighted only some I believe can help us to build a useful framework for a critical evaluation of the subject. Any serious study of what the Bible and Ellen White have to say about lifestyle issues has to (1) take into consideration the actual time and place in which she crafted those statements; (2) distinguish between universal principles and elements of time and space involved; (3) apply those principles consistently; (4) choose between the ideal and the real in carrying out counsels; and (5) avoid the Amish and the United Methodist extremes. I believe these five points can help us to build a healthy connection with the past from which we came, to the present in which we live, and the future to which we go.

## Endnotes

1. George R. Knight, *Angry Saints: Tensions and Possibilities in the Adventist Struggle Over Righteousness by Faith* (Hagerstown, Md.: Review and Herald®, 1989).

2. My personal recollection of George R. Knight's memorable statement at his seminar on "Historical Methodology" (Seventh-day Adventist Theological Seminary, Andrews University, early 1990s).

3. George R. Knight, *I Used to Be Perfect: An Ex-legalist Looks at Law, Sin, and Grace* (Bose, Idaho: Pacific Press®, 1994), 9.

4. In order to develop a reliable historical approach, Knight urged that his students read David H. Fischer's *Historians' Fallacies: Toward a Logic of Historical Thought* (New York: Harper & Row, 1970).

5. My personal notes of George R. Knight's class "CHIS 673: Development of Seventh-day Adventist Lifestyle" (Seventh-day Adventist Theological Seminary, Andrews University, Winter 1991), on January 15, 1991.

6. Otto L. Bettmann, *The Good Old Days—They Were Terrible!* (New York: Random House, 1974).

7. Gary Land, ed., *The World of Ellen G. White* (Hagerstown, Md.: Review and Herald®, 1987).

8. George R. Knight, *Ellen White's World: A Fascinating Look at the Times in Which She Lived* (Hagerstown, Md.: Review and Herald®, 1998).

9. Cf. Francis D. Nichol, *Ellen G. White and Her Critics* (Washington, D.C.: Review and Herald®, 1951), 376, 377; Denton E. Rebok, *Believe His Prophets* (Washington, D.C.: Review and Herald®, 1956), 224–230.

10. Ellen G. White, *Testimony for the Church*, no. 18 (1869); republished in Ellen G. White, *Testimonies for the Church* (Mountain View, Calif.: Pacific Press®, 1948), 2:400.

11. Ellen G. White, *Counsels on Diet and Foods* (Washington, D.C.: Review and Herald®, 1938), 204.

12. George R. Knight, *Reading Ellen White: How to Understand and Apply Her Writings* (Hagerstown, Md.: Review and Herald®, 1997), 13, 14, 74–76.

13. Ibid., 77, 78, 81, 82, 100–102.

14. Ellen G. White, *Education* (Oakland, Calif.: Pacific Press®, 1903), 216, 217.

15. White, *Testimonies for the Church*, 8:51, 52.

16. Ellen G. White, "Dear Brother and Sister Burden," Letter 158 (October 8), 1902; published in

Ellen G. White, *Manuscript Releases* (Washington, D.C.: Ellen G. White Estate, 1981), vol. 1, 394.

17. White, *Testimonies for the Church*, 1:521.

18. See, e.g., *Fashion: The Definitive History of Costume and Style* (New York: DK, 2012); "Fame, Fads, and Folly: Looking Good and Having Fun," in *Time of Transition: The 70s* (Alexandria, Va.: Time-Life Books, n.d.), 83–95. Cf. Susan B. Kaiser, *The Social Psychology of Clothing: Symbolic Appearances in Context*, 2nd ed., rev. ed. (New York: Fairchild, 1997).

19. Knight, *Reading Ellen White*, 78.

20. Ibid., 81.

21. Knight, *Ellen White's World*, 141.

22. Ibid., 143.

23. Knight, *Reading Ellen White*, 102, 103.

24. My personal notes of Knight's class "CHIS 673: Development of Seventh-day Adventist Lifestyle," on January 29, 1991.

25. White, *Education*, 216, 217.

26. Knight, *Reading Ellen White*, 69, 74.

27. For a more comprehensive study of Ellen White's statements on proper attitude in prayer, see http://drc.whiteestate.org, search for "prayer position."

28. Ellen G. White, *Selected Messages* (Washington, D.C.: Review and Herald®, 1958), bk. 2, 311, 312, 316.

29. Knight, *Reading Ellen White*, 68.

30. George R. Knight, *The Fat Lady and the Kingdom: Adventist Mission Confronts the Challenges of Institutionalism and Secularization* (Boise, Idaho: Pacific Press®, 1995), 117.

31. My personal notes of Knight's class "CHIS 673: Development of Seventh-day Adventist Lifestyle," on January 22 and 24, 1991. Helpful insights about Ellen White's counsels on playing games can be found in Knight, *Reading Ellen White*, 73, 74.

32. Personal notes "CHIS 673: Development of Seventh-day Adventist Lifestyle," on March 7, 1991.

33. Ellen G. White, *Fundamentals of Christian Education* (Nashville: Southern Publishing Assn., 1923), 312.

34. Ellen G. White, "Our Work in Washington," *Adventist Review and Sabbath Herald*, May 26, 1904, 17; republished in *Life Sketches of Ellen G. White* (Mountain View, Calif.: Pacific Press®, 1923), 397.

35. White, *Testimonies for the Church*, 9:201.

36. George R. Knight, *Myths in Adventism: An Interpretative Study of Ellen White, Education, and Related Issues* (Hagerstown, Md.: Review and Herald®, 1985), 24.

37. Knight, *Reading Ellen White*, 92.

38. My personal recollection of George R. Knight's statement in one of his classes (Seventh-day Adventist Theological Seminary, Andrews University, early 1990s).

39. David O. Moberg, *The Church as a Social Institution: The Sociology of American Religion* (Englewood Cliffs, N.J.: Prentice-Hall, 1962), 118–124. See also Ernst Troeltsch, *The Social Teaching of the Christian Churches*, 2 vols., trans. Olive Wyon (New York: Macmillan, 1931); Jacques Ellul, *The Subversion of Christianity*, trans. Geoffrey W. Bromiley (Grand Rapids: Eerdmans, 1986).

40. Knight, *The Fat Lady and the Kingdom*, 17–35; republished in George R. Knight, *If I Were the Devil: Seeing Through the Enemy's Smokescreen: Contemporary Challenges Facing Adventism* (Hagerstown, Md.: Review and Herald®, 2007), 28–31, 41–54.

41. George R. Knight, *The Apocalyptic Vision and the Neutering of Adventism* (Hagerstown, Md.: Review and Herald®, 2008), 19; emphasis in the original.

42. Knight, *The Fat Lady and the Kingdom*, 123.

43. Ibid.; emphasis in the original.

44. My personal recollection of George R. Knight's statement in one of his classes (Seventh-day Adventist Theological Seminary, Andrews University, early 1990s).

# Chapter 18

# Daily Devotionals and Grace for the Church

Theodore N. Levterov

Among his numerous writings, Dr. George R. Knight has written four volumes of daily devotional readings: *Walking With Jesus on the Mount of Blessing*,[1] *Walking With Paul Through the Book of Romans*,[2] *Lest We Forget*,[3] and *Turn Your Eyes Upon Jesus*.[4] His primary reading audience is Seventh-day Adventist, although other Christians may benefit from them as well. Composed between 1996 and 2008, they carry theological themes that frequently appeared in other works of Knight during the same time period. It is through these popular devotional books, however, that he has been able to have a much wider impact on the Seventh-day Adventist audience.

Daily devotional books have a long history in Adventism. They began with the publication of daily devotional columns in the *Adventist Review* of the 1860s. Then just after the turn of the century, the youth department of the church drawing on the late nineteenth-century Keswick tradition began sponsoring a "Morning Watch" program for young people through the publishing of a list of memory texts and short prayers in a "Morning Watch Calendar."[5] In 1945, these materials were expanded into a book with each page containing a series of inspirational thoughts for each day. Through the years, the annual daily devotional volumes became very popular achieving much higher circulation numbers than regular publications. They proved a profitable venture both for church publishing houses and for the fortunate writers chosen to author the texts. George with his creative and entrepreneurial gifts saw this avenue as a very effective way of influencing the church and didn't wait for an invitation. He initiated several proposals for the series and on three occasions successfully persuaded the Review and Herald® Publishing Association to buy into his proposals.[6] His other works, as valuable as they may be, have necessarily had smaller circulations, characterized as they are by a more scholarly orientation and addressing technical theological issues. Smaller groups, such as interested church members, pastors, church leaders, theological students, Adventist historians, and others who have had a particular interest in Seventh-day Adventist theology and history have appreciated such works, but not the wider circle of Seventh-day Adventist believers. The devotional volumes provided a way of reaching this larger audience.

Knight's devotional volumes divide into two categories: biblical (theological) and historical. *Walking With Jesus on the Mount of Blessing* and *Walking With Paul Through the Book of Romans* belong to the theological realm. His third devotional, *Lest We Forget,* is historical in nature while the fourth, *Turn Your Eyes Upon Jesus,* is again a biblical study tracing the life of Christ from eternity in the past through to eternity in the future. In the first two devotionals, Knight is more concerned with Adventist beliefs, traditions, and lifestyle. His history devotional, on the other hand, examines the development of Seventh-day Adventist ideals and beliefs and their relevance for the denomination as it searches for its identity in the twenty-first century. Each volume of readings, (one reading for each day of the year), nevertheless, has its own purpose to educate, inspire, and help Adventist believers in their faith journey as they still wait for the return of Jesus Christ.

My purpose in this essay is to briefly examine Knight's first three devotionals and discuss their significance within the context of the larger body of his literary work.[7] First, we will examine the *Walking With Jesus* and *Walking With Paul* devotionals and consider some of their major theological themes. We will also refer to some of Knight's other books that discuss and expand his concerns on similar theological topics.

Second, we will examine his third devotional, *Lest We Forget,* and see its different nature and importance in relation to Seventh-day Adventism. The essay will finish with short concluding remarks.

## Biblical (theological) devotionals

As noted above, George Knight's first two devotionals are biblical studies. *Walking With Jesus,* published in 1996, is a comprehensive overview of Matthew 5–7 and is devoted to Jesus' first sermon as He began His early ministry. Knight examines the 111 verses and illustrates how Jesus covers "nearly every aspect of Christian belief and living" and puts them in "the framework of the gospel."[8] He also connects Jesus' sermon to other scriptures, not only to cover the 365 days of the year, but also to shed further light on the theological concepts that he discusses.

*Walking With Paul,* published in 2002, is a verse-by-verse exploration of the book of Romans. Knight finds such a study important since the book of Romans is considered to be one of the most influential Christian documents that have transformed Christianity and its followers. Similar to his first devotional volume, Knight points out that Romans "covers all the essential aspects of Christian belief and living . . . within the framework of the gospel."[9]

One can immediately note the similarity of purpose between the two works. Knight is not only concerned with explaining his theological views but also with giving practical applications to theological questions related to Christian living. To achieve his goals, he often uses personal, family, or church illustrations. The examples are usually drawn from his pastoral and teaching experience or simply from his personal spiritual journey in Adventism. One can learn a lot about Knight simply by reading though his illustrations. He identifies with believers, particularly from the Seventh-day Adventist Christian tradition. His witty, yet profound approach to each reading is designed to captivate the reader's attention and make the spiritual lesson apt and unforgettable. George's choice of titles also reflects his ability to easily capture the reader's attention. After all, who could forget such titles as "Saint George of Berrien Springs,"[10] "Spiritual Arteriosclerosis,"[11] "Saved From Even 'Vegetarian Sins,' "[12] "Adventist Thought Police,"[13] and others. The titles may be amusing, but the lessons are deep. The following are some examples of theological issues and their practical applications that seem important for Knight as one reads through his first two devotionals.

## Grace and law

A major theological concern for Knight is the relationship between God's grace and the law in the context of salvation. This is not surprising, however, since he is addressing an issue that has been a point of discussion within Christianity for centuries. The question is even more appealing to Seventh-day Adventists who are particularly interested in the law of God. After all, it is the emphasis on the Ten Commandments (and especially the fourth commandment) that has been one of their distinguishing characteristics among the rest of the Protestant world. Knight uses the devotionals to explain his view on the issue and notes two major points.

First, he makes a contrast between God's grace and His law in the realm of salvation. While he reminds readers that salvation is by grace alone he also reassures them that the law is "good" and that keeping the commandments of God is beneficial. He even, somewhat surprisingly, (or not so surprisingly), praises the Pharisees as being "good" people because of their dedication to studying and keeping God's law. "Most Christians need to revise their picture of the Pharisees," he writes. "They [the Pharisees] were not merely good men; they were the best of men. . . . Here was a people totally dedicated to serving God from the time they arose in the morning to the time they retired at night."[14] Yet the Pharisees had a problem. They were "good people," but they "weren't good enough."[15] The fact is that Jesus was extremely critical towards their religion because it was legalistic and "did not come from the heart."[16]

Knight is clearly addressing an issue within his own faith community. Adventists have always emphasized the importance of keeping the commandments of God but the danger has always been that they might become a legalistic church that keeps the rules but neglects the love of Jesus. His devotionals contain unfortunate examples describing such "zealous" Adventists whose harsh passion for the law has made others leave the Adventist community. "The result," he observes, after one such story, is that "multitudes have gone elsewhere. And from reading the New Testament, I believe that Jesus would have gone with them."[17]

His point is clear. It is the other religions, including erroneous approaches to Christianity, that claim salvation based on "self-effort, self righteousness, and self-trust."[18] True Christians, on the other hand, will always realize their inadequacy and their need of Jesus.[19]

A second point that Knight makes between God's grace and the law is related to their function. Like James 1:23–25 Knight sees the law as "a mirror." Its function is to show what is right or wrong with our appearance, but it cannot change who we are. And "so it is with God's law," George explains. "When I compare myself with the law, I find that I have problems in my life. But the law cannot correct those problems. It has another function: to tell me I am a sinner. The law points out my problems and needs, but it does not solve them."[20] In another place, he writes again that while the law is good for "some things, it is worthless as a way to earn salvation. . . . The law ought to wake us up to the fact that we must have grace. The tragedy is that we sometimes try to make it a substitute for grace."[21] God's law points out our sins, but it is His grace that cleanses and transforms us. And this is not a "cheap grace," as some may conclude, Knight argues. "Costly grace demands that we give up everything for Jesus as we respond to His love and devote our lives to doing God's will."[22]

As one may suspect, Knight has written other books on the topics of grace and law. *Angry Saints* is a historical account of the Seventh-day Adventist struggle with the tension between grace and the law that came out in full force at the Minneapolis General Conference in 1888.[23] Seventh-day Adventists needed to be reminded of the danger of legalistic religion. The law was important, but Jesus and his righteousness were to be the focus of their theology. Interestingly, as George points out, Ellen White's own writings also experienced a change after the Minneapolis conference. Her most Christ-oriented books such as *Christ's Object Lessons, The Desire of Ages, Steps to Christ,* and others came as a result of the Minneapolis crisis.[24]

Similar ideas about the relationship between grace and law also appear in *The Pharisee's Guide to Perfect Holiness,*[25] in which Knight uses the example of the Pharisees from the time of Jesus to point out contemporary dangers for Seventh-day Adventists. Adventists in the twenty-first century need to know (a) the dangers associated with legalistic religion, and (b) the need to keep Jesus and grace at the center of their theology. Obviously, the right understanding of grace versus the law seems to be essential for Knight.

## SIN and sin(s)

Another distinctive emphasis is Knight's explanation of sin. Contrary to many, he does not consider sin only as an action. Sin, for him, has two faces. One is what he calls SIN (with capital letters), reflecting the condition of the human heart. This is the rebellious attitude that one has towards God and His love. Out of this condition comes "sin(s)" (with small letters), the actual, visible sinful acts that we do. Thus, the SIN problem is much deeper than people observe on the surface.

Knight argues that Jesus gives the same description of SIN and sins in Matthew 5.[26] "It is that insight that Jesus is building upon in the Sermon on the Mount," he writes. "Sin is much more than meets the eye. . . . Just because I have avoided performing the action does not mean that I am right with God."[27] Clearly, for Knight, the major problem of humanity is its SIN condition rather than the mere sinful act.

In a daily reading entitled "There Is More to Sin Than Meets the Eye," he illustrates what he means. "When did Eve sin," he asks, "when she took the fruit or before she took the fruit?" Then he explains: "Something happened in Eve's head and heart before she took the fruit. By the time she had taken the fruit, she had already sinned. . . . Before reaching for the fruit, she had chosen her own will over the will of God. She had put herself on the throne of her life, at the center of her universe, thus displacing God. In actuality, she had focused her love on her self rather than on God. And that is the core of sin."

"Eve committed sin when she loved herself and her desire more than she loved God and His will. She committed sin in her heart. And that sin in her heart led to the taking and eating of the fruit. Sin in the heart leads to sins in terms of action."[28]

Knight's view is intriguing and profound. In its very nature, SIN is love, love of yourself more than God. After all, the love of self has led even good church members to have what Knight calls "vegetarian sins." They may "appear good in their own eyes," but such people "suffer from the *sin of goodness,* the most hopeless of all sins."[29]

Again, his points are particularly relevant to Seventh-day Adventists as they cope with the tension between their desire to live according to God's principles and their sinful nature. As Paul writes, "For I do not do the good I want, but the evil I do not want is what I do. Now if I do what I do not want, it is no longer I that do it, but sin which dwells within me" (Romans 7:19, RSV).[30] Knight who knows the tension himself reminds his readers that it is through their helplessness that they are driven to Jesus and to the "foot of the cross."[31]

We can study Knight's view of SIN and sins in more depth in some of his other writings such as *The Pharisees Guide to Perfect Holiness* and *I Used to Be Perfect*.[32] These books have entire sections dealing with this issue. No doubt, the right understanding of sin is important since it affects one's view on such theological topics as salvation, the law of God, perfection, and others.

## Perfection and its meaning

Another prominent theme for Knight is the meaning of Christian perfection. Using Matthew 5, he notes that perfection has nothing to do with becoming "sinless" but rather with being more loving like God. George is certain that we must interpret Matthew 5:48 ("be ye therefore perfect, even as your Father which is in heaven is perfect") within the larger context of Matthew 5:21–47. He explains: "Jesus is not dealing with abstractions here. Being like the Father means loving one's enemies, just as God loves His enemies. . . . God demands of His children supernatural love for *all* people. Just as the Father so loved the world that He gave His Son to die for people who were ungodly and His enemies, so are Christians to love even those who despitefully use them. That is the ultimate in God-likeness in Godliness."[33]

Knight notes that the idea of perfection as "flawless sinlessness" came into Christianity from the apostasy of the medieval church that accepted Greek philosophical ideas rather than from the Hebrew Scriptures. It was this idea of sinless perfection, he observes, that gave birth to monasticism.[34] In his biography of Joseph Bates, George notes that perfectionism entered Adventism through the teachings of this founder and took some time to correct.[35] Adventists came to understand that perfection has to do with becoming more loving rather than being sinless.

Of course, Knight's view of perfection does not invalidate the growth of a Christian. Similar to John Wesley and Ellen White, he believes in what he calls "progressive sanctification,"[36] but not in sinless perfection. Perfection for him "is more like a line than a point."[37]

His other books discuss these themes in more detail. For example, *I Used to Be Perfect* and *The Pharisee's Guide to Perfect Holiness* have entire sections expounding the issue of perfection.[38] In his books of daily devotional readings, Knight is engaged in a dialectic and even here there is a marked polemic in his writing. For example, he takes the opportunity to deal with a statement from the writings of Ellen White used by some Adventists to argue for "sinless" perfection.[39] By examining the entire context of the statement, he shows that such a reading is a misreading. Ellen White, he declares, is in full agreement with Jesus' idea of perfection found in Matthew 5:48. She appeals for becoming more loving like Jesus rather than becoming "sinless."

Understanding perfection seems to be crucial for Seventh-day Adventists since many, including Knight himself, have experienced "spiritual agony" in their struggle to become sinless and perfect. That has been not only unhealthy but has led many to "utter frustration and discouragement."[40] Knight, himself, left the church for a while because he failed to reach perfection. His personal story of trying to become the "first perfect Christian since Christ" is not only interesting but contains profound lessons for others.[41] It seems that it was his agonizing experience that has driven him to correct the often-misunderstood meaning of biblical perfection. Thus Knight's first two devotionals are full of theological lessons that he deems important for Seventh-day Adventists today.

## A historical devotional

*Lest We Forget* is the third of Knight's devotionals in the popular genre. But it was the first ever to entirely focus on the theme of history and represented an innovative departure in its approach to the series. Knight saw the opportunity of sharing his enthusiasm for Adventist history with the masses. Published in 2008, it provides a step-by-step history of the Advent movement from 1844 until the present. It comes later in Knight's career when he is more concerned with the issue of Seventh-day Adventist identity. As he notes, for example, in the first daily meditation, when a church forgets its own history it loses its "sense of identity," and then its "mission and purpose."[42] Thus his main goal is to inspire and remind his church of its unique mission to the world.

The devotional covers many important developments in Adventist history. Knight begins with the story of William Miller and the Millerite movement. Then he goes through the Great Disappointment and the appearance of Sabbatarian Adventism that grew and organized into the Seventh-day Adventist denomination in 1863. George also reveals intriguing stories about James and Ellen White, Joseph Bates, Uriah Smith, J. N. Andrews, and many other leaders.

Following their official organization in 1863, Seventh-day Adventists developed their distinctive lifestyle and established their publishing, health, and educational institutions. Those became the landmarks for Adventists around the world. Today the Adventists have the largest Protestant health and educational systems in the world.

Next, Knight reveals how the movement went through several crises (theological and organizational) but continued to grow. Today the Seventh-day Adventist denomination is a global community with more than seventeen million members. The globalization, of course, has its own challenges but as Knight seems to point out, the church can continue to expand as long as it does not forget its distinctive message, sound biblical principles, working organizational structure, and a sense of prophetic mission. That "forgetting," in Knight's opinion, however, is one of the "greatest temptations" for Seventh-day Adventism today.[43]

His third volume of devotional readings marks a significant shift in his concern for his community. While his earlier devotionals are concerned with Adventist theology, his third devotional deals with what he perceives as a crisis of Adventist identity. Although reflected in a number of his later writings, perhaps the best example is his *The Apocalyptic Vision and the Neutering of Adventism*.[44] Similar to the *Lest We Forget* devotional, the book reflects on the meaning and the relevance of Seventh-day Adventism and its prophetic mission to the world. Clearly, Knight has a burden for the future of his church, and this is an attempt to affirm its significance and role within the larger Christian world.

## Conclusions

After briefly examining the three devotional volumes of George R. Knight, we can draw several conclusions. First, his daily devotional readings have been a very effective means to introduce important theological concepts to a wider Adventist audience and to influence the church's thinking on questions such as grace, sin, law, Christian perfection, and sinlessness. My personal theological journey is a good example of this influence. Living under a severe communist regime for the first twenty years of my life, I was quite legalistic in my Christian beliefs and living. It was after I went to England in 1990 and began reading George Knight's books (including his devotionals) that my whole theology of salvation, grace, sin, and later perfection changed.

Later, I went to the Seventh-day Adventist Theological Seminary and took a number of classes from Dr. Knight. Every class was another eye-opener for me in the development of the history, theology, and lifestyle of Seventh day Adventism. I particularly remember discussing the issue of perfection with him, something that I wanted to understand further. What I appreciated the most in our conversations was his honesty with historical and theological facts related to the Adventist past and biblical interpretations. He did not "hide" the struggles and problems of theological disagreement and discussions. Knight never depicted an overidealistic picture of Adventism, its leaders, and its theological battles. At the same time, he masterfully used those examples as an inspiration for us, his students. After all, God had always worked with imperfect but willing people, he affirmed. I still remember his examples of Abraham, Moses, David, and Peter that clearly supported his narrative.

During my PhD studies, Dr. Knight as my chair, continued to teach me to be honest with historical facts and events. Although my research was not related to the topics discussed here, but dealt with the development of the Adventist understanding of Ellen White's prophetic gift (another controversial issue within the denomination), his challenge for honesty made my research, in my opinion, more valuable and profitable for the church at large. In fact, my own "picture" of the role and ministry of Ellen White within Seventh-day Adventist church has been enlightened and strengthened under George's guidance of my dissertation. Now I use my knowledge to help others to get a healthier picture of Ellen White's prophetic ministry and its role for the church today. I feel very fortunate to have studied under Dr. Knight. In reality, he became not only my teacher and my mentor, but also a friend for life. It is not surprising, therefore, that George Knight has to a large extent influenced my theological and historical concepts related to Adventism. I am indebted to him for that influence on me.

Second, the devotional readings show that Knight's theology at its heart was concerned with practical living. For him, true Christianity is not only what one believes, but also how one lives. He, of course, was not afraid to challenge well-settled beliefs within Seventh-day Adventism. George reminds the church that at the center of its beliefs must be the gospel of God's love and grace that is able to transform human hearts and minds.

Third, the devotional writings depict Knight as a scholar genuinely concerned for his own denomination. Reading through the devotionals one cannot escape the fact that even in his most critical analyses, he loves his church and wants it to be a place where people can see Jesus. As he often notes, the law and the doctrines are important, but outside of the context of the gospel, they become useless for any Christian or any denomination. That is why his appeal to become more loving like Jesus is so profound and relevant today. His last devotional volume, *Lest We Forget,* is also an appeal to the Seventh-day Adventist Church never to forget its prophetic purpose and mission. Indeed, George Knight loves his church with a passion, and his devotional readings are a clear example of this passion. The devotional volumes are a distinctive part of his legacy, an important part of his work, and have had a significant impact on Adventism at large.

## Endnotes

1. George R. Knight, *Walking With Jesus on the Mount of Blessing* (Hagerstown, Md.: Review and Herald®, 1996).

2. George R. Knight, *Walking With Paul Through the Book of Romans* (Hagerstown, Md.: Review and Herald®, 2002).

3. George R. Knight, *Lest We Forget* (Hagerstown, Md.: Review and Herald®, 2008).

4. This volume was published in 2013 for use in 2014.

5. The history of the "Morning Watch" tradition is traced in Gregory Johnston's dissertation "From Morning Watch to Quiet Time: The Historical and Theological Development of Private Devotionalism in Anglo-American Protestant Instruction, 1870–1940" (St. Louis University, 2007). An example of the genre is found in John Mott, *The Morning Watch* (New York: International Committee of Young Men's Christian Associations, 1898).

6. The annual Daily Devotional series is one of the few publishing opportunities in the church to actually secure a reasonable return on the labor writers invest in their work. The opportunity to author a volume in the Daily Devotional series is coveted.

7. Because *Turn Your Eyes Upon Jesus* was prepared and published after the time of the writing of this article I make only brief mention of it here.

8. George R. Knight, *Walking With Jesus,* 7.

9. Knight, *Walking With Paul,* 5.

10. Ibid., 20.

11. Ibid., 48.

12. Knight, *Walking With Jesus,* 195.

13. Ibid., 301.

14. Ibid., 116.

15. Ibid., 118.

16. Ibid.

17. Ibid., 119.

18. Knight, *Walking With Paul,* 178.

19. Ibid., 177.

20. Knight, *Walking With Jesus,* 106.

21. Knight, *Walking With Paul*, 110.

22. Ibid., 69.

23. George R. Knight, *Angry Saints: The Frightening Possibility of Being Adventist Without Being Christian* (Hagerstown, Md.: Review and Herald®, 1989).

24. Knight, *Lest We Forget*, 289.

25. George R. Knight, *The Pharisee's Guide to Perfect Holiness: A Study of Sin and Salvation* (Boise, Idaho: Pacific Press®, 1992).

26. See, for example, the daily reading "Adultery Is More Than Adultery" in *Walking with Jesus*, 137.

27. Ibid., 139.

28. Ibid.

29. Knight, *Walking With Paul*, 45; See also Knight, *Walking With Jesus*, 13.

30. Knight, *Walking With Paul*, 185.

31. Knight, *Walking With Jesus*, 136.

32. George R. Knight, *I Used to Be Perfect: An Ex-legalist Looks at Law, Sin, and Grace* (Boise, Idaho: Pacific Press®, 1994).

33. Ibid., 179.

34. Ibid., 181.

35. George R. Knight, *Joseph Bates: The Real Founder of Seventh-day Adventism* (Hagerstown, Md.: Review and Herald®, 2004), 77–91, 117.

36. Knight, *Walking With Paul*, 185.

37. Knight, *Walking With Jesus*, 180.

38. See, for example, *The Pharisee's Guide*, 147–166; and *I Used to Be Perfect*, 65–79.

39. The statement appears in the book *Christ's Object Lessons*, page 69, and reads: "Christ is waiting with longing desire for the manifestation of Himself in His church. When the character of Christ shall be perfectly reproduced in His people then He will come to claim them as His own." Knight has argued, however, that the entire context of White's statement does not support the idea of becoming sinlessly perfect. See Knight, *Angry Saints*, 145–150; *I Used to Be Perfect*, 83–92; *The Pharisee's Guide*, 190–193.

40. Knight, *The Pharisee's Guide*, 193, 195.

41. Knight, *I Used to Be Perfect*, 80, 81, 85–87.

42. Knight, *Lest We Forget*, 9.

43. Ibid., 373.

44. George R. Knight, *The Apocalyptic Vision and the Neutering of Adventism: Are We Erasing Our Relevancy?* (Hagerstown, Md.: Review and Herald®, 2008).

# Chapter 19

# An Academic "Mutt's"* Search for Meaning

## George R. Knight

*O*verwhelmed and *humbled* are two words that best express my emotions upon reading the essays in this book. I had no idea that my rather circuitous life had, at least in the minds of their authors, made some of these contributions. Most days, I was just trying to survive and discover the meaning of life.

Of course, those activities led me to share my journey with others as I imparted the findings of my wanderings in the classroom, the pulpit, and my writings. But in doing so I had no feeling of making a contribution. I was merely doing my job and trying to find answers. Interestingly enough, while I have a keen sense of the historical past and its meaning for today, I have not until recently had much

---

* "Mutt . . . 1. A mongrel dog. 2. A fool (shortened from muttonhead)."

"Mongrel . . . 1. An animal or plant produced by the crossing of different breeds or varieties. . . . 2. Anything produced by the mixture of incongruous things, adj. of mixed breed, race, origin, or character. Often used derogatively."

perception about how people's current personal journeys and struggles (including my own) might impact or transform ideas and perspectives as the present slides into the future.

The future, of course, will be the final judge on whether any of us has made a difference. And the good news for those of us who have been teachers is that our most important legacy to that future is the students whom we have had a part in educating. The sign of a good teacher is that he or she has produced students that can move beyond the findings and conclusions of their mentor as they push beyond his or her work, either by extending and expounding upon it or by indicating which hypotheses were faulty or led nowhere. I have to admit that I am a restless idea person who jumped from one idea and one field to another, leaving all of them open to development far beyond my limited thoughts.

Before going any further, I would like to express my gratitude to those who have taken the time to write these essays. Some of them have been students for whom I served as their dissertation chair, others were students who I helped guide in their doctoral studies, while yet others were academic friends and colleagues. Two of them were classmates at Pacific Union College and later colleagues at Andrews University and three were my editors and publishers. To all I extend my appreciation. And that extension is especially heartfelt to Gilbert Valentine and Woodrow Whidden, who contributed much of their valuable time to this project as its editors.

I should note that several of the biographical details mentioned in the essays are different from what I remember, which makes me wonder about the reliability of the memories of even first-person witnesses. And that, as might be expected, brings me to the frontier of a "sermon" on historical method. But, thankfully, that is not the purpose of this essay.

I must say that it is difficult to know how to respond to the chapters in this festschrift. But most of them need no response. While I might have said some things differently, the essays are well written and make their points in a satisfactory way. There were two or three authors who did call for a response. And respond I will near the end of my remarks.

In the meantime, I will provide some autobiographical material that will help my readers see some of the factors and people who helped shape my academic journey. In the process, I will share some thoughts on "muttiness," teaching, writing, and leading the rather precarious life of a "provocateur." Near the end of this piece, I will offer a few responses to the essays and provide some thoughts on my future and on the topic of why I did things the way I did and what I would do if I had a second life to live.

Meanwhile, I need to say that I am more uncomfortable writing about myself than I expected. I have written tens of thousands of words over the past forty years, but now I am bordering on speechlessness. In many ways it would have been easier if this *festschrift* followed the usual "surprise" model. But, on the other hand, it is probably a good exercise to help my friends and readers (and wife) see what makes me tick. At least I hope so. With that halting thought, I will begin my autobiographical presentation.

## The BIG meeting

June 1976 witnessed my arrival at Andrews University. A couple of weeks before, I had been granted my doctoral degree in the history and philosophy of education and completed my principalship of Houston Junior Academy. Yet I was almost totally unprepared for what would hit me in the rapid pace of my first summer term of teaching. The course in the history of education in the United States posed no problem (outside of my having no class notes), but the one on the philosophy of Seventh-day Adventist education left me wondering what I was supposed to do. I had never had such a course and there was no book on the topic. And now Andrews expected me to develop one and teach it in a few short intensive weeks, all the while developing notes for the equally intensive course on American educational history. I was stressed.

The fall term was easier in that I had more time to develop notes, but the unknown material was even more threatening. Once again, I had one course (the general philosophy of education) for which I was well prepared. But the other one put me to the stretch in ways I didn't like. How could I develop a graduate course in the history of Adventist education when there were no books covering the field or even pointing to its shape? To put it mildly, I was uncomfortable.

But it got worse. Sometime in November I got a call to report to the office of the graduate dean. I expected a quiet little meeting between the two of us as he offered help to a beginning professor—a nice thought blown to bits as I entered the room. There, sitting in a circle, was the academic vice president, the graduate dean, the dean of Arts and Sciences, and the chair of the Department of Education (there was no School of Education at that time).

They had only one question: What was I doing? It seemed to me that the answer should have been obvious. I was researching and making class notes every day so that I would have something to present the next! In short, I told them the truth: that I was swimming hard and barely keeping my head above water.

That is not the answer they wanted. They wanted to know what I was *doing*. Mystified, I requested clarification. They wanted to know what I was writing. Again the answer should have been obvious—class notes. Then they knocked me flat by announcing that they had brought me to the university to write and publish.

That caught me by surprise. I had never published anything and had just finished writing my dissertation, which nobody in that circle had ever seen. What gave those experienced professors the idea that I could write was beyond me and still is. Perhaps they were desperate. They had recently established a doctorate in education and needed published professors to give it credibility.

But why me? I didn't want to write or publish. I had never even thought about those activities, although my doctoral advisor had sought to push me in that direction. I hadn't gotten a doctorate so that I could write. What I really desired was to get paid for reading the rest of my life, my idea of academic Nirvana. But four of the most important individuals in my professional world were challenging that vision of the good life.

What to do became the issue. I told them that if that is what they wanted, I would write. I then notified them that I expected them, in turn, to keep off of my back with extra teaching and administrative duties. I would teach my load and write, but they needed to look elsewhere if they had an emergency.

With that we had a gentlemen's agreement (it was an all-male circle) and I left the office totally bewildered. I had never heard of such a meeting with a new professor before that time, and I have not heard of one since. I am not sure what inspired that close-door session. But I do know that it was a major turning point in my life. I left the dean's office with a new and troubling vision.

The vision was clear enough. But it lacked content. How should I go about my new assignment? That question dominated my thoughts during the winter term of the 1976–1977 school year. The initial answer came in three flavors. First, I outlined the book proposal that Ron Knott reflected on. There was no adequate textbook in the philosophy of Adventist education. So I would write one for my own course. That would work since I taught it four times a year and in six years would have about one thousand students—enough to justify a short run at the budding Andrews University Press.

But the press's board had broader ideas. They suggested that I write it for the larger Christian market rather than merely for Adventists. That was one of the most fruitful suggestions in my career. I followed it and the rest is history as *Philosophy and Education* found its way into classrooms throughout the evangelical world, while its secular adaptation, *Issues and Alternatives in Educational Philosophy*, became widely adopted by state institutions and certain hyper-Calvinistic schools that had difficulties with my underlying Arminian presuppositions.

My second initiative during that first winter at Andrews (while I was teaching full time) was to write four articles in four weeks: two for Adventist publishers and two for the secular market. All four were accepted. And all four gave direction to my future publishing interests. The first, interestingly enough, was a cosmological essay that carried "A Search for Meaning" as its original title. And, as noted in the title of this autobiographical piece, that topic has consistently stood at the center of my intellectual journey. I desperately want to make sense out of a world that is in many ways meaningless.

The *Journal of Adventist Education* published the second article as "Redemptive Discipline." The fallout from that rather pedestrian topic shocked me. Within a week of publication I received a phone call from the National Catholic Education Association. They had read it and wanted to know if I would serve on their speaking circuit.

*Why not?* I thought. So the next two or three years found me periodically lecturing to large audiences of Roman Catholic educators on the topic of school discipline. It was great. I got to read Ellen White quotes to those good brothers and sisters, and they paid me a nice honorarium. In the meantime, I got to fellowship with the other speakers and the meeting organizers. There I sat among priests and nuns and an occasional bishop or two, most of them drinking alcoholic beverages and smoking, all the while cracking jokes about the Catholic Church and its clergy as I ate peanuts, drank cold water, and thought how similar their jokes were to those of Adventists concerning their own community.

Now I have to beware of where I share my dealings with Roman Catholics. After all, in some Adventist circles I am already suspect as being an undercover Jesuit. Some have pointed out in print that no one except an infiltrating agent would conclude some of his books with the Latin phrase *"soli deo gloria."* Flawless Adventist logic, except I am not sure why an undercover agent would flag his presence by using Latin—unless he was especially diabolical and subtle and was trying to throw people off his track by being open.

The third article found its way into print in the influential and hard-to-break-into *Phi Delta Kappan*. Titled "Reschooling Society: A New Road to Utopia," it built upon a play of words in the title of the radical educational anarchist Ivan Illich's *Deschooling Society*, an iconoclastic book making big waves at the time. Needless to say, my article was revolutionary, offering a proposal for recreating the educational world by turning it upside down.

The third initiative flowing out of the "Big Meeting" was a book I would edit. Utilizing the research expertise of professors older than I, the idea was that I would get credit for editing an important book without any work. That, I soon discovered, came near to being the apex of stupidity. I never worked harder on a book or had one that took longer to see print. By the time *Early Adventist Educators* finally came out, I had authored two of my own. And, as Gil Valentine (my research assistant at the time) has pointed out, I swore off of the editing business forever. Of course, such swearing didn't make it forever. I soon found myself as research editor for the *Journal of Adventist Education* and later as co-editor with Kenneth Strand of *Andrews University Seminary Studies*. Subsequent years found me editing several individual volumes and four series of books: the Bible Amplifier commentary (fifteen vols.), the Adventist Classic Library (seven vols.), the Library of Adventist Theology, with Woodrow Whidden as co-editor (four vols., before I turned the series over to Woody), and the Adventist Pioneer Series (nine vols., published or in press with another twenty on the schedule). The one thing that has changed in my editing is that I have learned the politics of the job. Namely, asking only people who can do the job right and get it done on time.

In concluding this section, all I can say after nearly forty years since the "Big Meeting" is that it was a major turning point in my life. Nothing has been the same since that intimidating session in the graduate dean's office. But how did I get there in the first place? To that topic I now turn.

## Thoughts on "muttiness"

My academic journey is about as twisted as everything else in my life. That thought calls for some reflection on the title of this autobiographical contribution: "An Academic 'Mutt's' Search for Meaning." As pointed out in my note on the first page of this essay, "mutt" has two basic meanings: (1) "mongrel" and (2) "fool," "muttonhead," or "blockhead." Since I tend to shy away from the implications of the second meaning, I prefer to focus on the first. Thus, I pointed out that the formal definition of "mongrel" highlights the fact that it represents the "crossing of different breeds" the "mixture of incongruous things." That definition describes my academic journey. As I wandered down the corridors of this and that discipline in my search for meaning, I could only look wistfully over the fence at those who had highly specialized pedigrees from Harvard or Princeton or Yale.

But looking back, it seems to me in retrospect that being an academic mutt is not all that bad. As I see it, the world of scholarship embraces two basic types. On the one hand are those highly specialized individuals who dedicate their life to understanding and explaining in infinite detail the implications of such topics as the word *kai* in John 3:16. I found myself bored with that one after 13.86 seconds and had to move on to less specialized endeavors. That brings me to type two in the academic world: those individuals who are driven to study almost everything as they try to fit the pieces of their world together in a meaningful manner.

Needless to say, I fit into the second category, in spite of momentary lapses into thinking about the joys at the other end of the spectrum. I am a dabbler who would like to know everything if time permitted. Most of my readers are aware of my studies in history, theology, philosophy, and biblical studies. But more unknown are my years as a high school math teacher, my exploration into the formal study of marine engineering as a collegiate midshipman in one of the government merchant marine academies, my equivalent of one year of graduate education in the realms of psychological and social theory, my study in inferential statistics, my several years of teaching a graduate course in sociology (not social theory), or my endless fascination with such fields as intelligent design. The upshot of all that diversionary activity is that I live in a world without academic boundaries. While understanding the basic shape and methodologies of each discipline, I tend to work across fields without respect for defining borders. And anyone who looks at my vita soon discovers that I quickly get bored with one area and jump to another. The end result tends to breadth rather than the depth of our above-mentioned *kai* expert. The good news is that I have come to the conclusion that the scholarly world needs both types of academics.

My own journey began in an agnostic framework. In my high school years, in the face of exposure to mindless macroevolution, I had come to the conclusion that I didn't have enough faith to be an atheist. That resulted in my choosing the agnostic route of not being able to know ultimate meaning with any certainty. Christianity wasn't really an option. My father had been quite clear that all Christians were hypocrites, and he also espoused the Freudian doctrine that only weaklings need a father figure (god).*

Those conclusions didn't leave me with too many options in my youthful search for meaning. The most attractive of them was hedonism—if it feels good do it. Pleasure is the meaning and end of life. Of course, in my childhood years I did find myself in cosmological speculations that led to the very definite and vivid conclusion that our planet was the center of the universe, my town was the center of the planet, my home was the center of my town, and that I was the center of my home. Such musings of a childish mind had all kinds of utility and pointed toward a life of searching for the meaning of existence.

My hedonistic period came to an abrupt halt when at nineteen years of age I attended a series of evangelistic meetings in Eureka, California, and joined the Seventh-day Adventist Church. That led to a new stage in my search. I soon realized that the rest of the members of the church were all messed up. Concluding that they weren't trying hard enough, I soon promised God out loud that I would be the first perfect Christian since Jesus. Whidden infers that I did so tongue in cheek. Not so. I did it with a "clear head" and the endless energy of my birthright. I had not the slightest doubt that I could do it. After all, I had spent nineteen years doing evil and had had no problem. I figured doing good was just exerting my energies in the other direction.

In the meantime, in my search for meaning I read everything I could about the Bible and Adventism, with a special focus on the writings of Ellen White. September 1962 found that search taking a jump forward when I enrolled as a

---

* For those with an interest in the "hard facts" of my journey, it should be noted that I was born on October 16, 1941, in Ross, California, a small town about fifteen miles above San Francisco. But my parents soon moved thirty-five miles north to Santa Rosa, where I graduated from high school in 1959. Then followed an aborted attempt at college, a stint in the army, and a return to the retail grocery business, which I had first entered at the age of fourteen. As the oldest son of a family of four (two of each sex), my conversion to Christianity was a shock to my salesman father. That was bad enough, but my three siblings followed my example. Fortunately, my father, over time, has made peace with the "wayward course" of his children. My housewife mother, on the other hand, seems to have been happy all along with our choices.

theology major at Pacific Union College. The energizing power of my new belief system propelled me that first term from my previous position of existing near the bottom of my class to the top. That was an utter shock to me. But I had finally found something powerful enough to ignite my latent intellectual abilities. Study became both a joy and a driving need that provided new directions for my perfectionistic tendencies.

At Pacific Union College, I came close to avoiding the world of academic "mutthood." My full intention was to major in theology with a minor in biblical languages. But such high mindedness came to an abrupt halt two years into my program. I woke up one morning in September 1964 and decided that it was a waste of time to use two more years in an undergraduate program.

The result: I completed the work for the junior and senior years in the next nine months and, with a couple of summer correspondence courses, graduated in August 1965. But there was a second outcome. I no longer had enough linear time to complete a biblical languages minor, so opted for one in history. Having taken no courses in history up to that point, I did the entire minor in nine months. In the process, I found myself deeply influenced by the insightful and provocative Walter Utt, whose sequence in Russian history and seminar in the philosophy of history widened my horizons in unanticipated ways.

I had now completed my BA, but had also taken the first step from purity of pedigree to "muttiness." But it wasn't too late to correct the problem. I spent my next two years at the newly created Andrews University where I earned an MA in 1966 and a BD (later MDiv) in 1967, both with an emphasis on theology and Christian philosophy. During those years I began to toy with the idea of doing a PhD in the area of biblical inspiration and hermeneutics. I obviously had something besides further mongrelization in my sights.

But it was not to happen. By the spring of 1969, my perfectionism had taken its toll. The plain fact was that I was as messed up as ever and so were the churches I was pastoring on the Texas Gulf Coast. Disillusioned, I resigned from the ministry, decided that "Christianity" had led me astray, planned on giving it all up, and was accepted for a high-paying administrative post with a fast track to the higher levels of one of America's large corporations.

There was only one problem with that solution. I had no interest in what I perceived to be the mindless world of business. I then contemplated becoming an MD, but that solution looked like a rat race. Next came a meandering toward dentistry, but it didn't seem to fit my personality. I finally decided to attend the University of Texas and work toward a doctorate in American history. But who would hire me? I had no desire to work for the church, and the market at the height of affirmative action was almost nonexistent for young white males; a generation that was beginning to pay for the discriminatory practices of it forbearers.

In the end, I chose to do a degree in a professional field in which I could enjoy my study of the liberal arts while finding better opportunities for employment. I knew absolutely nothing about the history and philosophy of education, but it looked like my best option. But how to support my family during the years of study became a real issue. I had no friends or sponsors and I knew little of financial aid for graduate students. Tuition was no problem since residents of Texas, thanks to oil revenues, paid only one hundred dollars per year for a full program of doctoral studies. But there were other considerations, such as eating and a place to live.

The solution to the problem was to "use" the church that I believed had so wrongly used me to make it through. I would drop them when I had my degree. It was a cold-blooded decision in my hour of necessity. The result was seven years in the Adventist educational system, first in a two-room school and later as third-grade teacher and then principle of a metropolitan junior academy. One result was that I discovered that I genuinely loved teaching. I should note in passing that even though I was in a state of spiritual anarchy during those years, I did, for some reason, have a genuine desire for the spiritual health of my students and the welfare of the schools. Thus one might say that even though I was in a spiritual vacuum, I was not yet absolutely degenerate.

My years at the University of Houston were crucial to my academic development. It was there that I learned to use every working minute to its maximum efficiency, even rising at four in the morning for seven years to reach my goals. Of necessity, efficiency in time usage became a way of life that set me up for my productive years in the world of writing and speaking.

Equally important was my provocative major professor, Joshua Weinstein. The most accurate description of Josh is that he was a Jewish atheistic existentialist. He smashed religion every day in class and if I, as a reconditioned agnostic, could have shouted "Amen," I would have done so. Josh was a big-idea sort of teacher. He helped me see the shape of philosophy and how esoteric ideas impacted everyday life, whether those ideas be in Hitler's *Mein Kampf* played out in the Holocaust or those of Plato, Locke, and Dewey applied to education.

Josh really wasn't much help as a graduate advisor. I still remember asking what I should read as I worked toward my comprehensive exams. His reply was as clear as it was foggy: "Read the library." That admonition sent me into a three-year reading frenzy in which I not only had to develop my own list of crucial primary and secondary works but to go through an average of three books per week during that period. Nor was he much more helpful in guiding my dissertation. When I submitted my first chapter of eighty pages, he marked the first three and told me to do the rest the same way. Needless to say, not many of his doctoral students graduated. But those who did had been schooled in the art of self-sufficiency.

I will never forget one conversation with Josh. I was taking his course on the history of nineteenth-century American education, for which I had to write a major research paper. Upon his asking what I was going to write on, I enthusiastically replied: Horace Mann. Great topic, I thought. Here was a person who had a more likely potential than Lincoln, yet chose to get kicked around as America's foremost educational reformer and eventually die an early death because of the stress. Josh's reply hit me hard. "So what? What are you going to do? Copy a chapter out of some book?"

That nasty little conversation was a turning point in my writing journey. For the first time I began to recognize clearly the difference between having a topic and a clear purpose and how purpose relates to investigative hypotheses. I chose to write my paper on the reasons Mann provided in his own writings as to why he gave up what would have been a fruitful political career for the unrewarding path of educational reform. When I had finished I knew that for the first time I had written well. And I have never forgotten the lesson. My students can testify that I am an absolute nut on the centrality of purpose as being determinative in all good writing, from title, to outline, to notes, to bibliography, and all else. I had discovered a major key to effective writing. Without a clear purpose the project is dead in the water.

The next step in my development came with my dissertation. By that time I knew how to write. The crucial element was now my topic: "An Analysis of the Educational Theory of George S. Counts." Counts was the revolutionary of revolutionaries in the American educational world of the first half of the twentieth century. His 1932 *Dare the Schools Build a New Social Order?* caught the usually obedient educational world by surprise and put Counts at the head of a movement that came to be known as social reconstructionism. Building upon crises in the social/economic/political order of the 1930s, he urged educators to proactively take the lead toward social change. A well-informed student of not only American culture, but also that of the Soviets (he read Russian and had spent a great deal of time visiting the new Soviet experiment and studying its economic and educational ideals) and the rising National Socialists, he developed a truly revolutionary philosophy of education.

Perhaps no individual has affected my academic life as much as Counts (1889–1974), even though I never met him. But I did trace his intellectual development from the 1920s, in which he focused on domestic (often local) threats to American values; through the 1930s, in which he realized that the issues and solutions had shifted to national economic, social, and political threats; and into the postwar world, when he realized that international threats made international solutions the only answer in preserving the essence of American culture. The final chapter dealt with the implications of Counts' explorations in revolutionary educational theory for the explosive ideas and philosophies being agitated in the early 1970s.

The topic, of course, put me deep into the revolutionary literatures of socialism and alternate ways of doing things. Those ideas and my reactions to them became a part of my identity. But Counts's educational profile also impacted me. He was interdisciplinary in the best sense of the word. In his PhD program at the University of Chicago, he did almost as much work in the social sciences as he did in the history and philosophy of education. Particularly important was the influence of Albion W. Small, the first person to be appointed professor of sociology in the United States and a leader in the field. Professorships at Yale and Chicago eventually led Counts in 1927 to what was then the most influential American institution in the field of education—Teachers College, Columbia University. There he helped form a group of educators known as the Frontier Thinkers, a collection of high-powered individuals out to change the world. At Columbia, Counts also came under the collegial influence of historian Charles A. Beard and philosopher John Dewey. He was especially attracted to Dewey's social theories for the reform of society. Beard had even a more profound influence on Counts, who was deeply influenced by the historian's ideas of economic determinism in history and his pragmatic urge to make history serve society by curing its social ills.

My years studying the work of Counts left an indelible impression on me.

He was, as noted above, interdisciplinary in the best sense of the word, and thus provided a role model for me as a budding academic. Beyond that, his theme of maintaining identity across a backdrop of changing times and his revolutionary and iconoclastic ideas helped frame my way of looking at the world and how to relate to it. As Ben McArthur points out, I also have sought a "usable past" in my study of Adventist history and how that history can help the church fulfill its earthly mission. Brian Strayer said it as well as anyone when he labeled me a "revisionist utilitarian historian."

In summary, I am one of those students whose doctoral dissertation was a shaping event. Not only did I meet a highly successful educational mutt, but I was profoundly influenced by his ideas. You don't have to look far in my writings to find shades of Counts's impact.

Academic "mutthood" was not my ideal. And at times it has generated in me an inferiority complex. But, looking back, it was probably the best thing that ever happened to me educationally. By helping me to be able to see "outside the box," it gave me perspectives I never would have gained had I achieved the pedigree I desired. I do not believe it should be the route for most scholars, but it served me well when I returned to the academic world of theology and church history. After all, one source of creativity is the ability to utilize the insights of several disciplines to analyze problems and propose solutions. In that sense my "muttiness" has been a blessing as I have continued to search for meaning.

That topic brings me to my "reconversion" to Christianity. It was a progressive experience in early 1975. I had studied philosophy to discover the answer to the meaning of life, but by that time had come to the unbearably frustrating conclusion that it held no ultimate answers. I had hit the brick wall of what I will call the philosophical loop. Namely, that a person cannot have an epistemology (understanding of the sources of truth and their validity) without first having a metaphysics (a theory of ultimate reality). Yet one cannot have a valid metaphysics without first having a valid epistemology. In short, I had come to realize that all individuals (whether they be religious or secular, scientists or business people), of necessity, live by a faith in presuppositions that are not subject to ultimate proof.

That was bad enough. But I also had come face to face with the shortcomings of those revolutionary philosophies that had done so much to shape my life for five years. To put it mildly, I was deep into idealistic Marxism (not Leninism or Stalinism), socialism, and their derivatives in the revolutionary era of the late

1960s and early 1970s. It would, I believed, be wonderful if people put into the common pot all they could while taking out only what they needed. Heaven on earth is possible in such a society. But, I thought as I sat at my desk one day, these theories have been around for thousands of years and yet they have never worked. What is the problem? I asked myself. The answer flashed across my over-heated brain in Technicolor: these revolutionary philosophies fail when applied to the everyday world because of a flawed anthropology. They begin with the basic premises that human nature is basically good and that if you create the right social conditions that goodness will take over to establish the ideal social order.

There, I almost shouted to myself, is the problem!—an inadequate anthropology that allows no understanding of that human perversion that the Bible defines as sin and human selfishness; the root problem of the world, the disabler of all those wonderful revolutionary ideologies. In actuality, people don't put in as much as they can and take out only what they need. Rather, they put in as little as possible and take out as much as they can. For me that insight was my first intellectual step back to Christianity, the only philosophy/theology that has an adequate doctrine of sin as self-centeredness. No other understanding has such explanatory power for comprehending the human problem and its possible solution as the issue of sin. At that time the problem of sin took a front row seat as one of the major pillars in my metaphysics. And, given the human inability to solve the world's problems, as demonstrated by my study of history and revolutionary philosophies, I soon began to conclude that the biblical teaching of the substitutionary death of Christ as the foundation for the gift of free grace offered the only adequate answer to the central human dilemma.

While that dawning had been the beginning of an intellectual conversion, it would take more than that to get me back into Christianity as a belief system and a way of life. But about the same time two other things took place. The first was Josh saying to me that if he weren't a Jew he would be a nobody. "But," I shot back, "you don't even like religion." "You don't understand," he noted. "You see, I am not merely one of those millions of people out there. I belong to the community. And because of that I have significance. They send me all over the world as a speaker. I count because I belong to the community, because I am a Jew." My only thought was that he could have said the same thing about being an Adventist. That conversation helped me see the difference between a person in a religious context who is there because of belief and conviction and those who are there primarily for social reasons. Josh helped me realize that a religious body is made up of those who believe and those who find it a comfortable social context for their way of life. With that insight I had begun to come to grips with some of the dynamics that had discouraged me in the churches I had pastored. But even with that recognition, I still wasn't ready to make peace with the church.

Then into my life came a man whom I had never wanted to see again. Robert Olson, then director of the Ellen G. White Estate, had been my first Bible teacher. Somehow someone had invited him to my house. He apparently knew my problem, but never said one word about it all afternoon. He merely exuded the sweet love of Jesus and a firm confidence in his faith. When he left I told my wife that he had what I needed. That day I met Christ in Robert Olson and my life has never been the same.

After that series of events, I was ready to recommit myself to Christianity. And not just any form of Christianity, but the Adventist way. After all, even in my apostasy I always believed that Adventism held the closest approximation to the teaching of the Bible of any Christian body. To be sure, the denomination's theology is not perfect, but it is the closest approach to Scripture that I could find. Thus it was that I had made peace with Adventism, but not yet its ministry.

The next year, as described above, found me teaching at Andrews University. One fortuitous reality was that nobody knew me outside of the university. I received few calls to speak and my writing was still minimal. As a result, I had nearly a decade of what I like to think of as post-doctoral education as I read widely in a broad variety of disciplines. That extensive reading has proved to be a massive well from which I have continued to draw over the years as the pressures of deadlines has limited my time for the broad reading that I would like to return to.

## Thoughts on teaching

As a kid I didn't like school, hardly ever did my homework, and had no particular love for teachers. To be one came near the very bottom of my wish list. That made it all the more surprising to me when, after resigning from pastoral ministry, I tried teaching in a two-room school in rural San Marcos, Texas, and discovered I loved it. Of course, having only seven or eight students probably helped. It was a relaxed situation in which some of the students occasionally rode horses to school and after school shooting expeditions periodically flavored the experience. Since San Marcos I have taught at every level except the two most important grades (first and second), for which I felt I did not have sufficient talent. I loved elementary, disliked junior high, and was indifferent to secondary. But after seven years of classroom teaching, it was in the university that I found my true vocational home.

Teaching was my thing. I liked working with individuals still flexible enough to have or learn a new thought—as opposed to work in the churches where many never were tempted by such things. Through the years I had a lot of calls out of teaching, many to the "higher" levels in the work of the church. More specifically, I had offers for vice presidencies in the publishing work, higher education, and even the hospital system (not as VP of chaplaincy). I never was, however, invited to the presidency of a conference. But Neal Wilson did phone one day, asking if I would be willing to take the lead position in a major General Conference organization, or if I was too wedded to my position at Andrews University to let go. Wilson surmised correctly. I had by that time found a worldwide pulpit for teaching, writing, and lecturing with a great deal of freedom in what I did and said. My answer two days later was clear and with no regrets. Administration or anything that looked like it is not for me. I had served nearly five years as a school administrator and was bored nearly to death. Or, as I frequently noted to my students, I had served my time in hell and had no desire to return. Now, please don't get me wrong. I admire and appreciate the valuable work of those who have the calling and talent of administration. But mine is the gift of teaching. And I have painfully watched too many good teachers and pastors "advance" to administration only to demonstrate mediocrity. We need to take more seriously what the Bible has to say on the gifts of the Spirit.

My biggest problem in teaching at Andrews was a lack of preparation for most of the courses I taught. My thirty years there were divided into nine years as a specialist in the history and philosophy of education and twenty-one years in church history, both graduate faculty positions. In the educational field, I was well prepared in the general history and philosophy courses, but had never taken classwork in the history or philosophy of Adventist education, the sociology of education, or the two-term course I taught in historical research methods. It got worse when I arrived at the seminary. While I had read widely and written in the field, I had taken no coursework in any of the specialized courses that I taught. In fact, I had avoided church history in my seminary years, except for the three required courses. And those in early church and Calvinism hardly prepared me for teaching the history of religion in America, the history of religious liberty, or modern church. I was least prepared in Adventist history. Yet I soon found myself preparing to teach a course in the development of Adventist lifestyle and a similar one in the denomination's theology. It is true that I had taken the required seminary course titled "Studies in Adventist History," but it was a joke taught by a man released from the faculty at the end of the year.

Well then, you might be thinking, how could I presume to be an "expert" in fields I never studied? Here we have a flashback to Josh and his admonition for me "to read the library." Nearly all of us moderns forget that for most of history people became specialists through massive and intensive reading. The twentieth century finds models of that approach in such influential thinkers as Reinhold Niebuhr and F. F. Bruce, neither of whom held an earned doctoral degree. But they knew how to read. Of course, I had the degree, but in the wrong field. It is only by the strange quirks of history that I ended up basically directing the PhD program in Adventist studies for two decades. I might add that it was the historical studies of my students in the field of education that recommended me for the Adventist studies position. By the time I transferred to the seminary, I had chaired more doctoral dissertations in Adventist history than any other individual. But, as Brian Strayer pointed out, I had learned by doing and helping others to do.

My teaching at Andrews fell into two basic categories: general classroom lecturing and preparing doctoral students. In the first area, Jerry Moon is quite correct that I did teach from a pile of yellow sheets. But I did so in two ways. One was with fairly well-developed manuscripts (such as my courses in religious liberty and the development of religion in America). A second approach was detailed outlines keyed to a raft of marked primary documents that accompanied me to class. The latter was my approach in my signature courses, including those on Adventist theology and lifestyle and the philosophy and history of Adventist education.

Anyone who examines my outline notes in the future will wonder what I did teach. The problem is this: The first time I taught a course I gave a lot of care to developing the structure for the material and to filling in the sections of the outline to the best of my current knowledge. But further growth on my part did not generally lead to a new set of notes. Rather, it led to additions in the margins all over the place, often in different colors of ink as I repeatedly annotated. And eventually there were quite a few pages that represented nothing said in class. But the pages were important because they provided the stimulus for what I wanted to say but hadn't committed to paper. I have provided this information as a warning to any future researcher who seeks to discover the content of my courses from my class notes. To put it bluntly, some of them are royally messed up. But they worked for me.

As to my preparation of doctoral students, Gil Valentine is quite accurate when he writes that it was a mutual voyage of discovery. It was a symbiotic relationship in which we all learned together, with my research and writing often taking place in the same fields as theirs as we plowed through undeveloped or underdeveloped areas in Adventist history. It was no accident that I dedicated my first major published work in Adventist history (*From 1888 to Apostasy*) "to Allan Lindsay, Gilbert Valentine, Arnold Reye, and Warren Ashworth—doctoral students who were my teachers in the researching and writing of Adventist biography."

While it is true that we all grew together, after my first years at Andrews I began to provide more help for structuring the growth process. In the School of Education that turned out to be a two-term course in the methods of documentary research, while in the seminary it found expression in my writing seminar. Actually, it wasn't a writing course but a content seminar that I utilized as a writing seminar for doctoral majors and minors in Adventist studies. In many ways it was a move in self-defense of my time and sanity. I told the students early on that if they could not write a doctoral level paper of twenty pages, there was no way they could do so at four hundred. In that seminar, all my pervasive perfectionism came to the fore, even, as some of the essays in this book have pointed out, to the extent of having students critique each others' papers by going to the library and checking the word-for-word accuracy and Turabian-level format flawlessness in both their bibliographic information and the quotations themselves. Shock was the usual result. But it taught them. The paper itself had to be a unified production all the way from purpose to bibliographic content and detail. Of necessity, the papers were limited in scope, but not in what I expected. This was doctoral boot camp and when faced with it more than one student opted to major in some other field. And all too many took two or more years to finally produce the needed quality. It was all a great waste of paper as the editions rolled by. But when completed the students understood what it meant to be a researcher and writer. The end result was that I saved massive amounts of time and the students produced better quality dissertations.

Before moving on, I should note that I frankly told students that the worst chapter in their dissertation would be the first. That is where we had to battle out the level of expectancy and would have the most rewrites. After a successful first chapter, each one would be easier and better if the student was really developing properly. And, as noted by Moon, I set for myself a one-week turn around time. I considered it to be a sin of the highest magnitude to delay getting a student's paper back. Their time was valuable and I had been hired at great expense to them to be their servant and guide. I had the same policy in exams, even for large classes that had an essay, except here I nearly always got the results back the next class period. Such an approach, however, meant that I had to lay aside my own research and writing until I accomplished what I was hired to do. It also meant that I needed to provide my travel schedule to my dissertation students if they were about to give birth to a chapter.

As to teaching style, several essays have alluded to the fact that I took pleasure in shocking students in my presentations. I confess to such a perverse practice. But it did have the salutary result of stimulating thought and catching their attention. No one fell asleep. In such an approach, however, one risks being misunderstood, especially by those who are not paying close attention or who are mentally challenged or are beyond the hope of growth.

I desired my students to think things through. Also near the beginning of every course I pointed out that some of them would not agree with all my positions. That, I indicated, was fine with me. After all, some mornings I wake up and am not sure if I agree with myself. The important point, however, was not agreement or disagreement, but knowing, based upon valid evidence, *why* one takes a position. I didn't want mindless responses of any sort, but thought-through ones.

## Thoughts on writing

Writing, along with public speaking, is another thing I never wanted to do. My lowest grades were in English and I still can't diagram the structure of a sentence. But I can read. And it is safe to say that I learned to write by reading a vast variety of others' writings and paying attention to what they did and how they did it.

Through the years, writing has become a way of life. So much so that for the past thirty years I have never had a day without multiple looming deadlines. But that is OK. It motivates me, and I work best on a tight schedule.

Writing began rather late in my journey. I was almost forty when I published my first book. But within a few years, I was looking at one coming out every two years. But that soon got out of control, and I ended up doing one or two a year for nearly twenty years. I am currently, in the eighth year of my retirement, trying to get the victory over that addiction.

Where do the ideas come from? Everywhere! I have come to the place where I think in terms of books, often waking up with two or three already outlined in my head, but knowing full well I will develop hardly any of them. My classroom teaching has been the source of many of those I did write. Others have been stimulated by issues and controversies in the larger culture. And being one who dislikes confrontational debate, I tend to write out my ideas. Other people can relate to my books and articles as they please. But writing is how I tend to communicate. And in the process I sharpen my ideas and move into greater depth.

Several have pointed out that I have largely written to and often about Seventh-day Adventists. That was a conscious choice. There are levels of treatment for any topic. At the most basic level are explorations of neglected fields. That was the status for most significant topics in Adventism when I began serious work in the area. While significant work had been done, most of the big "research diamonds" were lying right on the surface and many major topics had been neglected. The first task was to rough out the facts and parameters and provide structures for understanding. Thus, in many ways, I see my contribution to be a beginning upon which others may build by either extending the ideas or constructively reacting and moving forward. In this exploratory process, I have sought to look at old topics in new ways (often with new presuppositions, insights, and data banks). As I see it, my task has been to help Adventists understand themselves. If I had another life I would extend the presentation to the larger scholarly and Christian world. Being somewhat doubtful of reincarnation, however, I will have to rely on the next generation to take the needed steps.

My writing habits are simple and, as Paul Evans would say, perfectionistic. Since my first wife broke me of workaholism, I generally have restricted myself to five eight or eight and a half hour workdays per week. And while I have maintained victory over unlimited workaholism, I am still a workaholic during my dedicated time. Don't ask me to do an errand or answer the phone while I am writing. Without extreme focus I can't produce. And I don't even begin without a three- or four-hour block. Blocking time is crucial to success. Beyond that, when I am writing (or reading) I take ten minutes of every hour to exercise, even if I don't feel the need. I like to think that that schedule keeps properly oxygenated blood flowing to my mental equipment. The alternative is what I call "burning the edge" of my brain. I have discovered that if I push too hard for too long I lose my efficiency and the ability to think at optimum clarity. And once the burning takes place, optimum efficiency usually cannot be recaptured. When I have crossed the line, I find it best to quit writing for the day and move on to working on my footnotes or to explore some issue that tomorrow's writing will raise.

Beverly Rumble has accurately noted that I am a technophobe. And she is right. I am very happy as a nineteenth-century person and write everything by hand. I also still tend to do research by traditional methodologies, even though I have not been adverse for the past twenty-five years to hiring people with greater abilities and interests to search data banks electronically if I deem the move to be potentially fruitful. Being a technophobe, of course, has rendered me largely obsolete. But who cares? Not me. I am more than happy to roll over and let others pick up the task.

As one might expect, there are those who suggest that I could accomplish more if I wrote with a computer. Really? It seems to me that the nasty little machines slow most people down as they install new programs or are tempted to check their e-mail or Facebook. But, some say, it makes revision easier. That is a good argument, but outside of word choices I rarely revise anything. My outline is clear, my notes are in order, and I know what needs to be said before I begin writing. On the other hand, I often don't know how to say it or how to work through a problem until my pen hits the paper. I think with a pen in my hand. My procedure is to write a manuscript, then pass it on to my typist (my wife since retirement) without reading it. I then read the typed manuscript once, make corrections, have them entered into the computer, and send it to the publisher. After that I spend a great deal of time rereading a copy with the editor's jottings, checking quotations, indexing, and so on.

But that wasn't always so. My first few books went through a much more painful process. In fact, after receiving back the critiques for my first book (*Philosophy and Education*) I was so devastated that I never wanted to write again. But after two or three weeks I got off of the floor and began the rewrite. The process was painful in the extreme. For the next few book manuscripts I asked three or four experts in the field to critique them before they went to the publisher. But with the growth of confidence I eventually just sent them on after completion.

I do fear, however, that I will never be viewed as a great scholar. Partly because I use Adventist publishers, but even more so, as Strayer points out, because I do everything I can to make my work clear and readable. I use to tell my students, somewhat tongue-in-cheek, that to be recognized as really great, one needs to write a big book in such a way that no one understands it. Then you can spend the rest of your life writing books that explain the meaning. But if you want to be super great you write a book that no one can understand and refuse to explain it. That procedure develops schools of disciples who vie with each other in their explanations and keep your memory alive.

Readers will note that as time has gone by I have tended to write shorter volumes when I could have produced larger ones. The process began after I was authorized by my publisher to develop eight, four-hundred- to five-hundred-page volumes on the history of Adventism. I was excited, but soon concluded that no one would read them. At that point I opted to slice through that history with brief focused volumes. I introduced the series with my *Brief History of Seventh-day Adventists* and then produced short treatments on the development of Adventist theology and organization. There were to be more in the series, but I drifted on to other projects. The challenge in the approach is to accurately condense massive amounts of information. The same logic informed my four-volume Ellen White series. I could have written one six-hundred-page tome, but no one would have read it. Cut it up into four chunks, and in today's world you have bestsellers. People who avoid larger books will read short ones, even if the content is the same.

I probably don't need to say anything about my book titles. The trick is not to write a book but to get people to pick it up and actually read it. Many of my titles have been provocative enough to accomplish that purpose.

Regarding much of my writing, Whidden is onto something when he argues that "the real significance of the Jones biography is that it became the source from which would flow" not only my further work on 1888 but also that in the fields of Adventist history, Adventist theology, and biblical commentaries. In a sense he is correct. All of those fields were central to my work on Jones, which stimulated further activity in each of them. But the picture is more complicated in that I had been working on such topics as sin and salvation and issues related to Ellen White since my early college experience. And in terms of biblical studies, I had outlined a plan around 1980 in which I would study the entire Bible in depth over a period of thirty years at one hour a day. Thus, my work on Jones might best be seen as a watershed with streams flowing both in and out. What the Jones study did was to intensify my future work toward what were glaring areas of Adventist ignorance in the late nineteenth century and largely remain so today. Thus it is no accident that my next books dealt with issues in salvation, Ellen White, and biblical literacy, as well as further refining my understanding of the 1888 event and its implications.

All of my writings are in a sense autobiographical, since I was dealing with issues that I needed answers to in the face of my personal experience and the larger context of Adventism and religious culture in general. My first book, as earlier noted, came in response to the real need of not having an adequate text in the philosophy of Christian education. My next major production, *Myths in Adventism,* was in many ways an extension of my philosophy book, but an extension taking place in an Adventist context in which Ellen White was being dismembered. I felt that wiping away basic misunderstandings would set the stage for reconstructing the church's view of her work and place it on a new foundation.

In the biographical realm, it is probably no accident that I found a deep interest in the field. I suppose it all began when I was sent to first grade before my fifth birthday. My neural connections hadn't matured at that stage and I just couldn't do the work. That led to my not learning the alphabet until I memorized it in French in grade nine. And I didn't really grasp the art of reading until I was in grade seven when I discovered a host of biographies on characters in the American West. That early biographical reading got me started on a project that picked up in intensity over time. And by the time I arrived at Andrews I had come to realize the power of good biography to help us understand the world in which we live. It is no accident that I started out my doctoral students on that path or that I am closing out my career editing the most ambitious biographical project in Adventist history.

While on the topic of biography, I can't quite resist sharing an anecdote. While writing *Angry Saints* (developed as lectures for the 1888 centennial at the Annual Council of the General Conference in Nairobi, Kenya, and the commemorative meetings in Minneapolis) I couldn't help but notice how much the current General Conference president resembled G. I. Butler. So as I presented my paper, with Neal Wilson sitting at the center of the front row, I really worked Butler over. The unexpected sequel took place when Wilson came up to me in the lunch line, looked penetratingly into my eyes, and told me to stop talking about him.

Fortunately, at the conclusion he smiled. But he got the point and I lived to present my next few lectures. There is a utility to even biography. Individuals change but not personality types.

Anyone looking at my published corpus soon comes to realize that I tend to write in clusters, with often one book calling for another. That was so when I began my work on sin and salvation in what became *The Pharisee's Guide to Perfect Holiness*. Before beginning I realized that I couldn't really speak wisely about God's salvational work for and in us without first adequately presenting His work for us in the atonement and the cross. Thus, my writing of *My Gripe With God* before the *Pharisee's Guide*. That book was shortly followed by *I Used to Be Perfect*, provocative lectures on salvation presented at the 1992 Annual Council of the General Conference.

The same sort of cluster relationship holds in my Ellen White series. I originally wanted to extend my work in *Myths* by developing an introduction to Ellen White's hermeneutics, but soon realized that I couldn't adequately write *Reading Ellen White* until I had set her forth in context by introducing her biography, works, and theological themes in *Meeting Ellen White*. And those two books naturally called for the final two of the series.

In many ways my work on salvation stands at the center of my existential struggle. And at that center, as Whidden points out, is the person and work of Christ. The right and left wings of Adventism meet on the ground of Christ primarily being an example rather than a substitutionary sacrifice. That has led both groups to focus on ethics. That focus is good in itself, but ethics are not of much value without an effective Savior.

My work on Ellen White came in the wake of attacks on her life and work from a number of directions. In surveying the situation it appeared to me that both her admirers and her detractors all too often shared the same erroneous presuppositions—often related to ideas of inerrancy, verbal inspiration, falsely equating inspiration with revelation, and the supposed character perfection of prophets. Along that last line, one major scholar jump-started his career with the assumption that no prophetic claimant could be valid who apparently did not tell the truth about using certain works in her early health writings. Such can only be a problem if one assumes that prophets can't sin on important issues. That is not the biblical picture. After all, even telling a lie is pretty tame stuff next to Peter's cursing his Lord or David's affair with Bathsheba and the murders (plural) he ordered as a cover-up. Along another line, why the big to-do about the fact that Ellen White is reported as being at questionable meetings with Israel Damman? Any reader of her early biographical statements can't help but realize that her early ministry arose in the context of a web of ex-Millerite fanaticism from which the Sabbatarian group only gradually extricated itself. And why get shook up about her borrowing when she told her readers she did so. Beyond that, many of the works she borrowed from were familiar to her contemporary readers, some even being advertised in the *Review* and others being Adventist books, such as Smith's *Daniel and Revelation*. The borrowing may have come as a shock to my generation, but it couldn't have surprised hers to any great extent. The difference is the mythology about her that developed largely from the 1920s through the 1960s. We need to move beyond the misconceptions that fuel both sides of the Ellen White struggle and begin anew by bringing more adequate understandings to our study of topics related to the prophet and her work.

The biggest disappointment in my writing career has been the two commentary series I have been involved in. Gerald Wheeler makes a valid point when he notes that I followed William Barclay's model in my Exploring commentaries. But in the process I wanted to be more exegetically faithful to the text. The largest difference between us, however, is that his series was a smashing success while mine failed to find an adequate market, as had the earlier commentary, which I edited (the Bible Amplifier). The disappointing conclusion I derived from those extensive endeavors, in the light of my publishing history, is that book-buying Adventists are immensely more interested in Ellen White than they are in Bible study. With that lesson learned, I am finally giving up on the improving-the-biblical-literacy-of-Adventists front, and after seven volumes will probably pull the plug on my Exploring series, a project that I had hoped would take me well into my senility after forty or so volumes.

One area where I like to think I have had a bit of success in helping to shape the denomination's future is in my twenty-year advocacy of trimming down the denomination's administrative structure. That journey began in February 1991, when the *Adventist Review* published my "Fat Lady and the Kingdom," an article that called for the church to slim down in every area. After fielding responses for many weeks (all of them positive except those which objected to the admittedly disgusting title), the editors noted that that article had received more feedback than anything they had published and that the time had come to cease printing anymore of the continuing flow of letters. That beachhead was followed by an on-going series of articles and presentations and found voice in the concluding section of *Organizing to Beat the Devil* in 2001. Then in 2005 and 2006 came the General Conference Commission on Ministries, Services, and Structures. Preliminary to its first formal meeting, Jan Paulson invited me to meet with all the General Conference officers and the presidents of the world divisions at a Florida retreat. I had been granted thirty minutes to make my presentation, but my sixty-page paper formed the agenda for nearly four hours in this important pre-meeting. My task was to seek to bring relative harmony among the leadership by demonstrating that the current structure was not inspired but in the past had been pragmatically adapted to meet the needs of an expanding mission (a thesis greatly informed by the doctoral dissertations of Andrew Mustard and Barry Oliver).

The good news is that the eventual result of the commission's work was a vote to reduce the "necessary" levels of structure by fully recognizing the "union of churches" model. Thus, local conferences became an option that could be dispensed with. The bad news about the vote is that by and large its revolutionary promise has not been recognized or implemented. My guess is that it won't be until the system is faced with financial disaster. And in that sequence the denomination will be following its historic pattern of waiting until it is too late to gain major financial and missiological advantages from the changes.

Now I have to admit that I don't know if my agitation made any impact on this change. But in my ego-inflated heart I like to think that I might have. Of course, the possibility of flattening the structure of the church is just one thing that needs to be done. But it is a beginning.

One category of my writings that I should comment upon is that of my four daily devotionals. I viewed the massive multilanguage circulation of those books as a first-class teaching opportunity. As a result, I crafted each of them to be a pedagogical tool as I explored the meaning and implications of the Sermon on the Mount, the book of Romans, Adventist history, and the life of Christ. The most interesting responses came in relation to *Lest We Forget*, a history of Adventism broken down into 365 one-page readings. Many said they read the whole book in a day or a week. And some wondered why this story hadn't been told before. I tried to explain that I had already written a dozen books on the topic, but had had a difficult time getting people to read them. But enough said on that topic. The exchanges merely illustrate the didactic power of the devotional format in popularizing serious academic content.

My writing career just kind of grew as I moved from one topic to another. Given the large number of fields I have written in, it may seem rather disjointed. But viewed from the inside, I can assure you that it was a unified journey as I continued to struggle to find meaning in terms of both my personal life and the mixed up world in which I find myself.

In concluding my thoughts on writing, I should add a word about the translations of my books. To be honest, I have no idea how many there are. Much of it is done without permission, and I only learn of many translations as I travel around the world or by hearsay from others. "Borrowing" of copyrighted works is largely unpoliced in Adventism. I do have a ballpark idea regarding the number of languages that my books have been translated into, but even that is a guess. I have confirmed about forty languages (i.e., I have copies), have heard of a dozen more, and guess that there are yet others. All in all, my best estimate is sixty or so. Maybe in eternity I can come to more definite conclusions, if I still have any interest in the topic.

## Thoughts on being a provocateur

As to being a provocateur, I don't think I was born that way. On the other hand, it is not something that I have consciously worked at. It probably stems from the fun I have in playing with words, but even more so from a profound insecurity that fears people will fall asleep while I am talking. Shocking statements elicit interest and a provocative style keeps people focused. Of course, sometimes I give off unwanted side messages. As a result, I no longer preach my sermon entitled "Why I Don't Like Adventists." In that presentation I was quick to explain that I liked Adventists who were Christian, but if they were only Adventists I wanted to be as far away from them as possible. But by that time I had lost some I wanted to reach.

Paul Evans is correct when he notes that I do not nicely fit into any of the usual categories, such as liberal or conservative, and that I don't really belong to any of the denomination's established theological camps. An alternate title to this festschrift was *Thoughtful Maverick*. That is pretty close to how I view myself.

Ben McArthur has pointed out that I am basically moderate on all theological positions. And I think that is so. I have tried to define myself in the light of Jesus, who I see as a radical wine-skin-smashing conservative (not fundamentalist or traditionalist—the labels we too often confuse with conservative). He demonstrates His approach in the Sermon on the Mount, in which He repeatedly takes traditional teachings ("You have heard it said"), extracts the underlying principle, and sets forth a meaning ("But I say to you") that goes back to (i.e., conserves) the essence of the Old Testament ideal on the topic. Thus, my description of Him as a "radical conservative," the model I have sought to emulate.

One outcome of such a style is that it got Jesus crucified as the traditionalists (Pharisees) and liberals (Sadducees) of His day found a common enemy. While I don't think anybody is out to crucify me, my provocative style (as Evans, Moon, and others have pointed out) has created enemies on both sides of many theological controversies.

Another thing related to my style is what some consider my remarkable survival after making so many provocative statements in the face of many Adventists (including leaders) who don't like that approach. Bertil Wiklander (president of the Trans-European Division) first brought the survival issue to my consciousness at the 1998 Annual Council at Iguassu Falls, Brazil. He mentioned that a number of the leadership could not figure out how I had survived in light of my approach.

I suppose the answer is that most people recognize my pastoral concern for the church and cannot deny that I have based my positions firmly on scripture, the writings of Ellen White, and the lessons of Adventist history. Along another line, McArthur points out a fact that I early perceived. Namely, that such early revisionist works as *Myths* took place in the context of a more radical revisionism that tended to rejection of both Ellen White's role and the essence of Adventism. Thus McArthur makes a good point when he notes that without Ron Numbers and Walter Rea there would be no George Knight. The facts were on the table and people were ready for a moderate voice that was both revisionist and constructive. The time was right for my survival.

As a result, it is true that while my style is provocative, no one questions my loyalty. That came forth loud and clear the night before my "If I Were the Devil" presentation at the 2000 General Conference session in Toronto. That evening I went to Phil Follett's room (the vice president who had contacted me to participate) to give him a copy (unrequested) of my talk. Being a little worried about some of the content, I suggested that he read it first. He declined, adding that "those of us in the presidential circle don't like what you say, but we know you are right."

I should point out that one leader did question my loyalty in the wake of the Merikay Silver legal debacle. Because of the financial outfall, injustices were being formulated for selective pay scale classifications to moderate the cost of the settlement. I got wind of what was truly a secret and formed a short-lived but victorious Adventist labor union. One of my superiors called me on the carpet, questioning my loyalty. I responded that there are two types of loyalty—that of Martin Luther and that of the cardinals and archbishops who supported Rome. I let him know that my model was that of Luther. I then inquired as to his brand of loyalty.

The good news, for me at least, is that I have survived in spite of my provocative style.

## Thoughts about responding to my critics, friendly and otherwise

Why such a nice guy and clear thinker as I should have any critics is beyond me. But such is the case.

Let me start out by reporting the fact that I honestly and profoundly do not like controversy (especially over religious topics), even though I have been inundated with it for nearly forty years. As a result, I seek to avoid becoming involved in public debates and generally choose not to respond to my critics. I have no burden to argue about what I have written. In spite of perceptions, I love peace and acting agreeably, even when I am in disagreement.

One unfortunate exception to my general policy took place in the late 1980s after the Jones biography came out. The response began to form when I met (for the first time) the editor of the very aggressive *Adventist Currents*. He noted that he admired very much my *Myths* but disliked the Jones book. As a result, he told me that he had commissioned someone to "do a job on me and the book." I had previously heard that the attack was coming and now decided to ask why he hadn't done a piece on *Myths* since he liked it so much. He unequivocally told me that they "never did anything good" in the magazine. I replied that he should change the title to *Muddy Currents* and predicted his literary venture would have a brief life (which it did).

But while we were talking I asked if he would publish my response to the "job" they were performing on me. His response was affirmative. The result was a sequence that went from "Knight's Darkest Hour: Biography as Indictment" to my "A Spark in the Dark: A Reply to a Sermonette Masquerading as a Critique" to "A Fizzle in the Drizzle: A Reply to a Confession Masquerading as a Rebuttal." In actuality, I made no attempt at a rebuttal, but focused on the fact that the supposed critique was really a sermon setting forth the agenda they wanted to hear. My thought was that if they were so concerned they should write their own book on the topic. After all, it is a free country. But what I really took away from the sequence was the desire to avoid activities that manage to generate massive amounts of heat while generating no light.

My real aim in the church was to be a mediator between the right and left wings of the Adventist world. And in that I was successful in 1985 with *Myths*. Many were the letters of appreciation from both sides of the Adventist aisle. But two years later *From 1888 to Apostasy: The Case of A. T. Jones* had the polar opposite affect. Here I touched the patron saint of more than one group. Not only was I attacked by the radical, anti-organizational, extreme left, but all sorts of right-wing perfectionistic groups came out of the woodwork, including the periodical *Watchman What of the Night?* which classified me as the hierarchy's "hired assassin," while the 1888 Message Study Committee circulated a forty-three-page booklet exposing me and my evil ways to all the world. Thus with the Jones book my career as a mediatory voice came to an abrupt halt.

That is enough space for my "attackers." Now I need to say a few words about some of the thoughtful issues raised by my friends in this *festschrift*. Perhaps the most serious from a historian's point of view is that I failed to treat the early years of Jones. I admit to that flaw in my generally perfect character.

The shortcoming can be looked at from several perspectives: (1) that I was lazy or short on time, (2) that I am more interested in historical ideas and actions than in their underlying motivations, (3) that I have a congenital deformity that, while recognizing the importance of the early years, is not overly impressed with the explanatory power of Freudian concerns, or (4), my preferred response, that I have been generous enough to leave significant biographical territory for the next researcher in the field. But when all is said and done, I confess again my historiographical shortcoming.

On the other hand, I make no such confessions for my use of the conflict model in the Jones book. Conflict is what it was and all the participants, including Ellen White, knew it and used conflict language.

Regarding the suggestion that I didn't come out with a different picture of Ellen White in relation to Jones, all I really care to say at this point is that Jones was so extreme on nearly every topic that it was difficult for her to go wrong in her responses to him. That does not mean that I see Ellen White in the traditional hagiographic way. After all, it does appear that she fudged on the truth in her denial of the awareness and/or use of certain documents in her early health reform writings. And it is hard not to sympathize with Kellogg and others when private rebukes were made public. And then there is my lecture presented all over the world as "Another Look at the Vegetarian Virgin Mary" (although I often, of necessity, mask the title until part way through the presentation) and my open treatment of her marital, parenting, and other difficulties in *Walking With Ellen White* (1999).

The issues raised by Jon Dybdahl are of a different sort. He misread me in the area of victory and Adventist statistics. My argument was completely contexted in the post-Millerite world in which all groups failed except the Sabbatarians. The reason for the difference, I argued, was that the other movements lacked sufficient organization for extended outreach and without the apocalyptic imperative of prophecy had insufficient motivation for sustained mission to the world. In terms of general statistical success, I agree with Dybdahl and have published in other places the dismal percentage of success for what is still a small religious body in a very large world (currently about one-quarter of 1 percent). His call for analysis in relation to the charismatic movement is an excellent suggestion.

Jon also questioned how I would present the apocalyptic message to Hindus. I don't think I would. At least that is not where I would begin. The first step is always to present Christ as the unique way to salvation. That, in itself, is a massively difficult challenge in the Hindu world. Any treatment of the apocalyptic vision is a subsequent part of the educating task. Underlying my overall argument on the importance of the apocalyptic vision is that its primary purpose is for the motivation of the sending body to go to all the world. The reality is that the receiving people may or may not have the requisite information to even understand the apocalyptic vision. And that understanding it is certainly not necessary for their salvation.

On a slightly different missiological topic, I see no fault in beginning Adventist mission in new areas with already established church groups. Paul and others repeatedly set that model forth in the book of Acts. The problem is not where to begin, but in failing to move beyond the established Christian groups.

In closing this section, I suggest that constructive criticism serves a crucial purpose in the academic world. After all, every author's perspective (including my own I suppose) is less than complete, and of necessity the contribution of any given book is restricted by its purpose and space limitations.

Scholarship should be a dynamic process in which individuals, in the light of those who have gone before on a topic, make ever-closer approximations of its "truth." The progressiveness of good scholarship can be represented by the Hegelian dialectic. That is, one person's thesis, leads to another writer's antithesis, which hopefully eventuates into a third person's synthesis, which in turn becomes a new thesis as knowledge expands and seeks better understandings.

The "unfinishedness" and incomplete nature of scholarship is also represented by my words to students at the completion of a course: "Hopefully, this is not the end but the beginning of an ongoing exploration of ideas that have challenged you or that you think were handled inadequately." And with that I need to conclude with the admonition to all of my readers to write your own book. I will undoubtedly learn from it, whether you agree or disagree with me.

## And what about my future?

I have been working more or less intently since the age of eight when I stepped into the world of work by hocking newspapers on a street corner for five cents a hit (my take was 1 1/3 cents). I have written more than any "normal person" should desire, and for the past twenty years I have spent some part of roughly 10 percent of my days in an airplane (that works out to nearly two years of partial days). I am tired of traveling, tired of writing, tired of constant motion. What I would really like to do is stop and start smelling the roses before I receive my final earthly call to push up daisies and tulips. My ideal is to stop, but I'm not sure I have the fortitude to do so. I will know the answer in about ten years.

Meanwhile, although I am glad I spent my present life the way I did, if I had another one, as noted previously, I would undoubtedly reach out in my writings to the world beyond the restricted Adventist circle. For me that new challenge would build upon my work of trying to help Adventists understand themselves.

I have no doubt that I could put out another ten or twenty books before my brain finally turns to jelly. And if so, the following are some of the unfinished projects close to my heart and mind.

Among those most likely of completion are the following:

1. An extension that I have been working on in the area of my work in soteriology, tentatively titled *Knight's Revised Standard Vegetarian Version of the Bible and the Flavors of Salvation.*
2. A book on the stages of the development of Adventist educational thought. Once again, this manuscript is almost ready for final development.
3. A collection of my seminal articles on Adventist education.
4. A similar collection related to Ellen White.

Beyond those are other projects in various stages of development:

1. A commentary on Daniel.
2. An autobiography titled *Born Naked,* although a portion of the Adventist population thinks that the title of Michael Moore's autobiography, *Here Comes Trouble,* would be more appropriate.
3. A book titled *Becoming Peculiar: Studies in Adventist Lifestyle,* a refinement of my class presentations on the topic.
4. A volume expanding to book length my publications on the stages of Adventist mission development.
5. Filling out the promise of further work on a four-volume expansion of my analysis of Adventist historical theology, as hinted at in the preface to *A Search for Identity.*
6. And last, the project I would most value, a three-volume treatment of inspiration that would include its development in the history of the Christian church, a theological study of the topic, and an inductive study of Scripture to develop a truly biblical understanding of inspiration and hermeneutics. That last volume is the most crucial, since endless controversy has resulted from superimposing theories on the Bible instead of examining the internal evidences, which are much more plentiful than most people realize.

I don't know if I will do any of those books. But I still wake with new ideas ready to be developed. I enjoy the stimulating sensation for about fifteen minutes and then calm down enough to get busy with those parts of my life that have suffered neglect.

## And what have I learned in my search for meaning?

I could say with Solomon that it is all vanity. But I would phrase it differently. I think it all boils down to two conclusions.

First, I have observed that plants grow best in manure and that I have been up to my armpits in it for more than seventy years, in spite of the fact that some nearsighted individuals view me as moving from one success to another.

Second, that my life flashes forth one crucial message: "Saved by grace!" And that, in the words of Ecclesiastes, is "the conclusion of the whole matter" in a "muttish" search for meaning in a seemingly meaningless universe.

# Selected Bibliography

# of George R. Knight

(As of June 2014)

## Books authored

*Philosophy and Education: An Introduction in Christian Perspective.* Berrien Springs, Mich.: Andrews University Press, 1980. 2nd ed. 1989, 3rd ed. 1998, 4th ed. 2006. Also translated and published in Korean (1987), Romanian (1998), Portuguese (2001), Spanish (2002), German (2003), French (2004), Indonesian (2008), and Russian (forthcoming).

*Issues and Alternatives in Educational Philosophy.* Berrien Springs, Mich.: Andrews University Press, 1982. 2nd ed. 1989. 3rd ed. 1998. 4th ed. 2008. Also translated and published in Chinese (1995, 2002; 4th ed., forthcoming).

*Myths in Adventism: An Interpretive Study of Ellen White, Education, and Related Issues.* Washington, D.C.: Review and Herald® Publishing Assn., 1985. Twenty-fifth anniversary ed., Review and Herald®, 2010. Also translated and published in Portuguese (2010) and French and Russian (forthcoming).

*From 1888 to Apostasy: The Case of A. T. Jones.* Washington, D.C.: Review and Herald® Publishing Assn., 1987.

*Angry Saints: Tensions and Possibilities in the Adventist Struggle Over Righteousness by Faith.* Washington, D.C.: Review and Herald® Publishing Assn., 1989. Reprint by Pacific Press® forthcoming. Also translated and published in German (2010).

*My Gripe With God: A Study in Divine Justice and the Problem of the Cross.* Washington, D.C.: Review and Herald® Publishing Assn., 1990. Also translated and published in Russian (1998) and Romanian (forthcoming).

*The Pharisee's Guide to Perfect Holiness: A Study of Sin and Salvation.* Boise, Idaho: Pacific Press® Publishing Assn., 1992. Also translated and published in German (1997), Korean (1997), and Spanish (1998).

*Anticipating the Advent: A Brief History of Seventh-day Adventism.* Boise, Idaho: Pacific Press® Publishing Assn., 1993. Also translated and published in German (1994), Italian (1994), Danish (1995), and Japanese (1995).

*Millennial Fever and the End of the World: A Study of Millerite Adventism.* Boise, Idaho: Pacific Press® Publishing Assn., 1993. Also translated and published in Russian (forthcoming 2014).

*Matthew: The Gospel of the Kingdom.* Boise, Idaho: Pacific Press® Publishing Assn., 1994. Translated and published in Spanish in Inter-America (1997) and South America (1998).

*I Used to Be Perfect: An Ex-Idealist Looks at Law, Sin, and Grace.* Boise, Idaho: Pacific Press® Publishing Assn., 1994. Second edition published as *I Used to Be Perfect: A Study of Sin and Salvation.* Berrien Springs, Mich.: Andrews University Press, 2001. Also translated and published in Japanese (1995), French (1998 and 2004), Latvian (2002), Estonian (2002), Romanian (2005), Czech (2005), Korean (2009), Chinese (2012), and Spanish (2013).

*The Fat Lady and the Kingdom: Adventist Mission Confronts the Challenges of Secularization and Institutionalism.* Boise, Idaho: Pacific Press® Publishing Assn., 1995.

Also translated and published in Korean (2000) and German (2004).

*Meeting Ellen White: An Introduction to Her Life, Writings, and Major Themes.* Hagerstown, Md.: Review and Herald® Publishing Assn., 1996. Also translated and published in German (1998), Serbian (1998), Croatian (1999), Korean (2000), Hungarian (2000), Czech (2000), Spanish (2001 and 2012), Italian (1998), Bulgarian (n.d.), Portuguese (2006), Russian (2006), Dutch (2008), and French (forthcoming).

*Walking With Jesus on the Mount of Blessing.* Hagerstown, Md.: Review and Herald® Publishing Assn., 1996, by Signs Publishing Co., Warburton, Australia, 1996 and by Oriental Watchman Publishing House, Pune, India, 1998. Also translated and published in Korean (1996); Romanian, Russian, and Croatian (1997); Ukrainian, Serbian, and Latvian (1998); Portuguese (2000); Estonian (2004); Czech (2008); and Spanish (forthcoming 2014).

*Reading Ellen White: How to Understand and Apply Her Writings.* Hagerstown, Md.: Review and Herald® Publishing Assn., 1997. Also translated and published in German (1998), French (1999 and 2008), Latvian (1999), Czech (2000), Korean (2000), Hungarian (2001), Bulgarian (n.d.), Spanish (2004 and 2012), Russian (2006), Japanese (2007), Dutch (2008), Chinese (2012), and Portuguese (forthcoming 2014).

*A User-Friendly Guide to the 1888 Message.* Hagerstown, Md.: Review and Herald® Publishing Assn., 1998. Also translated and published in Portuguese (2003) and Russian (2003).

*Ellen White's World.* Hagerstown, Md.: Review and Herald® Publishing Assn., 1998. Also translated and published either in whole or in part in Korean (2000), Czech (2000), German (2001), Hungarian (2002), Bulgarian (n.d.), Russian (2006), Czech (2008), and Spanish (2012).

*Ellen White and Her Writings.* Never published in English but translated and published in Norwegian (1999) and in Finnish (2000).

*A Brief History of Seventh-day Adventists* (published as a revised version of

*Anticipating the Advent*) Hagerstown, Md.: Review and Herald® Publishing Assn., 1999. 2nd ed. 2004, 3rd ed. 2012. Also translated and published in Portuguese (2000), Croatian (2002), Czech (2003), Spanish (2005), Dutch (2006), and Thai and French (forthcoming).

*Walking With Ellen White: The Human Interest Story.* Hagerstown, Md.: Review and Herald® Publishing Assn., 1999. Also translated and published in whole or in part in Korean (2000), German (2001), Hungarian (2001), Bulgarian (n.d.), Spanish in Inter-America (2006) and South America (2010), Russian (2006), Spanish (2012), and French (forthcoming).

*A Search for Identity: The Development of Seventh-day Adventist Beliefs.* Hagerstown, Md.: Review and Herald® Publishing Assn., 2000. Also translated and published either in whole or in part in German, Finnish, and Italian (2002); Portuguese and Danish (2005); Dutch (2006); Spanish, Czech, and Korean (2007); French (2008); Russian (2009); Norwegian (2011); Japanese (2013); and Croatian (forthcoming).

*Organizing to Beat the Devil: The Development of Seventh-day Adventist Organization.* Hagerstown, Md.: Review and Herald® Publishing Assn., 2001. Also translated and published in Spanish (2007) and Russian (forthcoming).

*Walking With Paul Through Romans.* Hagerstown, Md.: Review and Herald® Publishing Assn., 2002. Also translated and published in Spanish and French (2002); Korean, Indonesian, and Croatian (2003); Bulgarian (n.d.); Latvian (2004); Serbian (2005); Polish (2011); and Estonian (2013).

*Exploring Hebrews.* Hagerstown, Md.: Review and Herald® Publishing Assn., 2003. Also translated and published in Chinese (2009) and Slovene (forthcoming).

*Joseph Bates: The Real Founder of Seventh-day Adventism.* Hagerstown, Md.: Review and Herald® Publishing Assn., 2004. Also translated and published in German (2007) and Korean (2013).

*Exploring Mark.* Hagerstown, Md.: Review and Herald® Publishing Assn., 2004. Also translated and published in German (2005), Chinese (2009), and Slovene (forthcoming).

*Exploring Galatians and Ephesians.* Hagerstown, Md.: Review and Herald® Publishing Assn., 2005. Also translated in whole or in part in German (2005), Chinese (2009), and Slovene (forthcoming).

*Organizing for Mission and Growth: The Development of Adventist Church Structure* (previously published as *Organizing to Beat the Devil*). Hagerstown, Md.: Review and Herald® Publishing Assn., 2006. Also translated and published in French (forthcoming).

*Exploring Ecclesiastes and Song of Solomon.* Hagerstown, Md.: Review and Herald® Publishing Assn., 2006. Also translated and published in Slovene (forthcoming).

*If I Were the Devil! Adventism's Mission, Structures, and Challenges for the 21st Century.* Hagerstown, Md.: Review and Herald® Publishing Assn., 2007. Also translated and published in Spanish and Romanian (forthcoming).

*The Cross of Christ: God's Work for Us.* Hagerstown, Md.: Review and Herald® Publishing Assn., 2008. (Revised version of *My Gripe With God.*) Also translated and published in Spanish (2009); and Russian, Spanish in Inter-America, and Danish (2010).

*Lest We Forget.* Hagerstown, Md.: Review and Herald® Publishing Assn., 2008. Also translated and published in Latvian and Korean (2009); Chinese (2010); Portuguese and Russian (2011); French, Spanish, and Papiamento (2013); Danish, Finnish, and new Portugese translation (forthcoming).

*The Apocalyptic Vision and the Neutering of Adventism.* Hagerstown, Md.: Review and Herald® Publishing Assn., 2008. Rev. ed. 2009. Also translated and published in Spanish and Romanian (2009); Portuguese, French, Czech, and Russian (2010); German (2011); Chinese (2012); and Korean (forthcoming).

*Sin and Salvation: God's Work for Us and in Us.* Hagerstown, Md.: Review and Herald® Publishing Assn., 2008. (Revised version of *The Pharisee's Guide to Perfect Holiness.*) Also translated and published in Portuguese (forthcoming).

*Exploring the Letters of John and Jude.* Hagerstown, Md.: Review and Herald® Publishing Assn., 2009.

*Exploring Romans.* Hagerstown, Md.: Review and Herald® Publishing Assn., 2010.

*William Miller and the Rise of Adventism.* Nampa, Idaho, Pacific Press® Publishing Assn., 2010. (Revised version of *Millennial Fever and the End of the World: A Study of Millerite Adventism.*) Also translated and published in Portuguese (forthcoming).

*Alonzo T. Jones: Point Man on Adventism's Charismatic Frontier.* Hagerstown, Md.: Review and Herald® Publishing Assn., 2011.

*The Truth.* Doral, Florida: Associación Publicadora Interamericana. Simultaneously published in French and Spanish (2012).

*Exploring Thessalonians.* Hagerstown, Md.: Review and Herald® Publishing Assn., 2012.

*Turn Your Eyes Upon Jesus.* Hagerstown, Md.: Review and Herald® Publishing Assn., 2013. Also translated and published in Latvian (forthcoming).

*Educating for Eternity: An Adventist Philosophy of Education.* Berrien Springs, Mich.: Andrews University Press, forthcoming.

## Books edited

*Early Adventist Educators.* Berrien Springs, Mich.: Andrews University Press, 1983.

*Die Adventisten und Hamburg: Von der Ortsgemeinde zur internationalen Bewegung.* Edited jointly with with Baldur E. Pfeiffer and Lothar Träder, Frankfurt am Main: Peter Lang, 1992.

*1844 and the Rise of Sabbatarian Adventism.* Hagerstown, Md.: Review and Herald® Publishing Assn., 1994.

*Seventh-day Adventists Answer Questions on Doctrine,* critical ed. Berrien Springs, Mich.: Andrews University Press, 2003.

## Book series edited as general editor

### *Abundant Life Bible Amplifier Commentary Series*

*Hebrews: Full Assurance for Christians Today,* by William G. Johnsson. Boise, Idaho: Pacific Press® Publishing Assn., 1994. Translated and published in Korean (1999) and German (2003).

*Exodus: God Creates a People,* by Jon L. Dybdahl. Boise, Idaho: Pacific Press® Publishing Assn., 1994. Translated and published in Spanish (1995 and 1997).

*Timothy and Titus: Counsel to Young Pastors for Struggling Churches,* by Charles E. Bradford. Boise, Idaho: Pacific Press® Publishing Assn., 1994. Translated and published in Spanish (1997).

*Matthew: The Gospel of the Kingdom,* by George R. Knight. Boise, Idaho: Pacific Press® Publishing Assn., 1994. Translated and published in Spanish (1997 and 1998).

*John: Jesus Gives Life to a New Generation,* by Jon Paulien. Boise, Idaho: Pacific Press® Publishing Assn., 1995. Translated and published in German (2000) and Spanish (2001).

*Peter and Jude: Living in Dangerous Times,* by Robert M. Johnston. Boise, Idaho: Pacific Press® Publishing Assn., 1995. Translated and published in Spanish (2006).

*Samuel: From the Danger of Chaos to the Danger of Power,* by Alden Thompson. Boise, Idaho: Pacific Press® Publishing Assn., 1995. Translated and published in Spanish (2002).

*Romans: Mercy for All,* by John C. Brunt. Boise, Idaho: Pacific Press® Publishing Assn., 1996. Translated and published in German (1999).

*Daniel 1-7: Prophecy as History,* by William H. Shea. Boise, Idaho: Pacific Press® Publishing Assn., 1996. Translated and published in German (1998) and Korean (1999).

*Daniel 7-12: Prophecies of the End Time,* by William H. Shea. Boise, Idaho: Pacific Press® Publishing Assn., 1996. Published in German (1998).

*Hosea-Micah: A Call to Radical Reform,* by John L. Dybdahl. Boise, Idaho: Pacific Press® Publishing Assn., 1996.

*James: True Religion in Suffering,* by Pedrito Maynard-Reid. Boise, Idaho: Pacific Press® Publishing Assn., 1996. Translated and published in Spanish (1999).

*Ezekiel: Through Crisis to Victory,* by Robert K. McIver. Boise, Idaho: Pacific Press® Publishing Assn., 1997.

*First Corinthians: The Essentials and Nonessentials of Christian Living,* by W. Larry Richards. Boise, Idaho: Pacific Press® Publishing Assn., 1997.

*Second Corinthians: God's Way Is the Best Way,* by W. Larry Richards. Boise, Idaho: Pacific Press® Publishing Assn., 1998.

## Adventist Classic Library Series

*Life Incidents, in Connection With the Great Advent Movement,* by James White. Historical introduction by Jerry Moon. Berrien Springs, Mich.: Andrews University Press, 2003.

*Seventh-day Adventists Answer Questions on Doctrine.* Critical notes and historical and theological introduction by George R. Knight. Berrien Springs, Mich.: Andrews University Press, 2003. Also translated and published in Portuguese and Spanish (2009) and Romanian (forthcoming).

*Autobiography of Joseph Bates.* Historical introduction by Gary Land. Berrien Springs, Mich.: Andrews University Press, 2004.

*Memoirs of William Miller.* Historical introduction by Merlin D. Burt. Berrien Springs, Mich.: Andrews University Press, 2005.

*Historical Sketches of the Foreign Missions of the Seventh-day Adventists.* Historical introduction by George R. Knight. Berrien Springs, Mich.: Andrews University Press, 2005.

*Earliest Seventh-day Adventist Periodicals.* Historical introduction by George R. Knight. Berrien Springs, Mich.: Andrews University Press, 2005.

*History of the Second Advent Message and Mission, Doctrine and People,* by Isaac C. Wellcome. Historical introduction by Gary Land. Berrien Springs, Mich.: Andrews University Press, 2008.

## Adventist Pioneer Series

*James White: Innovator and Overcomer,* by Gerald Wheeler. Hagerstown, Md.: Review and Herald® Publishing Assn., 2003. Also translated and published in German (2006).

*Joseph Bates: The Real Founder of Seventh-day Adventism,* by George R. Knight. Hagerstown, Md.: Review and Herald® Publishing Assn., 2004. Also translated and published in German (2008).

*W. W. Prescott: Forgotten Giant of Adventism's Second Generation,* by Gilbert M. Valentine. Hagerstown, Md.: Review and Herald® Publishing Assn., 2005.

*John Harvey Kellogg, M.D.: Pioneering Health Reformer,* by Richard W. Schwarz. Hagerstown, Md.: Review and Herald® Publishing Assn., 2006.

*E. J. Waggoner: From the Physician of Good News to the Agent of Division,* by Woodrow W. Whidden II. Hagerstown, Md.: Review and Herald® Publishing Assn., 2008.

*Lewis C. Sheafe: Apostle to Black America,* by Douglas Morgan. Hagerstown, Md.: Review and Herald® Publishing Assn., 2010.

*Alonzo T. Jones: Point Man on Adventism's Charismatic Frontier,* by George R. Knight. Hagerstown, Md.: Review and Herald® Publishing Assn., 2011.

*J. N. Loughborough: Last of the Adventist Pioneers,* by Brian E. Strayer. Hagerstown, Md.: Review and Herald®, 2014.

*Uriah Smith: Editor-in-Chief,* by Gary Land. Hagerstown, Md.: Review and Herald®, forthcoming 2014.

## Library of Adventist Theology Series (series editor with Woodrow Whidden)

*The Cross of Christ: God's Work for Us,* by George R. Knight. Hagerstown, Md.: Review and Herald® Publishing Assn., 2008.

*Sin and Salvation: God's Work for Us and in Us,* by George R. Knight. Hagerstown, Md.: Review and Herald® Publishing Assn., 2008

*The Body of Christ: A Biblical Understanding of the Church,* by Reinder Bruinsma. Hagerstown, Md.: Review and Herald® Publishing Assn., 2010.

*The Judgment and Assurance: The Dynamics of Personal Salvation,* by Woodrow Whidden. Hagerstown, Md.: Review and Herald® Publishing Assn., 2012.

## Book chapters authored

"The Transformation of Change and the Future Role of Education." In *Philosophy of the Humanistic Society,* edited by Alfred E. Koenig, 226, 227. Washington, D.C.: University Press of America, 1981.

"Early Adventists and Education." In *Early Adventist Educators,* edited by George R. Knight, 1–10. Berrien Springs, Mich.: Andrews University Press, 1983.

"Ellen G. White: Prophet." In *Early Adventist Educators,* 26–49.

"Frederick Griggs: Moderate." In *Early Adventist Educators,* 184–204. Co-authored with Arnold Reye.

"A Bibliography of Works Relating to Seventh-day Adventist Education." In *Early Adventist Educators,* 239–243.

"Seventh-day Adventist Education: A Historical Sketch and Profile." In *Religious Schooling in America,* edited by James C. Carper and Thomas C. Hunt, 85–109. Birmingham, Ala.: Religious Education Press, 1984.

"Seventh-day Adventist Schools." In *Religious Schools in America: A Selected*

*Bibliography,* edited by Thomas C. Hunt, James C. Carper, and Charles R, Kniker, 283–296. New York: Garland, 1986.

"The Transformation of Education." In *The World of Ellen White,* edited by Gary Land, 161–175. Washington, D.C.: Review and Herald® Publishing Assn., 1987.

"Seventh-day Adventist Colleges and Universities." In *Religious Colleges and Universities in America: A Selected Bibliography,* edited by Thomas C. Hunt, James C. Carper, and Charles R. Kniker, 277–285. New York: Garland, 1988.

"Seventh-day Adventist Seminaries." In *Religious Seminaries in America: A Selected Bibliography,* edited by Thomas C. Hunt and James C. Carper, 170, 171. New York: Garland, 1989.

"From Shut Door to Worldwide Mission: The Dynamic Context of Early German Adventism." In *Die Adventisten und Hamburg: Von der Ortsgemeinde zur internationalen Bewegung,* edited by Baldur E. Pfeiffer, Lothar Träder, and George R. Knight, 46–69. Frankfurt am Main: Peter Lang, 1992.

"Amish, Methodists, Adventists and Changing Standards and Values: A Historical Perspective." In *Perspectives on Values,* edited by Bailey Gillespie, 176–213. La Sierra, Calif.: La Sierra University Press, 1993.

"Seventh-day Adventist Schooling in the United States." In *Religious Schools in the United States, K-12: A Source Book,* edited by James C. Carper and Thomas C. Hunt, 97–126. New York: Garland, 1993.

"Moving Beyond Reductionism: A Response to Peter DeBoer." In *Educating Christian Teachers for Responsible Discipleship,* edited by Peter DeBoer et al., 26–29. Washington, D.C.: University Press of America, 1993.

"A Reply to Martin Weber." In *Who's Got the Truth? Making Sense Out of Five Different Adventist Gospels,* by Martin Weber, 50–53. Silver Spring, Md.: Home Study International Press, 1994.

"Adventism's Missiological Quadrilateral: A Wholistic Approach to World Mission." In *The Development of the Seventh-day Adventist Church in Eastern Africa:*

*Past, Present, and Future,* edited by K. B. Elineema, 17–30. Dar es Salaam, Tanzania: University of Dar es Salaam Press, 1995.

"Caught Red-Handed." In *College Faith,* edited by Ronald Alan Knott, 46, 47. Boise, Idaho: Pacific Press® Publishing Assn., 1995.

"Seventh-day Adventist Higher Education in the United States." In *Religious Higher Education in the United States: A Source Book,* edited by Thomas C. Hunt and James C. Carper, 387–412. New York: Garland, 1996.

"Foreword." In *Christian Faith and Religious Freedom,* by V. Norskov Olsen, 7–10. Brushton, N.Y.: TEACH Services, 1996.

"Adventism and Military Service: Individual Conscience in Ethical Tension." In *Proclaim Peace: Christian Pacificism from Unexpected Quarters,* edited by Theron Schlabach and Richard T. Hughes, 157–171. Urbana, Ill.: University of Illinois Press, 1997.

"A Distasteful Answer to Prayer." In *God Answers Prayer,* edited by William Johnsson, 45–47. Silver Spring, Md.: *Adventist Review,* 1997.

"Early Adventists and Ordination: 1844–1863." In *Women in Ministry: Biblical and Historical Perspectives,* edited by Nancy Vyhmeister, 101–114. Berrien Springs, Mich.: Andrews University Press, 1998.

"Remnant Theology and World Mission." In *Adventist Mission Faces the 21st Century,* edited by Jon Dybdahl, 88–95. Hagerstown, Md.: Review and Herald® Publishing Assn., 1999.

"Blending Two Families: His and Hers." In *Maximum Marriage,* by Peggy and Roger Dudley, 89–93. Hagerstown, Md.: Review and Herald® Publishing Assn., 2003. Co-authored with with Bonnie Knight.

"Foreword." In *James White: Innovator and Overcomer,* by Gerald Wheeler, xi, xii. Hagerstown, Md.: Review and Herald® Publishing Assn., 2003.

"Preface to the Annotated Edition." In *Seventh-day Adventists Answer Questions on*

*Doctrine,* critical ed., edited by George R. Knight, xi, xii. Berrien Springs, Mich.: Andrews University Press, 2003.

"Historical and Theological Introduction." In *Seventh-day Adventists Answer Questions on Doctrine,* critical ed., edited by George R. Knight, xiii–xxxvi. Berrien Springs, Mich.: Andrews University Press, 2003.

"Introduzione." In Italian edition of Ellen White's *Last Day Events* (*Ultimi giorni: Come affrontare la crisi finale*), 5, 6. Firenze: Edizioni ADV, 2003.

"Joseph Bates: Originator of Seventh-day Adventist Mission Theory." In *Mission: A Man With a Vision,* edited by Rudi Maier, 3–10. Berrien Springs, Mich.: Andrews University Department of World Mission, 2005.

"Foreword." In *W. W. Prescott: Forgotten Giant of Adventism's Second Generation,* by Gilbert M. Valentine, 21, 22. Hagerstown, Md.: Review and Herald® Publishing Assn., 2005.

"Historical Introduction." In *Earliest Seventh-day Adventist Periodicals,* vii–xxxvi. Berrien Springs, Mich.: Andrews University Press, 2005.

"Historical Introduction." In *Historical Sketches of the Foreign Missions of the Seventh-day Adventists,* v–xxxv. Berrien Springs, Mich.: Andrews University Press, 2005.

"Foreword." In *Questions on Doctrine Revisited: Keys to the Doctrine of the Atonement and Experience of At-one-ment,* by A. Leroy Moore, 7, 8. Ithaca, Mich.: AB Publishing, 2005.

"Preface." In *People Are Human (Look What They Did to Ellen White),* by Graeme Bradford, 11–14. Warburton, Australia: Signs Publishing, 2006,

"Foreword." In *John Harvey Kellogg, M.D.: Pioneering Health Reformer,* by Richard W. Schwarz, 9, 10. Hagerstown, Md.: Review and Herald® Publishing Assn., 2006.

"Preface." In *The 19th Century Odyssey of John and Judith: From the Battlefields of the Civil War to Spiritual Battlefields on the Texas Frontier,* by G. Tom Carter, 5, 6. Silver Spring, Md.: Ministerial Association of Seventh-day Adventists, 2007.

"Foreword." In *E. J. Waggoner: From the Physician of Good News to the Agent of Division,* by Woodrow W. Whidden II, 15, 16. Hagerstown, Md.: Review and Herald® Publishing Assn., 2008.

"Visions and the Word: The Authority of Ellen White in Relationship to the Authority of Scripture in the Seventh-day Adventist Movement." In *By What Authority? The Vital Question of Religious Authority in Christianity,* edited by Robert L. Millet, 144–161. Macon, Ga.: Mercer University Press, 2010.

"Foreword." In *The Body of Christ: A Biblical Understanding of the Church,* by Reinder Bruinsma, 9. Hagerstown, Md.: Review and Herald® Publishing Assn., 2010. Co-authored with Woodrow W. Whidden.

"Apostolic Succession, the Great Commissions, and Adventist Mission in a 'Greek' World." In *Encountering God in Life and Mission,* edited by Rudi Maier, 189–199. Berrien Springs, Mich.: Department of World Mission, Andrews University, 2010.

"Foreword." In *Lewis C. Sheafe: Apostle to Black America,* by Douglas Morgan, 11, 12. Hagerstown, Md.: Review and Herald® Publishing Assn., 2010.

"Foreword." In *The Prophets and the Presidents,* by Gilbert M. Valentine, 11–13. Nampa, Idaho: Pacific Press® Publishing Assn., 2011.

"A Word to the Reader." In *The Judgment and Assurance: The Dynamics of Personal Salvation,* by Woodrow Whidden, 9, 10. Hagerstown, Md.: Review and Herald® Publishing Assn., 2012.

"Foreword." In *J. N. Loughborough: Last of the Adventist Pioneers,* by Brian Strayer. Hagerstown, Md.: Review and Herald® Publishing Assn., 2014.

"Foreword." In *The Close of Probation,* by Marvin Moore, 11, 12. Nampa, Idaho: Pacific Press® Publishing Assn., 2014.

"An Academic 'Mutt's' Search for Meaning." In *Adventist Maverick,* edited by Gilbert Valentine and Woodrow Whidden, 217–250. Nampa, Idaho: Pacific Press® Publishing Assn., 2014.

"Vorwort." In the German edition of *Continuity and Change in Adventist Teaching*, by Rolf J. Pöhler, Frankfurt am Main: Peter Lang, forthcoming.

"The Historical Development of Seventh-day Adventist Doctrine." In *Adventist Beliefs*, edited by Gerald Klingbeil, forthcoming.

"Hermeneutics: How to Read Ellen White's Writings." In *Ellen White's Writings*, edited by Merlin Burt, forthcoming.

"Foreword." In *A Man Called Roy*, by Shirley McGarrell, forthcoming.

"Walking With Jesus Every Day." In *Revival and Reformation: Spiritual Supplement*, forthcoming.

"Contemporary Prophetism, Modern Prophets, and the Bible: Two Divergent Paths and Their Meaning for the Twenty-First Century." In *The Holy Spirit in Adventist Theology*, edited by Alberto Timm, forthcoming.

"The Sinful Nature and Spiritual Inability." In *Contours of the Seventh-day Adventist Doctrine of Salvation*, edited by Martin Hanna, Darius Jankiewicz, and John Reeve. Berrien Springs, Mich.: Andrews University Press, forthcoming.

"The Grace That Comes Before Saving Grace." In *Contours of the Seventh-day Adventist Doctrine of Salvation*, edited by Martin Hanna, Darius Jankiewicz, and John Reeve. Berrien Springs, Mich.: Andrews University Press, forthcoming.

"Background and Roots of Seventh-day Adventist Theology." In *Studies in Adventist Theology*, edited by Eugene V. Zaitsev,, forthcoming. Co-authored with Alberto R. Timm.

"James White Finds the Answer: The Hermeneutical Key That Allowed Early Adventists to Make Decisions on Topics not Adequately Covered in Scripture." In *Women in Ministry*, edited by Nancy Vhymeister, Karen Abrahamson, and John Reeve. Berrien Springs, Mich.: Andrews University Press, forthcoming.

"The Issue of Time in Seventh-day Adventist History: Adventism's Only Problem." In *Issues in Adventist History*, edited by John Reeve, forthcoming.

"Foreword." In *Ellen G. White and the Gift of Prophecy: A User-Friendly Introduction to Her Prophetic Life and Ministry,* by Michael Campbell. Silver Spring, Md.: North American Division of Seventh-day Adventists, forthcoming.

"Foreword." In *Uriah Smith: Editor and Interpreter of Prophecy,* by Gary Land, Hagerstown, Md.: Review and Herald® Publishing Assn., forthcoming.

"Foreword." In *Escape From the Rocking Chair: What Every Adventist Should Know About Mission and Success,* by Abraham Guerrero, forthcoming.

"Faith in Tension, the Great War and Internationalism, and a Lost Part of Adventist Heritage." In *The Impact of World War I on Seventh-day Adventism,* edited by Rolf Pöhler et al. Friedensau, Germany: Theologische Hochschule Friedensau, forthcoming 2015.

"The Historical Development of Ellen White's Educational Philosophy." In *Essays in Honor of Merling K. Alomia,* edited by Joel Iparraguirre. Lima, Peru: Universidad Peruana Unión, Publicaciones y Difusión Cultural, forthcoming 2015.

"Foreword." In *Stephen Nelson Haskell: Son of New England, by* Gerald Wheeler. Nampa, Idaho: Pacific Press® Publishing Assn., forthcoming 2015.

## Entries authored for reference works

"Adventisten: I. Entstehung, Geschichte, Ausbreitung und Lehre." In *Die Religion in Geschichte und Geganwart,* vol. 1, 4th ed., edited by Hans Dieter Betz et al., 127–130. Tübingen, Germany: J. C. B. Mohr, 1998. Also published in English as "Adventists." In *Religion Past and Present: Encyclopedia of Theology and Religion,* vol. 1, edited by Hans Dieter Betz et al., 68–70. Leiden, Netherlands: Brill, 2007.

"Continental Philosophy of Education." In *Evangelical Dictionary of Christian Education,* edited by Michael J. Anthony, 175, 176. Grand Rapids, Mich.: Baker Academic, 2001.

"Seventh-day Adventist Education." In *Evangelical Dictionary of Christian Education,* 627, 628.

"Adventism." In *Encyclopedia of the Great Plains*, edited by David J. Wishart, 735. Lincoln, Neb.: University of Nebraska Press, 2004.

"White, Ellen G." In *Diccionario Ilustrado de Intérprete de la Fe*, edited by Justo L. González, 478, 479. Barcelona, Spain: Editorial Calidad en Literatura Evangélica, 2004. Co-authored with Edwin Hernandez. Also published in English as "White, Ellen G." In *Westminster Dictionary of Theologians*, trans. Suzanne E. Hoeferkamp Segovia, 354, 355. Louisville: Westminster John Knox Prress, 2006.

"Adventist and Millennialist Denominational Families." In *Encyclopedia of Religion in America*, vol. 1, edited by Charles H. Lippy and Peter W. Williams, 21–25. Washington, D.C.: CQ Press, 2010.

"Seventh-day Adventists." In *Encyclopedia of Religion in America*, vol. 4, 2065–2068.

"Inspiration of the Bible." In *Andrews Study Bible*, edited by Jon L. Dybdahl, xxv, xxvi. Berrien Springs, Mich.: Andrews University Press, 2010. Also "Message of the Bible," xxvii-xxx; "Reading the Bible," 1691, 1692; "Studying the Bible," 1693–1695; "Annotated Theme Index," 1700–1703.

"Ellen White's Writings" (major introductory essay). In *Ellen G. White Encyclopedia*, edited by Denis Fortin and Jerry Moon. Hagerstown, Md.: Review and Herald® Publishing Assn., 2014. Also "Bates, Joseph," "Canright, Dudley M.," "Canright, Lucretia," "Christian Connexion," "Church Organization," "City Mission," "Colcord, Willard A.," "Conflict of the Ages Series," "Competition," "Fitch, Charles," "General Conference Session of 1888," "Harbor Springs, Michigan," "Hillcrest School," "Interpreting Ellen White's Writings," "Jones, Alonzo T.," "Law of God," "Military Service," "Mormonism," "Oberlin College," "Rice, Anna C.," "Rice, J. D.," "The 'Scattering' and 'Gathering' Times."

## Journal and magazine articles authored

One hundred and fifty-two articles published between October 1977 and June 2014.

## Doctoral dissertations directed

"William Warren Prescott: Seventh-day Adventist Educator," by Gilbert Murray Valentine, PhD diss., 1982.

"Goodloe Harper Bell: Pioneer Seventh-day Adventist Christian Educator," by Allan G. Lindsay, EdD diss., 1982.

"Frederick Griggs: Seventh-day Adventist Educator and Administrator," by Arnold Colin Reye, PhD diss., 1984.

"Edward Alexander Sutherland and Seventh-day Adventist Educational Reform: The Denominational Years, 1890-1904," by Warren Sidney Ashworth, PhD diss., 1986.

"Alexander Hegius (ca. 1433-98): His Life, Philosophy, and Pedagogy," by John V. G. Matthews, PhD diss., 1988.

"The Historical Development of Seventh-day Adventist Eschatology, 1884-1895," by Roy Israel McGarrell, PhD diss., 1989.

"William Clarence (W. C.) White: His Relationship to Ellen G. White and Her Work," by Jerry Allan Moon, PhD diss., 1993.

"Enthusiasm and Charismatic Manifestations in Sabbatarian Adventism With Applications for the Seventh-day Adventist Church of the Late Twentieth Century," by James Michael Wilson, DMin diss., 1995.

"The Sanctuary and the Three Angels' Messages, 1844-1863: Integrating Factors in the Development of Seventh-day Adventist Doctrines," by Alberto R. Timm, PhD diss., 1995.

"The Colton Celebration Congregation: A Case Study in American Adventist Worship Renewal, 1986-1991," by Viviane Haenni, PhD diss., 1996.

"The Historical Background, Interconnected Development, and Integration of the Doctrines of the Sanctuary, the Sabbath, and Ellen G. White's Role in Sabbatarian Adventism From 1844 to 1849," by Merlin D. Burt, PhD diss., 2002.

"Reactions to the Seventh-day Adventist Evangelical Conferences and *Questions on Doctrine*, 1955-1971," by Juhyeuk Nam, PhD diss., 2005.

"The Development of the Seventh-day Adventist Understanding of Ellen G. White's Prophetic Gift, 1844-1889," by Theodore N. Levterov, PhD diss., 2011.

## Published book reviews

Seventy-four authored between 1979 and 2009.

## Awards and honors

*John Nevins Andrews Medallion* (for Academic Achievement), Andrews University, February 1989

*Andrews University Award for Excellence in Faculty Research* (1) June 1994, (2) May 1996, (3) April 1999

*Award of Excellence* (June 1996) from Excellence in Media for "Neither Ape nor Angel," *Signs of the Times*, March 1995

*Award of Merit* (June 1998) from the Associated Church Press for "The Infinite Hitler," *Signs of the Times*, July 1997

*Honored Alumnus of the Year Award*, Pacific Union College, April 20, 2002

*The Daniel A. Augsburger Excellence in Teaching Award*, Andrews University, March 9, 2003

*The Charles Elliott Weniger Award for Excellence*, by the Weniger Society, Loma Linda, California, January 30, 2010

# List of Contributors

Michael W. Campbell,
Assistant Professor of Adventist Studies,
Adventist International Institute of Advanced Studies, Cavite, Philippines

Jon L. Dybdahl,
Missionary Pastor, Professor, and Former University President,
Walla Walla, Washington

Paul M. Evans,
Assistant Professor,
Theology Department, Sahmyook University, Seoul, South Korea

Denis Fortin,
Professor of Historical Theology,
Seventh-day Adventist Theological Seminary, Berrien Springs, Michigan

Ronald A. Knott
Director,
Andrews University Press, Berrien Springs, Michigan

George R. Knight,
Professor Emeritus,
Andrews University, Berrien Springs, Michigan

Gary Land
Professor Emeritus
Andrews University, Berrien Springs, Michigan

Theodore N. Levterov,
Director, Ellen G. White Estate,
Loma Linda University, Loma Linda, California

Benjamin McArthur,
Professor of History,
Southern Adventist University, Chattanooga, Tennessee

Paul E. McGraw,
Professor of History,
Pacific Union College, Angwin, California

John V. G. Matthews,
Professor of Educational Administration and Religious Education,
Seventh-day Adventist Theological Seminary, Berrien Springs, Michigan

Jerry A. Moon
Professor of Church History,
Seventh-day Adventist Theological Seminary, Berrien Springs, Michigan

Barry D. Oliver,
President,
South Pacific Division of Seventh-day Adventists, Sydney, Australia

Arnold C. Reye,
Retired Administrator,
Brisbane, Queensland, Australia

Beverly J. Robinson-Rumble,
Editor, *Journal of Adventist Education,*
Washington, D.C.

Brian E. Strayer,
Professor of History,
Andrews University, Berrien Springs, Michigan

Alberto R. Timm,
Associate Director,
Ellen G. White Estate, Washington, D.C.

Gilbert M. Valentine,
Professor of Administration and Leadership,
La Sierra University, Riverside, California

Gerald Wheeler,
Book Editor,
Review and Herald® Publishing Association, Washington, D.C.

Woodrow W. Whidden,
Professor Emeritus,
Seventh-day Adventist Theological Seminary, Berrien Springs, Michigan